THE CAMBRIAN WAY

THE CAMBRIAN WAY

CLASSIC WALES MOUNTAIN TREK – SOUTH TO NORTH FROM CARDIFF TO CONWY

by George Tod with Richard Tyler

JUNIPER HOUSE, MURLEY MOSS,
OXENHOLME ROAD, KENDAL, CUMBRIA LA9 7RL
www.cicerone.co.uk

ROUTE SUMMARY TABLE

Stage	Start/finish
1	Cardiff to Machen
2	Machen to Pontypool
3	Pontypool to Abergavenny
4	Abergavenny to Capel-y-ffin
5	Capel-y-ffin to Crickhowel
6	Crickhowell to Storey Arms
7	Storey Arms to Glyntawe
8	Glyntawe to Llandovery
9	Llandovery to Tŷ'n-y-cornel
10	Tŷ'n-y-cornel to Claerddu
11	Claerddu to Ponterwyd
12	Ponterwyd to Dylife
13	Dylife to Dinas Mawddwy
14	Dinas Mawddwy to Bwlch Llyn Bach
15	Bwlch Llyn Bach to Barmouth
16	Barmouth to Cwm Bychan
17	Cwm Bychan to Maentwrog
18	Maentwrog to Beddgelert
19	Beddgelert to Pen-y-Pass
20	Pen-y-Pass to Llyn Ogwen
21	Llyn Ogwen to Conwy
Total	

* extra hour added for slow progress

Distance	Ascent	Descent	Time	Page
24.5km (15¼ miles)	480m (1570ft)	440m (1440ft)	6–7¼hr	38
18.5km (11½ miles)	830m (2720ft)	770m (2520ft)	5¾–6¾hr	48
20km (12¼ miles)	580m (1890ft)	640m (2080ft)	5–6¼hr	56
21.5km (13¼ miles)	1130m (3700ft)	870m (2850ft)	6¼–8hr	64
26.5km (16½ miles)	950m (3110ft)	1180m (3860ft)	7–9hr	71
33.5km (21 miles)	1720m (5630ft)	1370m (4490ft)	9¾–12½hr	79
19km (11¾ miles)	690m (2250ft)	930m (3040ft)	5–6¼hr	95
29.5km (18½ miles)	1360m (4460ft)	1500m (4930ft)	8¼–10¾hr	105
26km (16 miles)	870m (2850ft)	620m (2030ft)	6¾–8½hr	115
23.5km (14½ miles)	820m (2700ft)	690m (2250ft)	6¼–7¾hr	124
24km (14¾ miles)	910m (2970ft)	1140m (3740ft)	6½–8¼hr	133
23.5km (14½ miles)	920m (3030ft)	780m (2550ft)	6½–8¼hr	141
37km (23 miles)	1470m (4820ft)	1740m (5720ft)	10–12¾hr	149
15.5km (9½ miles)	1170m (3830ft)	980m (3210ft)	5–6¾hr	163
20km (12½ miles)	970m (3180ft)	1240m (4070ft)	5¾–7½hr	171
23km (14 miles)	1690m (5540ft)	1530m (5020ft)	8½–10¾hr*	180
16km (9¾ miles)	860m (2810ft)	1000m (3290ft)	5½–7hr*	196
22km (13½ miles)	1340m (4390ft)	1320m (4320ft)	7–8¾hr	205
17.5km (10¾ miles)	1390m (4560ft)	1060m (3490ft)	5¾–7¾hr	217
8.5km (5½ miles)	810m (2670ft)	870m (2860ft)	4–5hr*	224
30.5km (19 miles)	1580m (5180ft)	1870m (6120ft)	9–11½hr	230
479km (298 miles)	**22,460m (73,700ft)**	**22,480m (73,760ft)**	**136–174hr**	

13

Descent into Glyntawe (Stage 7; photo: Oliver Wicks)

INTRODUCTION

Llyn Caseg-fraith and Y Foel Goch from the rock-strewn Glyder Fach (Stage 20)

THE MOUNTAIN CONNOISSEURS' WALK

The Cambrian Way starts in the south of Wales at Cardiff Castle in the centre of the country's capital city and ends at Conwy, the mighty northern fortress of a town. Both castles were built in the 12th century by the Normans in an endeavour to keep the rebellious people of Wales under control. Between the two lies glorious verdant countryside featuring steep-sided valleys with streams and waterfalls, picturesque rolling hills, an abundance of high ridges and, in the north, rugged, cragged and challenging mountains. Much of the route runs through two national parks – Brecon Beacons and Snowdonia – as well as most of the areas in Wales that have been designated as wilderness.

Tempting as it may be, the Cambrian Way should not be the first outing attempted by the novice trekker. It is nearly 300 miles long and much of the route is in open access country, requiring good navigational skills. Some sections are long and remote, and accommodation can be rudimentary. While the mountains are not high, reaching a little over 1000m, the isolation and the challenge of the highest peaks require good mountain walking experience. Much of the route has been waymarked using the Cambrian Way Welsh hat symbol, but waymarks are not generally found on the mountain sections of the way. As the route follows public rights of way from footpaths to roads a whole variety of other waymarks will be found, but this can be at times misleading where

THE CAMBRIAN WAY TRUST

several paths meet. For those who are accustomed to such challenges, the Cambrian Way offers a superb long-distance walking experience.

Although the route traces many of the ancient trails used by the early settlers of Wales in the Stone and Bronze ages, the official route has its origins in the 1960s when a small group of members of Ramblers (formerly The Ramblers Association) decided to look at the formation of a south–north trail running through the upland areas of Wales. Agreement could not be reached and the project would have failed without the determination of Tony Drake, a

Looking towards Bwlch Siglen ('shaking pass') from the summit of Maesglase (Stage 14)

rambler with a passion for wild Wales. Over the following years he walked and climbed most of the Welsh ridges and mountains, searching out the optimum route. At the launch of the long-distance Offa's Dyke Path in 1971 he presented the initial plan for the trek and produced his first guidebook which, prior to the publication of this version, ran to seven editions. Sadly, Tony Drake died on 7 March 2012, leaving much of his estate for the continued development of the route. His work is carried on by the Cambrian Way Trust and Ramblers Cambrian Way Working Group.

The Cambrian Way is 479km (298 miles) in total with around 22,500m (73,700ft) of ascent. It starts in the middle of Cardiff at the main entrance to the impressive castle, and follows Afon (River) Taff initially through splendid parkland before rising to Castell Coch, a replica Norman castle. After leaving the city limits it passes through former coal mining valleys and enters Brecon Beacons National Park, traversing the iconic Pen y Fan mountain. It then leads through the Carmarthen Fans with their legendary Llyn y Fan Fach lake. Beyond the lush meadows around Llandovery the countryside becomes more remote and wild as the route enters the Elenydd region and crosses Pumlumon. After the town of Dinas Mawddwy and superb walking there is a challenging traverse of Cadair Idris, and a brief glimpse of the sea when crossing the Barmouth viaduct. A stiff ascent leads to the unyielding twin summits of Rhinog Fach and Rhinog Fawr where there are views north to the highest peaks in Wales, commanded by Snowdon. A long final day leads again over high peaks before descending to the coast at Conwy Castle.

The Welsh language

Wales has one of the oldest languages in Europe. Welsh was once spoken across England and Wales and in the southern half of Scotland; in fact, before it acquired its current meaning, the term 'Briton' was originally used to describe someone who spoke Welsh or one of its sister dialects. Around half a million people in Wales – 19% of the population – speak Welsh. The western half of Wales is where the language is spoken most; the Cambrian Way walker is most likely to hear the language spoken in Cardiff and in the more rural sections of the second half of the journey.

Those who are not familiar with Welsh will find initial difficulty in understanding signs, due to the lack of resemblance to English. Welsh is a phonetic language but has a different alphabet from English. However, place names in Welsh are frequently very descriptive, which can often assist in wayfinding. The glossary in Appendix B gives some useful examples. Cambria is an adjective which means relating to Wales.

A brief history of Wales

The early settlement of Wales started when the British Isles were still connected to mainland Europe in the period following the last great ice age, which ended around 12,000 years ago, with Stone Age and early Bronze Age people hunting and fishing in this land, so much of which had been covered by ice.

The Bronze Age people settled and farmed and there is little evidence of them having to resort to building forts, unlike the more warlike Iron Age people who arrived around 2000 years ago from central Europe. In the mountains on the Cambrian Way the walker will encounter hundreds of Bronze Age cairns – very often given the name *carn* – which marked ancient routes or were burial sites or sites of pagan worship. The Romans invaded Britain in the first century BC, conquering England and subsequently Wales. The Roman remains in Wales tend to be army camps, both temporary and permanent, unlike in England which was quite well settled for farming and city life. The route of Sarn Helen, one of the major Roman roads, is encountered on Stage 7 of the Cambrian Way.

With the fall of the Roman Empire in the fourth century AD the Romans withdrew, and the area we now know as England and Wales was made up of a number of independent kingdoms presided over by Welsh princes and Romano-British kings. Then invasion came by the Angles, Irish and Norse, and British power was concentrated in the southern part of Britain, in Wales and Cornwall. The Welsh language, which had been the language of much of Britain, was replaced in England by Germanic and Scandinavian languages, but was retained in Wales and Cornwall.

In this time, Wales and Ireland became the sanctuary for Christianity – hence so many place names in Wales starting with the word *Llan*, which indicates an early church settlement. For these countries the area around the Irish Sea is said to have enjoyed the 'golden age of the saints'.

In the mid 11th century the Normans invaded England and William of Normandy became king following the Battle of Hastings in 1066. The Normans subdued the English and established the barriers of the border countries of the Marches, which lay between England and Wales and Scotland. The Marcher Lords – the Norman Barons – were given fixed boundaries for their estates in England but open boundaries with the other two countries, which resulted in hundreds of years of conflict, evidenced by the numerous Welsh and English castles in Wales. A good example of these is Cardiff Castle at the start of the walk, which was built on the site of a Roman fort. Castell Coch, on the outskirts of Cardiff, is a wonderfully built Victorian replica of a Norman castle.

Under Edward I the Welsh were finally subdued following the death of Llywelyn Ein Llyw Olaf ('Llewelyn, our last prince of Wales'). Conwy Castle, at the Cambrian Way's end, is one of the great fortifications built by Edward. There was a serious uprising in the 15th century, led by Owain Glyndŵr, which was put down.

In the 16th century the Tudors, who were of Welsh origin, became the rulers of England and Wales and this assisted with the retention of the Welsh way of life and language, although the Acts of Union prohibited non-English speakers from holding public office in Wales and contributed to the anglicisation of the ruling classes.

During the reign of Henry VIII, the whole of Wales was annexed by England

The ruins of Abergavenny Castle (Stage 4)

and incorporated within the English legal system under the Laws in Wales Acts 1535–1542. Distinctive Welsh politics developed in the 19th century and the United Kingdom attained its only Welsh prime minister to date, David Lloyd George, in the early 20th century. At the end of the 20th century, the Government of Wales Act created a devolved parliament, the National Assembly for Wales, which now meets at the Senedd (Senate) in Cardiff Bay – this can be visited before commencing the walk.

GEOLOGY AND LANDSCAPE

Geology shapes landscapes. Much of Wales' rich geological history is showcased in the landscapes through which the Cambrian Way passes. What you see today is due to a host of different geological forces which have formed, altered and removed rocks over more than 500 million years.

A copy of the geological map and an accompanying chronological geology table can be downloaded for free from the Cicerone website: www. cicerone.co.uk/990.

Colliding continents

The main forces shaping the Welsh landscape arise from plate tectonics: the surface of the earth consists of rigid lithospheric plates which move very slowly over the underlying mantle. When plates carrying continents collide, mountain-building episodes (orogenies) are likely to occur. Wales has been caught up in three such events in the last 500 million years.

In the Cambrian Period southern Britain, including Wales, was part of the

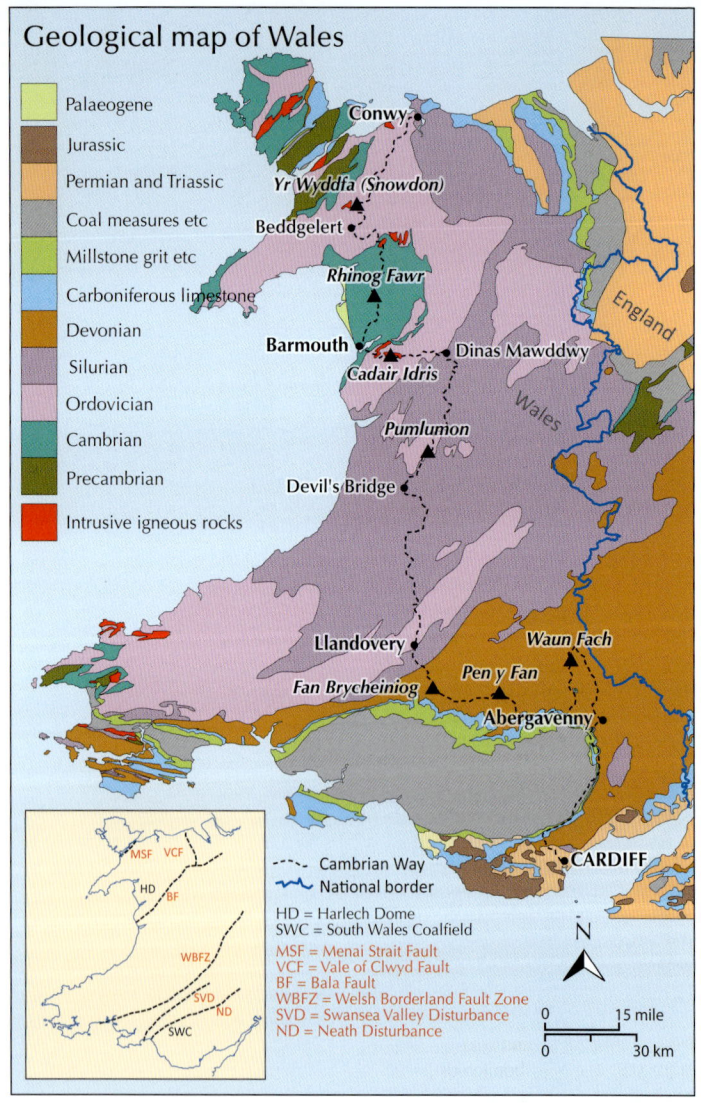

Geological map of Wales

- Palaeogene
- Jurassic
- Permian and Triassic
- Coal measures etc
- Millstone grit etc
- Carboniferous limestone
- Devonian
- Silurian
- Ordovician
- Cambrian
- Precambrian
- Intrusive igneous rocks

Conwy
Yr Wyddfa (Snowdon)
Beddgelert
Rhinog Fawr
Barmouth
Cadair Idris
Dinas Mawddwy
Pumlumon
Devil's Bridge
England
Wales
Llandovery
Waun Fach
Fan Brycheiniog
Pen y Fan
Abergavenny
CARDIFF

- - - - Cambrian Way
~~~~ National border

HD = Harlech Dome
SWC = South Wales Coalfield
MSF = Menai Strait Fault
VCF = Vale of Clwyd Fault
BF = Bala Fault
WBFZ = Welsh Borderland Fault Zone
SVD = Swansea Valley Disturbance
ND = Neath Disturbance

MSF VCF
HD
BF
WBFZ
SVD
ND
SWC

N

| 0 | | 15 mile |
| 0 | | 30 km |

microcontinent of East Avalonia, which lay near the South Pole and was starting to split away from the great southern landmass of Gondwana. This split opened a deep sea basin, now termed the Welsh Basin. Over the next 100 million years large volumes of mud and sand poured into this basin as East Avalonia moved north to collide with the great northern landmass of Laurentia (which included Scotland and the northern part of Ireland), creating Laurussia 425 million years ago.

The convergence of these continents and the closure of the Iapetus Ocean between them resulted in a series of violent underwater volcanic eruptions in the Welsh Basin. The igneous rocks erupted and intruded at that time now form many of the mountains in Snowdonia. This continental collision and lengthy mountain-building episode (Caledonian Orogeny) formed the Caledonian mountains stretching from Norway across northern Britain into North America.

These mountains were rapidly weathered and the eroded debris was carried south by great rivers to be deposited on a desert plain (latitude 20°S) and eventually uplifted to form the Old Red Sandstone landscape of South Wales.

Around 390 million years ago more plate tectonic movements (Acadian Orogeny) compressed the Welsh Basin so that its contents were folded, faulted and pushed upwards, creating the mountains of North and Mid Wales and the economically important slates.

Tropical seas, deltas and coal
At the start of the Carboniferous Period, much of South Wales – which by then lay just south of the equator – was flooded by a shallow tropical sea in which thick limestones formed. Deltas carrying sediment from the north eventually encroached into this sea and equatorial swamp forests grew on the delta tops. The forest vegetation rotted in the oxygen-poor swamps to form thick peat layers which were compressed into coal deposits over millions of years.

Around 300 million years ago Gondwana collided with Laurussia, producing Pangaea, the latest supercontinent. This collision raised the Variscan mountains, stretching from the Gulf of Mexico into Eastern Europe. The weight of these mountains across mainland Europe depressed the adjacent lithosphere of southern Britain into a series of basins, one of which is the South Wales Coal Basin, as it folded the Carboniferous deposits described above.

Desert rocks
Wales, along with most of Britain and Ireland, became a hot desert near the centre of Pangaea. Mud and silt derived from the Variscan mountains was carried north by flash floods to be deposited in ephemeral lakes and lagoons. These are now the rocks under Cardiff at the start of the Cambrian Way.

Wearing down and going up
There is much that remains unknown, but Wales may have sunk below sea level one or more times during the Jurassic and Cretaceous periods and its surface planed flat. However, over the past few tens of millions of years Wales has been lifted up above sea level once again. Rivers have since cut down deeply into this broad easterly

Snowdon's iconic summit, seen here from Bwlch Glas (Stage 19)

tilted plateau, aided by glaciers on many occasions during the Quaternary Period.

Ice and water

Ice put the finishing touches to the landscape. Wales was heavily glaciated at least eight times over the past 2.6 million years; ice sheets and valley glaciers covered most of the country. Ice eroded and sculpted the landscape, deepening valleys and carving sharp peaks, ridges and glacial cirques. When the ice melted, torrents of meltwater enlarged valleys and cave systems and triggered landslips.

GEOLOGICAL HIGHLIGHTS

The rocks are youngest in the south around Cardiff and get progressively older as the route continues north until the oldest Cambrian rocks are reached in the Rhinogau.

- From Castell Coch to the Blorenge you walk along the southern and eastern rim of the South Wales Coal Basin (Stages 1–3).
- As you descend the Blorenge you reach the Old Red Sandstone and stay on that until shortly before Myddfai, except above Llangattock, which is Carboniferous (Stages 4–5).
- The Brecon Beacons National Park west of the Gap Road in the Central Beacons is also designated Fforest Fawr UNESCO Global Geopark in light of its geological significance (Stage 6).

- Rhandirmwyn (Ordovician), Cwmystwyth and Dylife (Silurian) were major centres of lead mining (Stage 9).
- Glacial meltwater carved the steep-sided Ystwyth gorge (Stage 9).
- Cadair Idris is a magnificent mountain of mostly igneous rocks. Just SW of the summit are fantastic piles of pillow lavas. These form when hot basaltic lava is extruded under water, cools rapidly forming a 'skin' around itself, then buds another pillow, and so on (Stage 15).
- Ordovician slate was mined and quarried around Moelwyn Mawr and Cnicht (Stage 18).
- Snowdon is the climax of the walk and a geological climax too. Magma chambers in the vicinity of the present summit erupted explosively many times, emptying the chambers, which collapsed inwards forming a great caldera whose southern rim was south of Beddgelert and eastern rim near the Llanberis Pass. The caldera filled up with the products of more explosive eruptions. Fossil casts of marine shells were discovered at the summit, proving the eruptions were submarine (Stage 19).
- The summit plateau of the Glyderau is a blockfield formed by repeated freezing and thawing, which shatters the igneous rocks (Stage 20).
- The Sychnant Pass was cut by glacial meltwater (Stage 21).
- Igneous rocks continue underfoot until you enter Conwy, which sits on Ordovician gritstone (the castle is built of it too) (Stage 21).

PLANTS AND ANIMALS

Animals

In terms of the animals that will be seen en route, this could be summed up as sheep, sheep and more sheep given that there are around 11 million of them, mainly in the upland areas through which the Cambrian Way runs. It is worth comparing the large cross-breeds in the lowland areas with the small and lithe Welsh Mountain sheep in the hills. This gave rise to the old Welsh sheep stealer's rhyme: 'Mountain lambs are sweet, but lowland sheep are fatter, which is why we deem it meet to carry off the latter.' In the mountains there are usually few fences as flocks are 'hefted', whereby after many generations of breeding, herds learn to stick to their own territory.

A large variety of sheepdogs will be seen, usually border collies. The browner version of these are often Welsh collies which are descended from the dogs used by the drovers who, until the coming of the railways in the 19th century, used to drive the flocks to the markets, in some cases as far as London.

There are also cattle on the route. In the lowlands these will often be larger animals, usually in dairy herds, while in the mountains smaller animals are reared for beef. Small Welsh Black cattle may be seen on the hills.

Idwal Cottage in its picturesque position between Y Garn and Llyn Ogwen (Stage 21)

As in the Alps, it is still traditional in the mountain areas to take the sheep and cattle to graze on the higher hills in the spring and bring them back down in the autumn. In these seasons, sheep-gathering – in which the shepherds use quad bikes, dogs and even ponies for moving the animals for shearing and sorting – may be seen.

Semi-feral Welsh Mountain ponies will occasionally be found in small herds as these, with cattle, are often used for controlled grazing on the mountains. At one time the ponies were used in huge numbers for pulling coal trucks in the South Wales mines and lived underground, besides a two-week break in the fresh air during the miners' summer holidays.

There are still wild Welsh goats around Rhinog Fawr and Rhinog Fach near Harlech, and they can also still be seen in the remoter areas around Snowdon. One of these is selected as the mascot of the 1st Battalion, Royal Welsh (formerly the Royal Welch Fusiliers) and may be seen at special events such as rugby matches, leading their band.

Wild creatures that might be spotted along the way include rabbits, hares, mice, rats, voles, grey squirrels, foxes, badgers, weasels, stoats; and more rarely, otters, polecats and pine martens. Frogs, toads and newts are evident – especially in the spring mating season – and lizards, slow-worms, grass snakes and adders may be glimpsed, the latter having a poisonous bite. Spiders abound even in very high places. Summer sees an abundance of caterpillars, butterflies and, at night, moths. There are numerous species of fly, the biting versions of which are the horsefly, large and grey, and the tiny midge which will be found around water on summer evenings. Bees and wasps also abound.

There is a huge variety of bird-life, much of which in the mountains is made up of buzzards, kites, ravens, rooks, crows and magpies – mainly carrion birds. There is also a variety of hawks such as kestrels, sparrowhawks, hen harriers and goshawks as well as the fastest of all creatures, the peregrine falcon which can reach a diving speed of 389km/h (242mph). Smaller birds to watch out for are the flycatchers, red-starts, tree creepers and nuthatches, wrens and robins, blackbirds, thrushes, and finches and tits. On the high moors the skylark is often seen and heard singing high in the summer sky, while on the ground, stone and whinchats may be seen. At night the brown tawny and white barn owls will be heard, and if you're lucky you'll spot the ground-nesting short-eared owls in wild moorland areas.

Plant life

There is a rich variety of trees along the route of the Cambrian Way. Many of these will be found in forest areas, planted by the Forestry Commission or by the owners of private woodland; they consist mostly of larch and pine and are managed for use as fencing products or wood chip. There are some areas where there are collections of rare trees, particularly in Bute Park at the start of the walk. Otherwise, predominant species are oak, ash and birch. In the central section of the Cambrian Mountains there are hanging woods of sessile oak, often ancient forest which has over the centuries been coppiced for firewood, charcoal and tannin. There are also wet woods of alder, used in the past for making clogs and in the production of saltpetre for gunpowder.

Hedging is still used for enclosing fields and the common plants found include hawthorn, blackthorn and hazel, often intertwined with wild roses and honeysuckle. In the upland areas there are good examples of pleached or laid hedges, an ancient craft of inter-twining branches to form barriers. This, along with cutting, can prolong the life of a hedge for hundreds of years. In rocky areas substantial dry stone walls will be encountered. The ancient crafts of laying hedges and building dry stone walling are very much alive in Wales.

In the spring, bluebells and primroses as well as many other small flowers abound; and in high places wild whinberries (bilberries), cranberries and cowberries (lingonberries) can be found among the heather moorland during the summer and autumn. Tiny plants such as sundew and tormentil and many mosses and lichens grow around the paths and on the trees, and bog cotton is seen in the wetter areas. One of the more annoying plants found in the peat bogs is molinia grass, which grows in large tufts and is quite difficult to walk on – especially if you're wearing a heavy rucksack – as the tufts wobble.

WHEN TO GO

Wales is renowned for its rainfall and contributes much water to cities on the other side of the border in England, so walkers should always be prepared for wet weather. The route can be attempted at any time of the year but the higher mountains of the Snowdonia area are best avoided in the middle of winter due to wind, ice and snow. Likewise, in particularly rainy winters the central moorland sections can become very wet and difficult to cross. Some hostels close for the winter, but it is possible to find B&B accommodation throughout the year – although this of course should be checked in advance. Few factors are as predictable as daylight hours, and some of the longer sections would be difficult to complete during the winter months; however, the British weather being far less predictable, it is not unheard of to encounter glorious walking conditions very early or late in the year and unpleasant conditions in the middle of summer. Rhinog Fach and Rhinog Fawr and the mountains between them and Maentwrog can be testing at all times of the year in the event of poor visibility, rain or wind, or in very hot weather due to the lack of shade.

TRAVEL

Getting to Cardiff at the start of the Cambrian Way and from Conwy at the end is easy by road or rail. Cardiff is on the South Wales Main Line which offers connections with stations across the UK and a direct link with London. Conwy is on the North Wales Coast Line which runs from Crewe to Holyhead, Crewe being a major junction with good connections to both the north and south. The National Rail website (www. nationalrail.co.uk) and Trainline (www. thetrainline.com) allow you to compare options and make rail bookings, and both train and bus information can be found at www.traveline.cymru.

The Ffestiniog Railway, now a popular attraction, is seen towards the end of the Cambrian Way

Cardiff Castle, the starting point of the Cambrian Way, is around 800m (½ mile) north of the main railway station. At the end, Conwy station is less than 300m (¼ mile) west of the castle; or alternatively, Llandudno Junction, around 1.5km (1 mile) away on the other side of Afon Conwy, is on the same line and boasts more services.

Walkers travelling from abroad might consider flying into Cardiff Airport. Liverpool, Manchester and Birmingham are the nearest major international airports to Conwy at the end of the route.

In-between there are good bus services in the urban districts and on main roads in the countryside, should you want to leave the route in order to take advantage of wider accommodation options. If walking the route in sections rather than in one go, railways can be used to reach either Pontypool or Abergavenny (Stage 3) on the Newport to Hereford line; Llandovery (Stages 8 and 9) on the Heart of Wales Line from Swansea to Shrewsbury; Caersws or Machynlleth on the Shrewsbury to Aberystwyth line for Commins Coch (Stage 13) by bus; Barmouth (Stages 15 and 16) on the Cambrian Coast Line; and Harlech (an option for off-route accommodation on Stages 17 and 18), also on the Cambrian Coast Line.

Wales is famous for its little railways, old mining or quarrying lines now used as tourist attractions. There are opportunities to use these or to visit them on rest days. The lines that run close to the Cambrian Way are the Rheidol (Stage 11), Tal-y-llyn (Stages 14 and 15) and Ffestiniog and Welsh Highland (Stages 18 and 19) railways.

ACCOMMODATION

Wales is famed for its hospitality and great quality of food, very often locally sourced. There is a wide range of accommodation along the Cambrian Way, from youth hostels, bunkhouses, bothies and campsites to expensive hotels. There are many bed-and-breakfast establishments on the route. Wild camping in Wales is only allowed with the landowner's permission. There is a detailed accommodation list on the Cambrian Way website (www.cambrianway.org.uk), and in this guide there is an abbreviated list in Appendix D and a more general list of contacts in Appendix C.

With often quite long distances between accommodation it is unwise to arrive without booking in advance. It is safest to book for the whole route or the part of the route you're walking before setting off so that you can be assured of a bed for the night. However, this does restrict any flexibility that may be needed as a result of bad weather or fatigue, and if the walk (or part of it) has to be abandoned it may not be possible to recoup all of the money that has been paid in advance. Another option is to book one or two days ahead as you go along so that you always know that you have a bed for the night and won't have as much to lose should you need to cancel. The drawback of this is that you may be faced with paying higher prices when some places are fully booked.

When booking, it is also advisable to consider where food can be obtained for an evening meal, breakfast and packed lunch. Many rural pubs only serve meals at limited hours or not at all, so if you're hoping to obtain a meal it pays to check what's available locally when you book accommodation. See also the Trek Planner in this guide.

In some popular tourist areas prices can be high, especially for single occupancy, and sometimes bookings are only taken for a minimum two-night stay, although this may not apply to last-minute bookings if there are a number of empty rooms. Many of the smaller accommodation businesses do not take credit or debit cards, so sufficient cash will be needed.

At certain times of the year, such as public holidays, school holidays and weekends, popular places can get fully booked well in advance and youth hostels often have school parties making block bookings, particularly in the early summer. Booking ahead is therefore particularly important in the summer season – and note that some B&B businesses close during the winter. A number of towns have special events at certain times of the year which result in accommodation in a wide area being fully booked. Examples are the Abergavenny Food Festival in mid September, the Brecon Jazz Festival in mid August, the Hay-on-Wye Book Festival at the end of May, and the Royal Welsh Show at Builth Wells in the third week of July.

When the Cambrian Way was first created there were many more youth hostels than there are today, and the route was designed so that as many of these as possible could be used. Over the years, many small remote hostels have closed, and as a result the route has often been changed to take in places where other accommodation is available. Fortunately, to compensate for these closures, the number of independent hostels has grown, either by taking over the YHA hostels or by creating new ones, and the number of bunkhouses has also increased. Nevertheless, most of these are in the national parks and popular tourist areas, which leaves some of the wild and remote parts of the Cambrian Way with very few places to choose from. In some areas it is necessary to divert a long way from the route.

In the more remote areas, it is often the case that all accommodation is a long distance from the route – this is particularly the case on Stages 16 and 17 over the Rhinog mountains, where it may be necessary to go as much as 8 or 10km off-route. Some accommodation providers offer a pick-up service from the route, but it may still be necessary to walk a few kilometres to reach the nearest road. Taxis can also be used, although difficulties can arise with pick-up times when it is not easy to know exactly what time you will arrive at the pick-up point. It is often possible to get mobile phone reception on mountaintops where there are no obstacles blocking the signal, but once down into valleys there is frequently no reception at all, making it impossible to call for a taxi or to change the pick-up arrangements. Arrangements for accommodation therefore require careful advance planning.

KIT

Given the demands of the route, if walking the whole of the Cambrian Way in one go, a balance needs to be struck between staying warm and dry in moorland and mountain sections and staying cooler in the earlier sections until the Black Mountains are reached. Even in the summer it can become very cold at night in the moorland and mountain sections.

Pack weight should be between 7 and 10kg, depending on whether camping gear is being carried. It is well worth investing in lightweight equipment, as some of the mountain sections are difficult to negotiate with a large pack.

Although much of the southern section can be walked in good mountain shoes, boots are advisable for the later sections, as well as gaiters for the peat bogs in the mid moorland areas where streams will also need to be waded on occasion. Sun cream and insect repellent are advisable. Trekking poles can be very useful for the more mountainous and boggy sections. Safety items such as a first aid kit, torch, whistle, map and compass are essential. Sheets are not usually required for hostels but it is wise to a carry light silk inner lining and pillow cover. For bothies, a sleeping bag and mat will be needed. The logistics of washing and drying clothes over a three-week trek will need to be considered; liquid soap and a drying line are recommended, although many accommodation businesses will provide laundry services at a charge.

Cambrian Way waymark

WAYMARKING AND NAVIGATION

Much of the Cambrian Way is waymarked with the Welsh hat symbol or on marked public rights of way. Substantial parts of it are over open access country and mountain ridges and peaks where paths are not always clear. Often there can be a confusion of paths, many of which may be sheep tracks. For these reasons it is necessary to have good map-reading skills, particularly if visibility is bad.

Paths sometimes have legal diversions around private land or temporary diversions in case of repair or to avoid danger, so always take note of these. Information on diversions and comments from walkers can be found on the Cambrian Way website at www. cambrianway.org.uk.

Throughout this guide you will see references to checkpoints. There is nothing physically at these checkpoints; they just represent key points along the route and are a way of marking progress. They were introduced by Tony Drake as a way of defining completion of the whole route, but it is up to the individual to decide whether to follow these. In bad weather, mountain safety should take priority over reaching checkpoints.

This guide contains 1:50,000 maps which should be adequate especially if used in conjunction with GPS. Ensure that maps have been downloaded to your device before starting the walk. Without GPS there are many areas where the greater detail on a 1:25,000

map, such as field boundaries and names of local features and farms, make route finding much easier. The relevant Ordnance Survey sheet maps are listed at the beginning of each stage.

FOOD, WATER AND SUPPLIES

Being an upland route, there are long sections on which food and drink are not easily available without making detours off-route. The detours are not generally very long but a few remote sections require enough food to be carried for a few days. Except in long periods of dry weather, there are generally plenty of streams on or near the route to provide water, although there are many long moorland ridges where longer detours would be required to reach them. The maps give a rough idea of how close the route is to rivers and streams, but bear in mind that these can dry up through lack of rainfall. It is, therefore, advisable to carry enough water to last for the whole day in areas such as the Brecon Beacons, Pumlumon and the Carneddau. Water from streams carries risks from E. coli, especially where sheep or cattle graze, so ensure that all such water is treated, either by the addition of purification tablets or use of a water filter before drinking.

The route description in this guide gives indications as to where there are food shops, cafés or pubs on or near the route, and the Trek Planner should be checked carefully when planning the walk. Bear in mind, however, that shops, pubs and accommodation providers can change over time; it is advisable to look on the Cambrian Way website for up-to-date information or directly online for those places that have their own websites. If you're unsure as to whether meals or supplies are available, check with accommodation providers about the availability and opening times of places nearby.

Cash dispensers can be found in towns, and supermarkets will usually give cashback if using cards for purchases. ATMs in shops will be subject to opening hours and they may also charge a fee, so it is worth carrying sufficient cash for several days at a time.

Telephone kiosks are being phased out and often do not accept cash (although neither cash nor a phone card is required for 999 emergency calls).

EMERGENCIES

The emergency number 999 may be used even in areas of poor signal strength. If in the mountains, ask for the police and then mountain rescue or ambulance, depending on the circumstances. It is wise before starting out for the day to assess weather conditions and the nature of the route as indicated in this guide.

If possible, it is worth leaving the details of your proposed day's walk with your accommodation provider, including a note of the number of people in your group. Phoning ahead on the day and giving a proposed time of arrival is not only courteous but may save worry or, conversely, allow the alarm to be raised should one of your party suffer an accident or injury.

USING THIS GUIDE

The Cambrian Way for the purposes of this guide is divided into 21 main stages

starting from Cardiff. These include a number of alternative routes, mainly to access accommodation or for use in the event of bad weather. The main stages average around 23km (14 miles) a day, but Stages 6 and 21 are particularly long. The longer stages can be broken up, although they don't all feature accommodation in the middle. Cwm Bychan at the end of Stage 16 provides only a very basic campsite.

At the start of each stage, an information box sets out the distance, total ascent, walking time and the OS maps required. Availability of refreshments, public transport and accommodation is also indicated; for accommodation, the distance from the stage start is given, and if the accommodation lies significantly off-route, the distance from the Cambrian Way is given in brackets.

Distance, ascent and descent figures were calculated using online mapping, which gives more accuracy than the old method of counting contours. However, it is not an exact science – particularly for ascents and descents – and figures have been rounded off to the nearest 10 units (m or ft). GPS measurements may differ somewhat from these.

Times are calculated using Naismith's formula of 3mph plus 30min per 1000ft of ascent for the first figure, and 2½mph and 45min per 1000ft of ascent for the second figure – all rounded to the nearest 15min. Some areas where walking speed is considerably reduced by craggy terrain have had 1hr added to their times. These times do not allow for rest breaks or slow descents.

Following the stage information box there is a brief résumé of the day's

Stile above Pen Caenewydd (Stage 8; photo: Oliver Wicks)

walk, followed by a detailed description of the route. This includes a numbered sequence of checkpoints which occur at major landmarks. To assist in navigation, significant places and features which appear on the stage maps are shown in **bold** in the text. Information is also given about places of interest on the way.

At the back of the guide there are appendices intended to assist with route planning:

- Appendix A: The checkpoints
- Appendix B: Glossary of Welsh words
- Appendix C: Useful contacts
- Appendix D: Accommodation list.

GPX tracks

GPX tracks for the routes in this guidebook are available to download free at www.cicerone.co.uk/990/GPX. A GPS device is an excellent aid to navigation, but you should also carry a map and compass and know how to use them.

THE ROUTE

Glyder Fach and the shattered pinnacles of Castell y Gwynt (Stage 20)

STAGE 1
Cardiff to Machen

Start	Cardiff Castle (ST 181 765)
Finish	A468 near St John's Church, Machen (ST 212 892)
Distance	24.5km (15¼ miles)
Total ascent	480m (1570ft)
Total descent	440m (1440ft)
Time	6–7¼hr
Maps	OS Explorer 151 and 152; OS Landranger 171
Refreshments	Tongwynlais, Thornhill, Rudry
Public transport	Wide range of rail and bus services at Cardiff; bus service to Caerphilly from Machen
Accommodation	Cardiff; Rudry 19.5km (+1km); Draethen 22.5km (+1km); Caerphilly (+7km)

The walk starts with fine parkland on the banks of Afon Taff and continues with some canal bank and road walking over and under a large road interchange to climb to Castell Coch. Beyond this, there is ridge walking on forest tracks and farmland with fine views to the Brecon Beacons and the Severn Estuary before descending steeply to the old mining village of Machen.

Cardiff Castle may look relatively modern, but it is on the site of a third-century Roman fort and the original motte-and-bailey castle was built by the Normans in the 11th century. Huge changes were made in Victorian times to turn it into a fairytale castle, but the old castle keep has survived and the remains of old stonework can be seen at the base of the outside walls. The magnificent clock tower and many other parts were built by the Bute family with their great wealth derived from coal and iron. The Animal Wall in front of the castle, built in the 1890s, contained many grotesque gargoyles, but road widening after World War 1 meant that the whole wall was moved along the road towards the bridge and more animals were added. Weathering caused a lot of damage, so they were extensively restored in 2010.

Cardiff Castle's impressive entrance

Starting from the entrance to **Cardiff Castle**, which is Checkpoint 1, go W towards Afon Taff for 300 metres to find the gates of Bute Park on the right. ▶

It is planned to place a plaque here to mark the Cambrian Way.

Alternative route along the west bank
Very early starters might find that the park gates are locked (they are open from 7.30am until 30 minutes before sunset). However, the west bank route through Sophia Gardens is almost equally attractive. Return to the east bank after 200 metres by a suspension footbridge.

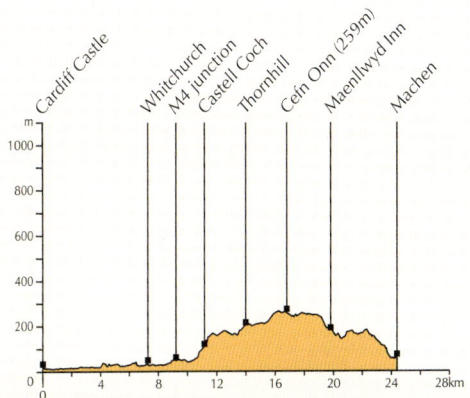

Easy wide paths lead through Bute Park, and there is a choice of walking by the riverside or through formal gardens. After 1.2km the path enters woodland lining the riverbank, passing a weir and footbridge 700 metres further along where the Taff Trail crosses the river to join the Cambrian Way. The route follows the river as it turns to the west for a further 1km, at which point cross the Gabalfa bridge to visit Llandaff Cathedral. ◄ Across the bridge, take the riverside path W for 600 metres, passing by Cardiff University, then turn left and walk across playing fields for 150 metres to reach the **cathedral**.

If short of time, this diversion can be omitted by continuing along the Taff Trail to rejoin the route at Whitchurch.

Head WNW from the cathedral for 400 metres, going near to the river but round to the left of Llandaff Rowing Club, then join the A4054 road near Llandaff Bridge. It is possible to return to the east bank of the Taff by crossing here, but the route follows the west bank along Radyr Court Road, a minor riverside road.

Glamorgan Canal Nature Reserve (photo: Oliver Wicks)

After 900 metres do not turn left under a railway bridge but continue along a riverside path for a further 950 metres, swinging from NW to NE round a bend in the river. The next

bridge is a railway bridge with a pedestrian walkway at the far side; cross the bridge and follow a path NE, with trees on the left and a housing estate on the right, for 200 metres until it joins Ty-Mawr Road through a residential area of **Whitchurch**. ▶

After 250 metres bear left, where Ty-Mawr Road joins the wider Forest Farm road, and follow this for 150 metres. Then, do not follow the Taff Trail, which continues along the riverbank – instead look out for the entrance to the Glamorgan Canal Nature Reserve on the right, and follow the left bank of the disused canal for 1.4km

Look out for the restored Melingriffith water pump on the left shortly after joining the road.

Map continues on page 44

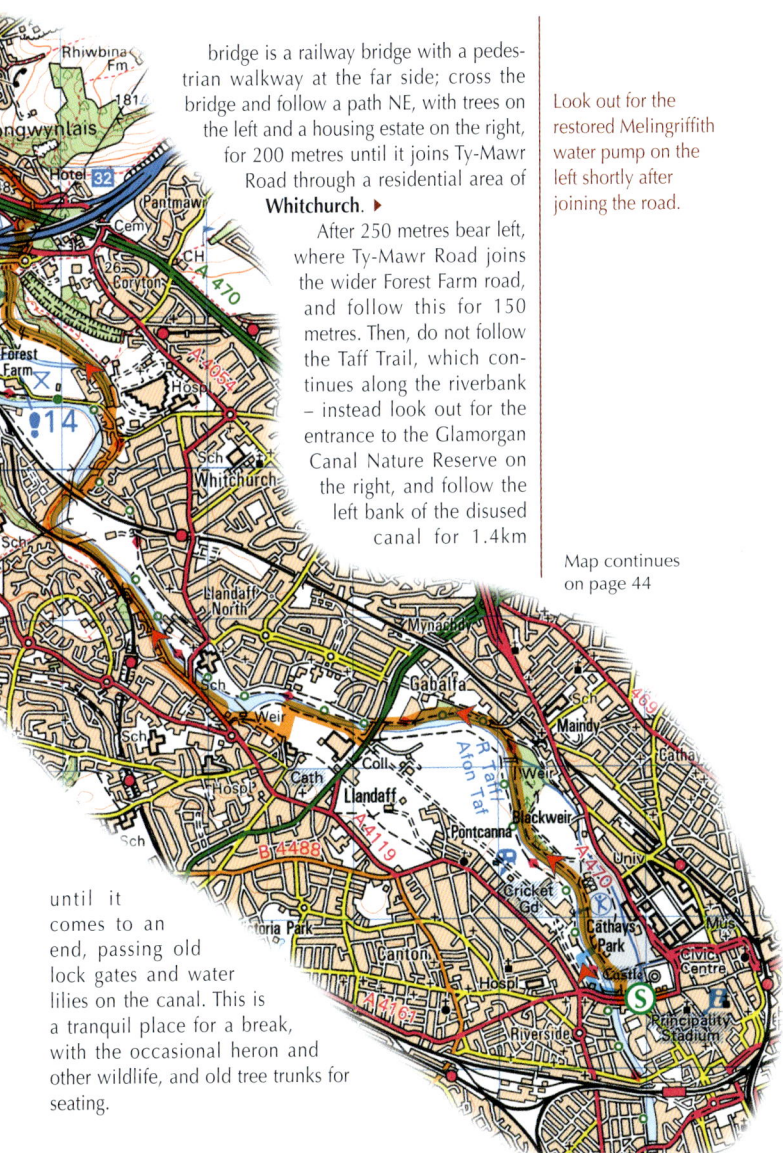

until it comes to an end, passing old lock gates and water lilies on the canal. This is a tranquil place for a break, with the occasional heron and other wildlife, and old tree trunks for seating.

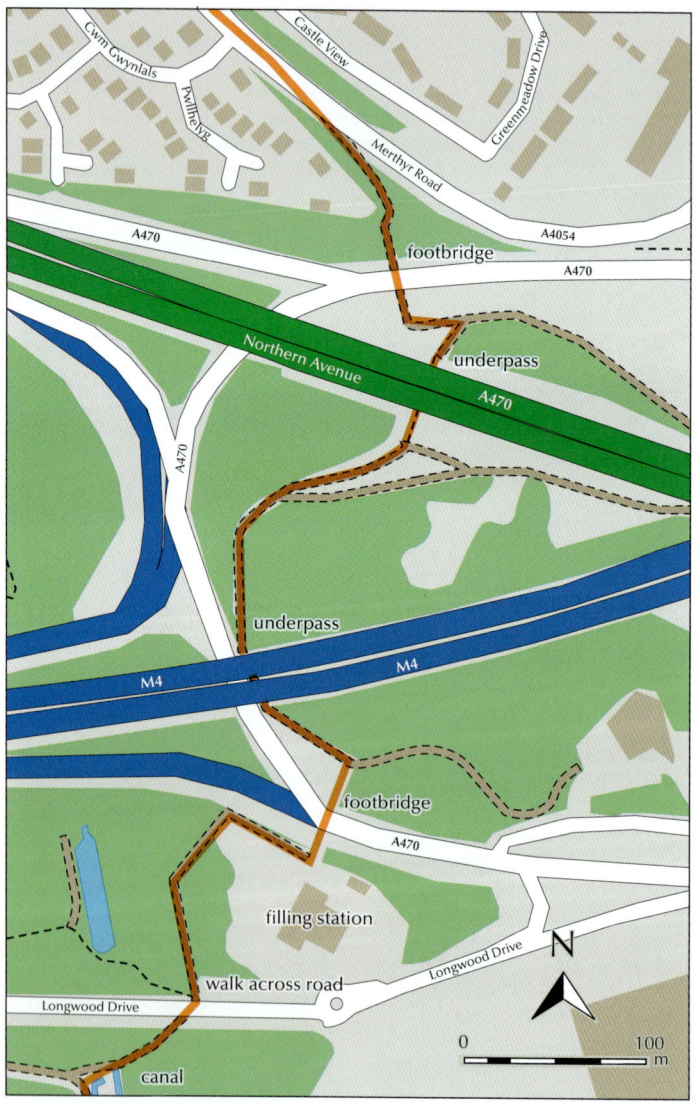

At the end of the canal, climb a steep bank with steps to the busy M4 motorway intersection. A series of pedestrian walkways and bridges cross this 'spaghetti' junction (see map). First cross a road then pass behind a petrol station to reach a footbridge – from which there is a view of Castell Coch ('red castle') on the hillside ahead – then take two underpasses and cross over a footbridge to reach the A4054 (Merthyr Road), a total of 700 metres from the canal. Follow the A4054 NW for 700 metres into **Tongwynlais**. ▶

There are pubs, shops and a fish-and-chip shop in Tongwynlais, and hotels and B&Bs near the M4 interchange.

Turn right in the centre of Tongwynlais and head N up Mill Road, which then becomes Castle Road. Ignore any turnings until you reach the main entrance gate for vehicles after 600 metres, then turn sharp left past car parks and continue for 350 metres to reach **Castell Coch**, which is Checkpoint 2.

> **Castell Coch** is a fairytale-style Victorian castle built on Norman foundations. It was a complete ruin until 1870, at which point it was rebuilt as a country residence for the 3rd Marquess of Bute. The internal decor is lavish and worth a visit. It is now owned by Cadw, the Welsh body that looks after historical buildings, and it is open to the public most months of the year. See https://cadw.gov.wales for details.

From the castle, turn sharp right on a path going NE up the fairly steep hillside through the forest, another part of the Taff Trail. Do not follow the Taff Trail where it turns left after 300 metres, but keep straight on along the main forest track, which climbs more gently and provides easier walking for 1.6km through Fforest-fawr ('big forest'), first heading N then NE. A number of tracks join or cross but keep to the main track. ▶

Unfortunately, there are no views here, although there are some points of interest along the way.

> At ST 136 836, The Arches or **Three Bears Caves** can be seen on the left along with an explanatory board telling of their history as three mine entrances, or adits. The site is now in use as a setting for a number of film and TV scenes in productions that include *Doctor Who*, *Merlin*, *Sherlock*, *Harry Potter* and *Robin Hood*. A short way after this is the start of a Sculpture Trail running parallel to the main route; an interesting alternative that adds very little extra distance.

Three Bears Caves

At the end of the Sculpture Trail there is a car park and 150 metres further on the track joins Hoel-Y-Fforest, a minor road coming up the valley from Tongwynlais. Cross the road and turn sharp right near an information board along a track into Fforestganol ('central forest'), heading SSE then S through the forest along the eastern side of the valley. Look out for a path on the left heading ESE up the hillside, ignoring the first path after 100 metres and taking the better path after 200 metres (not shown on OS maps). This joins a road in 100 metres after going up some steps.

Turn right along the road and walk for a short way until a track forks off sharp left at **Bwlch-y-cwm** ('pass of the valley'). Take the track, which follows the ridge NNE through woodland at first and past a quarry on the left, entering an area with fewer trees and better views of the country-side. The way goes in and out of small sections of woodland, passing a farm on the right and a few gates before reaching the Ridgeway Golf Course at **Thornhill** after 1.5km.

The right of way goes through the middle of the course, so beware of flying golf balls! ▶ At this point the Rhymney Valley Ridgeway Walk joins the Cambrian Way. A 300-metre walk down the golf course access road leads to the **A469** Thornhill Road. The Travellers' Rest pub is about 100 metres to the right, but the route goes across the road past a large farm where it continues to follow the Ridgeway Walk.

Go E along the edge of woodland for 800 metres with some views to the right between the trees. Continue on the Ridgeway Walk for the next 300 metres before passing below an overhead power line and entering more woodland, then turn left after a gate. Before descending very far, after 100 metres turn right to follow a track through the trees along the hillside. ▶ After 400 metres of fairly level walking along the gently sloping hillside, the main route forks left to go around an old quarry, but a path straight ahead leads to the edge of the quarry, which has some of the best views along the ridge, making it a fine place to take a rest.

The club's restaurant is on the route and is open to walkers.

The forest floor is carpeted with wild garlic, which has white flowers and a strong scent in early summer.

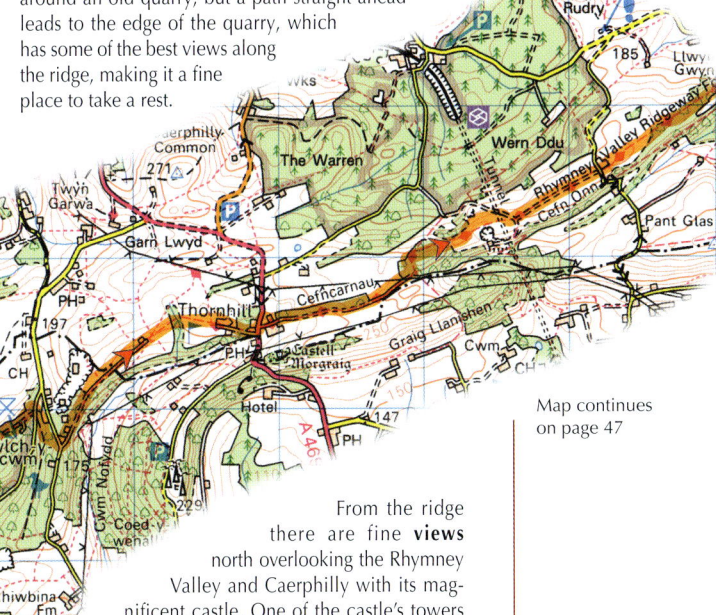

Map continues on page 47

From the ridge there are fine **views** north overlooking the Rhymney Valley and Caerphilly with its magnificent castle. One of the castle's towers leans at an angle that seems to defy gravity.

45

On a clear day it is even possible to see Pen y Fan in the Brecon Beacons – visited on Stage 6 of the walk, five days ahead. To the south is Cardiff and the Bristol Channel.

A short drop down the hillside from the quarry allows you to rejoin the route as it skirts around N of the quarry before climbing back up onto the ridge after 400 metres. (Ignore the right of way through the quarry shown on OS maps – it is impractical.) Follow the ridge for 200 metres ENE through patchy woodland to the open ridge of **Cefn Onn** ('ash tree ridge'). After 500 metres cross a minor road and continue along the ridge as it climbs and then steadily descends for 1.3km. ◄ Continue ahead along the track through the wood for a further 550 metres, dropping further to a dip with a wide metal gate across the track.

Here a path to the N leads down to Rudry (300 metres) for those seeking accommodation.

There is a **secret World War 2 bunker** at ST 199 865, up a small hill to the right, but this can easily be missed as it is somewhat hidden in the trees. It was a communication and operation centre in the event of an invasion, with a deep, well-concealed bunker and an aerial hidden in the trees. An information board shows what it looked like.

View from the old quarry on Cefn Onn

Continue W on the track and descend from the ridge after 350 metres to come out at a crossroads by the **Maenllwyd Inn**. Take the road going NE to the right of the inn for 400 metres, keeping to the right where a road forks off to the left. Where the road turns left towards Penhow Farm after a further 450 metres, turn right to enter the forest through an opening in the trees at SN 208 871 and take the forest track going ENE past old lead mines for 400 metres, shortly entering **Coed Cefn-pwll-du**. ▸ There are a number of forest tracks, but the route follows the main wide track as it swings N then W and N again, gradually descending to reach a minor road where the forest ends after 1.9km at ST 211 888.

For accommodation in Draethen (800 metres off-route), take the track that forks right at ST 212 873.

Cross the road and head NNE down a lane towards **Afon Rhymni** for 300 metres, passing houses on the right. At the end of the lane turn left and continue for 100 metres then turn right over the bridge and go straight ahead for 100 metres to the A468. Turn right and continue for 100 metres to the point where a road leads up past the **church** on the left.

This is **Machen**, the end of the stage. There are not many facilities here, but there is a bus service to Caerphilly and beyond (turn left instead of right along the A468 and continue for 150 metres to a bus stop past the school). There is also a convenience store on a road to the left past the church.

47

STAGE 2
Machen to Pontypool

Start	A468 near St John's Church, Machen (ST 212 892)
Finish	Pontypool Park entrance gates (SO 291 005)
Distance	18.5km (11½ miles)
Total ascent	830m (2720ft)
Total descent	770m (2520ft)
Time	5¾–6¾hr
Maps	OS Explorer 152; OS Landranger 171
Refreshments	Pubs and small shops in Crosskeys and Risca
Public transport	Bus service to Caerphilly from Machen; train service to Cardiff and Abergavenny from Pontypool
Accommodation	Crosskeys 5km; Henllys 8km (+1.5km); Pontypool (+1–3km)

This stage offers the first real taste of mountain scenery, starting with a steep climb. More ridge walking gives views to the Severn Estuary and the mining villages around Ebbw Vale. Some careful navigation is needed on the descent from Twmbarlwm to the road leading to Pontypool.

For anyone setting off from an earlier starting point, a bench beside the church makes a peaceful resting place.

Starting from the A468 at the bottom of Church Street in **Machen**, walk N for 150 metres to St John's Church. ◄ Just past the church, where the road bears left, take the smaller road on the right, passing a house on the left, then go over a footbridge leading into woodland. This is part of the Rhymney Valley Ridgeway Walk. About 150 metres from the footbridge, cross over a track and bear right up the main path leading E diagonally up the hillside – being careful not to get confused by paths that have been developed by mountain bikers.

It is fairly steep at first but gentler further on and there are not many views until you reach gaps in the trees further up. Continue in a fairly straight line for 1.2km, crossing a stile at the end of the forest. Here, the views open up and a steep grassy slope to the left leads to the summit of Mynydd Machen. Our route, however, takes a somewhat easier way

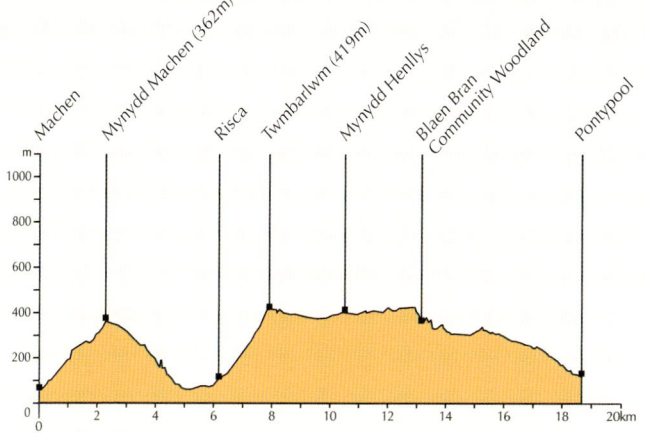

by continuing along the reasonably level path E then NE around the hillside for 200 metres then turning left to climb WNW up a track for 400 metres to the **summit** trig point, which is Checkpoint 3 at 362m (1192ft). This route gives better views of the valley overlooking Pontymister to the E which are lost at the summit.

Mynydd Machen is the highest point so far, giving a taste of the higher mountains to come. Next is the Iron Age hill fort of Twmbarlwm, E of Ebbw Vale and

Old spoil heap seen from Mynydd Machen

clearly visible ahead. Another interesting feature lies on the hilltop to the west, looking like the burial mound of a huge giant. It is actually a massive spoil heap, now gradually becoming grassed over.

There is some confusion as to what constitutes a mountain. It is often defined as being a hill that stands more than 2000ft (610m) above sea level; however, in areas where there are few of these, 1000ft (305m) often qualifies. The Welsh word *mynydd* means mountain, and there are

Map continues on page 55

many hills named as Mynydd, even ones that are less than 1000ft high. These names relate more to their appearance than actual height.

Continue NNW from the summit along a good track, passing a mast on the right. After 400 metres head W towards the spoil heap, then bear right after 300 metres to descend diagonally down the hillside for a further 450 metres to reach a minor road. Turn right along the road and continue for 150 metres, looking out for a footpath sign to the left, where the route enters a field east of a farmhouse. ▶

OS maps show the right of way through the farm, but this has been diverted.

Follow the left-hand edge of the field N for about 70 metres, then turn ENE and continue down the field for 100 metres, looking out for a gate leading into woodland. Go through the gate and follow the track E for 250 metres, heading diagonally down the hillside to reach a wide forest track. Go left along the track for about 10 metres then turn sharp right down the path (which is easy to miss) that continues E down the hillside for 150 metres until it meets a minor road. The path exits the forest onto the access road to a large house.

Go right (E) along the access road for 30 metres to join the road that zigzags down the hillside. Turn left and go downhill for 30 metres to reach a path heading off to the left; take this and skirt around the western edge of the forest for 170 metres to meet the road again. Cross the road and take the path going E for 40 metres before turning N and continuing for 100 metres to join the road again. This time follow the road NE, then E as it runs parallel to the main A467 before turning N through an underpass after 150 metres. This leads to a bridge over Afon Ebbw and into **Crosskeys** along Blackvein Road.

Crosskeys has a hotel near the railway station and there are pubs in both Crosskeys itself and in Risca, as well as small shops. There are also good transport services along the valley, with a regular commuter train service to Cardiff, allowing accommodation there to be used instead.

Cross over New Park Road and continue NE to the end of Blackvein Road in a further 150 metres. Bear right along the B4591 for 70 metres, then take the first turning left, going

NE up the hillside. Continue for 300 metres, following signs for the canal as you go uphill and over the railway line to join the towpath of the Monmouthshire and Brecon Canal. Turn right and follow the towpath for 400 metres to its end.

Turn left up the road, which goes fairly steeply uphill for 800 metres, first N then NNE. Where the road meets a wide track, keep straight ahead to go up a steep track for 600 metres through woodland to the head of the pass at **Pegwn-y-bwlch**, crossing a wide forest track on the way.

> A number of forest tracks converge at **Pegwn-y-bwlch**, and the Cwmcarn Forest Drive gives access to the nearby car park. This is a very pleasant resting spot, with views back towards Risca and the nearby hills, as well as across the forested hills to the north. There is a stone plinth with a bronze sculpture of a raven emerging from under a book, this being the route of the Raven Walk.

From the pass, turn sharp right and continue up the steep open hillside for 500 metres, heading SE to the summit of **Twmbarlwm**. The summit is not seen immediately because of the rounded hillside, the first thing to come into view being the trig point just beyond the outer fortification ditch. The main mound is 200 metres E of the trig point, with a smaller, well-preserved circular ditch surrounding it. This fine viewpoint, with wide-ranging views, is Checkpoint 4 at 419m (1374ft).

> At the summit of Twmbarlwm there is a **hillfort** that is believed to have been built by the Silures, a Celtic tribe of the Iron Age. There is also the possibility that it was used as a Roman signal station. A Norman motte-and-bailey castle was then located at the eastern side, with a ditch and large mound to defend the level approach from that direction. It was restored in 1984 and is a scheduled ancient monument.

From Twmbarlwm continue NNE on a delightful ridge walk along **Mynydd Henllys**. It is fairly level on gentle grassy paths, making for easy walking and enabling a good pace to be maintained. ◄ Those seeking accommodation in Henllys should bear right at ST 253 940 after 1.7km where a track leads down to a minor road into the village (1.7km);

Mountain ponies often graze here and occasionally long-horned highland cattle.

*The attractive towpath alongside the Monmouth and Brecon Canal
(photo: Oliver Wicks)*

otherwise continue along the main ridge for a further 1.3km. The main ridge track then swings N to the flat-topped Mynydd Maen, but the Cambrian Way continues NNE along the hillside, roughly following the contour for 1km to around ST 263 958. Here the clear path starts to deviate to the left of the path marked on maps, which is very indistinct.

Continue to maintain your height on the hill for another 650 metres, gradually passing scrub on your right and swinging N to reach electricity pylons. The path then starts to descend, swinging round to the right where it becomes steeper and almost doubles back on itself as it meets the boundary fence of the woodland after 500 metres. Turn sharp left along the boundary track, heading around the hillside for 700 metres, initially going NNE before swinging round WNW, then N and NW. The track then turns sharp right at ST 264 973, and just past the bend is a metal kissing gate on the right with a sign for Blaen Bran Community Woodland.

To avoid the kissing gate
The kissing gate is very tight, as is the exit gate, making it difficult to squeeze through with a large rucksack. To avoid these, you could continue along the rougher track by the common boundary. The tracks rejoin after 1.6km.

On entering the Woodland Walk, keep to the higher track, which runs parallel to and about 200 metres S of the common boundary. ◀ After 1.2km, exit via another kissing gate and continue NE for 400 metres, at which point the boundary track is rejoined. Continue NE, following close to the mountain road for a further 1.2km as it swings NNE. There are wide grass verges and footpaths beside the road, which is generally quiet anyway.

This track is evenly surfaced, and there are better views of the Blaen Bran reservoirs as well as some wooden sculptures.

Where the road turns left, take the smaller Prescoch Lane that goes to the right. The building on the corner was the Lamb Inn, but this closed in 2014 and like many rural pubs its future is uncertain. Follow the lane for 250 metres, heading E then swinging N. The lane then turns right and sharp left again before going in a straight line NNE for 1km towards Pontypool. There are footpaths that avoid some road walking, but these are often overgrown.

After passing some houses on the right and descending steeply downhill, the lane does a zigzag left and right then joins Cwmynyscoy Road close to a large roundabout on the right. Go across the round-about, where the road becomes Rockhill Road, then go underneath the flyover of the **A472** and straight on for 150 metres to the Pontymoile entrance into Pontypool Park, where this section ends.

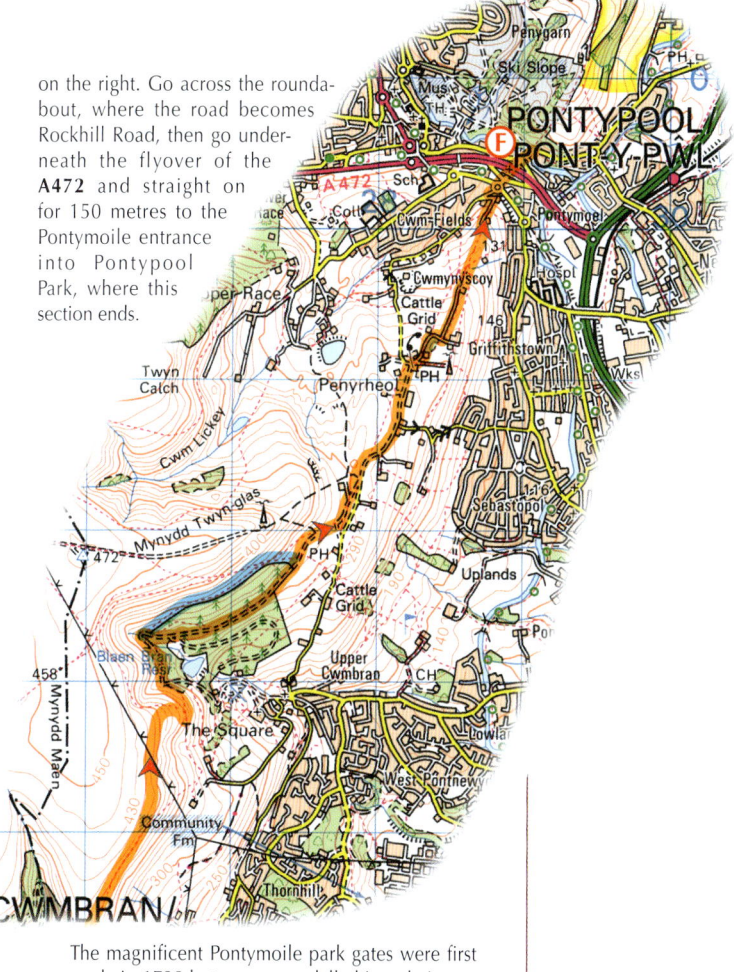

The magnificent Pontymoile park gates were first made in 1720 but were remodelled into their present form in 1835. They are now grade II listed and known as **The Sally Gates**. Sally was the nickname of the Duchess of Marlborough at that time.

Pontypool offers a few B&Bs, shops, pubs, takeaways and restaurants. The commuter rail service here also makes it possible to use accommodation in Cardiff or Abergavenny.

STAGE 3
Pontypool to Abergavenny

Start	Pontypool Park entrance gates (SO 291 005)
Finish	Abergavenny war memorial, Frogmore St (SO 297 145)
Distance	20km (12¼ miles)
Total ascent	580m (1890ft)
Total descent	640m (2080ft)
Time	5–6¼hr
Maps	OS Explorer OL 13; OS Landranger 171 and 161
Refreshments	None before Abergavenny
Public transport	Train service to Cardiff and North Wales from Pontypool and Abergavenny; bus services from Pontypool and Abergavenny
Accommodation	Abergavenny

A fine walk starting at the historic Pontypool Park with a climb under a ski run, past a shell grotto to a folly with magnificent ridge views. Somewhat more difficult boggy tracks lead into the Brecon Beacons National Park, and the route passes the grave of the legendary show-jumping horse Foxhunter. There are superb views beyond the Blorenge mountain-top and a very steep descent which needs careful navigation. An interesting descent under the Monmouthshire and Brecon Canal leads to the stage end at Abergavenny.

Starting out from the Pontymoile gates to **Pontypool** Park, enter the park along the wide path between lawns lined with woodland on both sides, heading WNW for 350 metres. Bear right, heading ENE uphill towards the **dry ski slope** and passing under a subway after 300 metres. Continue beyond the underpass for 250 metres then bear right off the main track towards a circular stone building 120 metres ahead on a track with trees on either side. This is the Grade II-listed Shell Grotto. ◄ Beyond the grotto take the path ENE down the hillside for 80 metres to join the main track leading up the ridge.

Unfortunately, the grotto is currently open on very few occasions, so is usually only visible from outside.

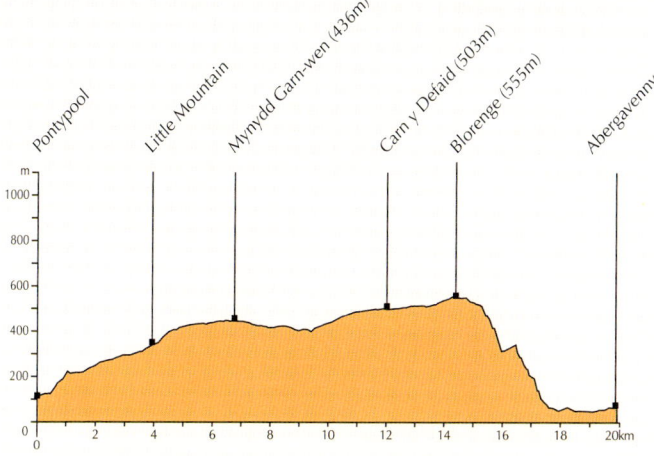

Follow the track N, climbing steadily upwards for 1.4km with a tower coming into view ahead. This is near a war memorial and is known as The Folly or Watchtower.

The **Folly** was originally built around 1765 as an observatory on the site of a Roman watchtower. It was demolished in 1940 to prevent its use as a landmark for enemy bombers. In the 1990s it was rebuilt and officially reopened in 1994. As its name suggests, it commands good views over the local area.

Continue along the track as it curves round NW and dips slightly to reach an old Roman road called Folly Lane after 350 metres. Cross the lane and go up a small rise where there is a junction of tracks. Take the track going WNW, skirting around the left of the hill called **Little Mountain** that is straight ahead. The track curves round NW then NNW, climbing steadily upwards for 650 metres before turning more sharply NNE towards a farm.

Take a rutted sunken track going N with trees on either side. This is fairly steep at first but soon becomes steadier as it follows the boundary wall, heading in a northerly direction up the ridge for 1km. The boundary wall ends at a junction of tracks; continue N up the ridge for 200 metres to the trig point on **Mynydd Garn-wen**. From there continue N for 550 metres to reach the actual summit at 436m (1430ft) with

Map continues
on page 61

wide distant views all around – although the flat top does not give views down into the valleys. ▶

After dropping gently N from summit for 300 metres, a junction of several paths and tracks is reached with some field boundaries to both left and right. Go past the wall on the right and then head directly N towards the highest point of the reasonably flat moor, gradually parting company with the boundary wall to the right. The paths are not clearly defined here, but it is generally possible to pick up on some for most of the way. The exact route does not matter as this is just cutting off a corner to rejoin the main track after 1.2km at around SO 289 063 on **Mynydd Garnclochdy**. (It is possible to follow clearer tracks around the eastern edge of the common which give better views.)

After joining the track, head NW for 800 metres, descending gently to a dip in the ridge. ▶ Avoid taking any of the paths to the right but keep heading NW, staying about 50–100 metres from the boundary for 1.4km to join a minor road at SO 275 076.

Follow the road NW for 300 metres as it swings round W, looking out for a small path up the hillside on the right that doubles back NE. Take the path and follow it for 200 metres as it swings N and joins a wider track. Keep heading upwards in a northerly direction for 2.2km to the summit of **Carn y Defaid** ('cairn of the sheep') at 503m (1650ft). The actual track is at variance with maps but there are marker posts most of the way. The terrain here is considerably different from the previous grassy common, with lots of rocks and stones among the heather, requiring care to avoid tripping and hence the going is slower.

Beyond the summit, twin aerial masts come into sight ahead, and the aim is to reach the road just to the right of these 1km ahead, going NW along a well-trodden path. At the road, turn left for a very short way to the **car park** for visitors to Foxhunter's Grave. ▶ Head N from the car park for 200 metres to where a plaque notes his achievements.

Bear right near the grave and head NE to join the main path to Blorenge. This may involve walking through heather but it is only for 70 metres. Follow the path for 1.1km NNE as it heads steadily upwards to the trig point and cairn on the summit of **Blorenge** at 559m (1833ft), which is Checkpoint 5. ▶ Continue NE then E for 800 metres to reach a magnificent viewpoint at the steep edge of the mountain, SO 278 122.

The walking all along this ridge is easy, over the grassy common with good paths and pleasant scenery.

A track turns off to the right at SO 280 068, leading to a road that reaches the Goose and Cuckoo Inn (1.3km) down the hillside.

Foxhunter was a famous showjumper, gaining Britain's only gold medal in the 1952 Olympic Games.

The summit itself can be rather disappointing as there are only distant views from this mound on a flat mountain-top. The best views lie ahead.

Heading out to the summit of Blorenge (photo: Oliver Wicks)

There are spectacular bird's-eye **views** over the town of Abergavenny and across to Sugar Loaf and the Black Mountains, giving a taste of what's to come in the next two sections of the walk. There is also a fine view of the Skirrid, west of Abergavenny, with its distinctive shape – although this is not on the route.

A few paths lead down from Blorenge, but the direct one should be avoided as it is very steep, making it difficult with a heavy pack. It also causes erosion.

Gentler descent of Blorenge

This adds about 1.9km of extra walking, albeit less taxing.

◄ Instead of turning E down the steep slope at SO 277 122, continue S along the path for 1km to where it meets a minor road by a cattle grid at SO 278 112. Take the track that forks left from the road, going ENE for 600 metres to reach the **Punchbowl**. Head NNW down to the lake for 250 metres, then NNE along the hillside for 400 metres to SO 284 120. Then follow the path heading NW and swinging N along the hillside for 800 metres to rejoin the main route at SO 284 123.

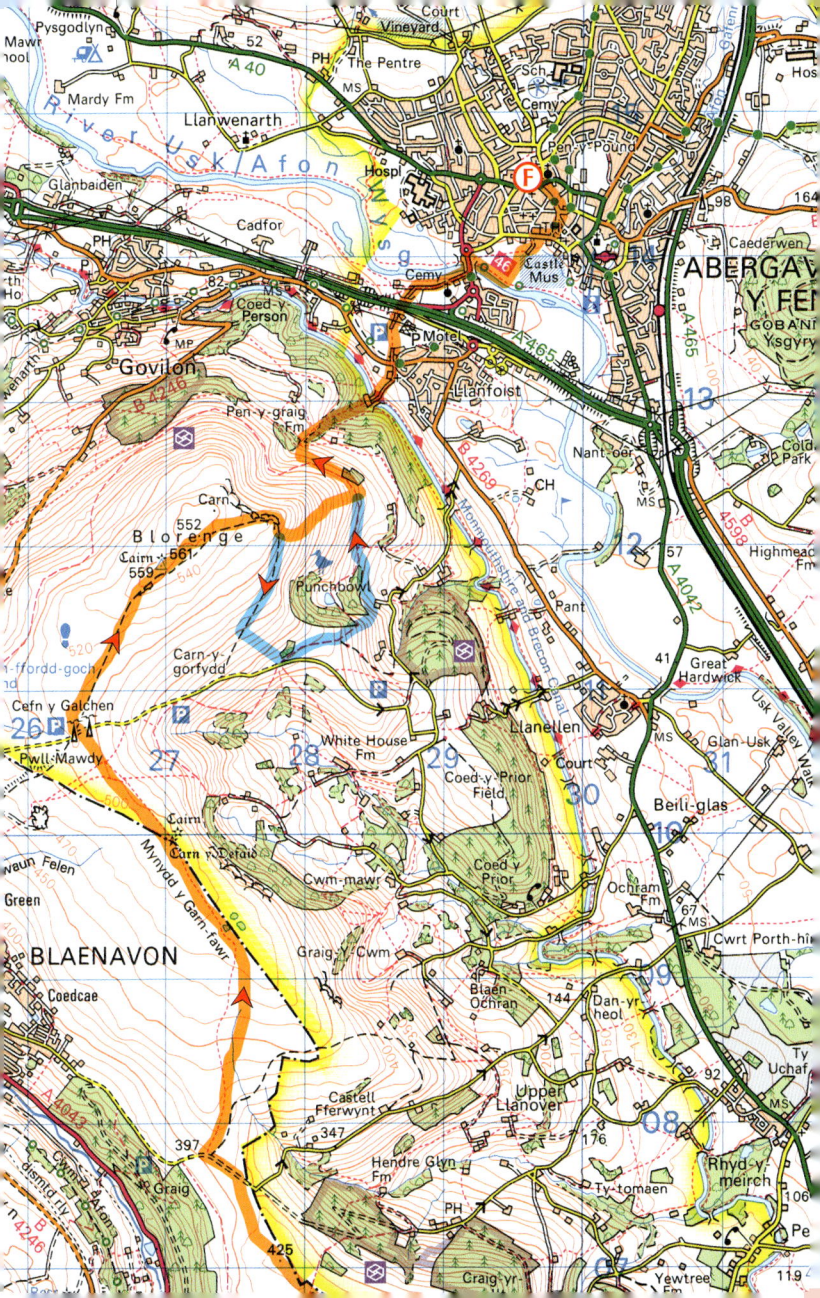

Abergavenny from Blorenge

It is possible to reach the valley of Cwm Craf directly from the wall by heading N but the way is generally thick with bracken.

The recommended route (if you do not opt for the gentler descent) is to take the path from SO 277 122 on the eastern edge of the mountain, following it as it swings S for 200 metres. Past a craggy area, turn ESE down the mountainside where the slope is less steep. The path isn't very clear, but it swings steadily round to the left for 300 metres to head NE towards the corner of a boundary wall. ◄

Continue NE for 100 metres, moving away from the wall to join a clear track, then head ENE for 250 metres to meet a right of way at SO 284 124 by the common boundary. ◄ Turn left and follow this track as it heads NNW then WNW on the level for 500 metres to a stile at Cwm Craf (SO 281 128) with several signs – this is where the gentler descent rejoins. Cross the stile and turn right down the hillside, heading NNE for 100 metres, then the track swings ENE down a steep narrow valley, entering woodland to reach the tunnel under the **canal** after a further 450 metres.

This is where the gentler descent rejoins the main route.

A **tunnel** goes under the Monmouthshire and Brecon Canal, and the interesting feature is that it not only goes under the canal but also under the house that's next to the canal. The tunnel is quite dark and steep, but light can be seen at the other end.

Follow the track through the tunnel where it becomes Church Lane, heading NNE into **Llanfoist** to reach the B4246 after 350 metres. Cross the B4246 and continue N for 400 metres and stay on the lane as it goes underneath the main A465 road. Continue NNE for 100 metres to the end of the lane and turn right along a minor road which goes past Llanfoist's **cemetery**, reaching the main gates after 150 metres.

Continue for 100 metres to the end of the road and turn left over the Usk Bridge. Immediately after crossing the river, turn right along the riverbank path and continue for 300 metres, then turn left on the path to reach the **castle** after a further 350 metres. ▶ From the castle, join Tudor Street just to the N and go left, soon turning right along Baker Street to its end in 150 metres. Turn left along Frogmore Street and follow this to its end where it meets the main A40 road at Pen-y-Pound by the war memorial near **Abergavenny** town centre after 400 metres.

Abergavenny has all the facilities of a busy market town, but beware that it can be especially busy during the Food Festival in mid September and during cycling festivals in June and July, making accommodation difficult to find.

Abergavenny Castle, built by the Normans around 1078, is now in ruins but has a museum with free admission.

Blorenge from Abergavenny

STAGE 4
Abergavenny to Capel-y-ffin

Start	Abergavenny war memorial, Frogmore St (SO 297 145)
Finish	Capel-y-ffin chapel (SO 255 315)
Distance	21.5km (13¼ miles)
Total ascent	1130m (3700ft)
Total descent	870m (2850ft)
Time	6¼–8hr
Maps	OS Explorer OL 13; OS Landranger 161
Refreshments	Llanthony (detour), Grange Trekking Centre, Capel-y-ffin
Public transport	Train and bus services from Abergavenny
Accommodation	Llanthony 14.5km (+2.5km); Grange Trekking Centre, Capel-y-ffin

The Cambrian Way takes a long loop round to Crickhowell and this section of the loop ends at Capel-y-ffin ('chapel of the border') in the heart of the Black Mountains. Some initial road walking gives way to tracks leading up to Sugar Loaf mountain, which involves a fairly steep climb and descent. The route goes down to Forest Coal Pit and then rises on paths through woodland to a series of small summits and a superb ridge, which narrows before dropping steeply to the valley.

Starting from the war memorial at **Abergavenny**, facing the chapel across the A40 road, head N for 300 metres along Pen-y-Pound Road past the right of the chapel. Turn left into Avenue Road and go W then NW for 900 metres to where it joins Chapel Lane and Pentre Road. ◄ Climb steadily as the road heads N. Continue for 300 metres, looking out for a footpath that bears off across fields to the left, heading NW; follow this path for 450 metres, heading for a stile at the top left corner near Home Farm.

The next turning to the right is Chain Road, leading to Smithy's Bunkhouse in Pantygelli (3.4km).

Take the minor road and continue NW for 450 metres, ignoring the road that turns right, and head round the left side of the ridge ahead. Bear right on a track that enters woodland at SO 284 162 and take a steady ascent NNW diagonally up

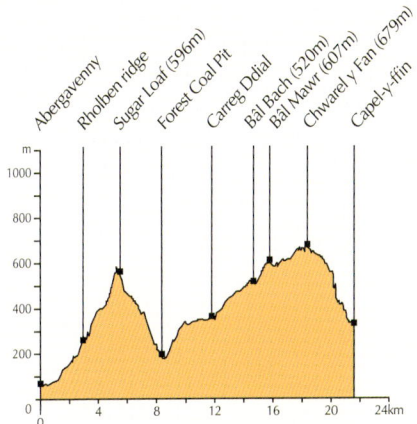

Abergavenny
Rholben ridge
Sugar Loaf (596m)
Forest Coal Pit
Carreg Ddial
Bâl Bach (520m)
Bâl Mawr (607m)
Chwarel y Fan (679m)
Capel-y-ffin
m
1000
800
600
400
200
0
0
4
8
12
16
20
24km

the **Rholben ridge** with St Mary's Vale below on the left. After 800 metres the trees thin out on the right and the track starts to come out onto the open hillside, although there are still a number of trees around.

The path gradually steepens as it makes its way onto the top of the ridge and along a grassy track through bracken,

Ascending Sugar Loaf

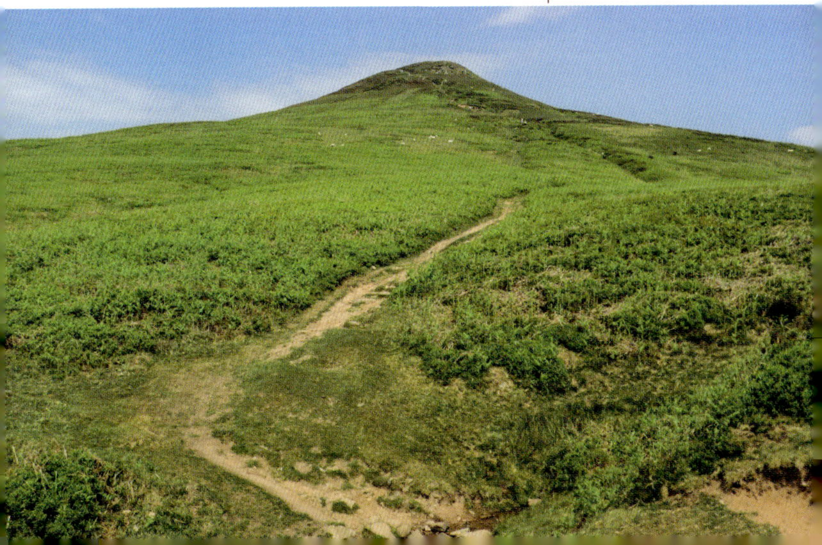

West of the summit are good views into the valley and across to Pen Allt-mawr and Pen Cerrig-calch, which are visited on the next stage.

and there are fine views back over Abergavenny and Blorenge, with the distinctive shape of Sugar Loaf ahead. Continue NNE up the ridge along the grassy track through bracken for 1.4km, then cross a small stream and continue for a further 650 metres of ascent to the summit. The climbing gets steeper over small crags near the top of the summit ridge then levels out towards the trig point of **Sugar Loaf**, which is Checkpoint 6 at 596m (1955ft). ◀

From the summit, go back E along the ridge and take the path leading down to the left, heading ENE as it drops from the summit, gradually turning NE and meeting up with a boundary formed by the remnants of a wall and a fence after 500 metres. Follow the boundary for 700 metres as it descends the ridge with a fine view of Skirrid to the right. The boundary then curves around to the right, but the path continues NE, joining another boundary going N after 500 metres. Follow this for 200 metres until this boundary also swings right and the path heads NNE for 250 metres over open ground towards trees. Keep left of the trees, heading N for a further 250 metres before bearing right down the hill for 150 metres to meet a minor road.

Turn left along the road and head NW for 100 metres, then turn right down a lane past the former post office in **Forest Coal Pit**.

> The name the hamlet of **Forest Coal Pit** is not derived from coal but from the charcoal that was used before coal for smelting iron. The local area produced this 'coal' for the ironworks at Glangrwyney when it was difficult to transport from further afield. There are remains of original hearths in the valley.

This path gets very boggy in wet weather, in which case it is better to go around W on the road and rejoin the route at Pontyspig Farm.

After a further 100 metres the lane reaches a T-junction with a building ahead; go over the stile just to the left of this and take the footpath running diagonally NW across the field and into the valley, running close to woodland on the right. ◀ After 300 metres, cross a stream via a footbridge at the bottom and continue NW on the path up the hillside, reaching the road at Pontyspig Farm (SO 285 210) after 150 metres.

Turn right (NE) along the road and you'll come to a junction of five roads after 100 metres. Take the lane opposite, which climbs steeply NE then N for 500 metres and is lined with trees. Continue up the lane, passing Fferm Newydd and ignoring any lanes to left or right, heading NNE uphill for 750 metres. The slope eases off as the top of the ridge is reached and the walking becomes a lot easier for the next 700 metres. The lane then becomes a track which leads to Carreg Ddial ('revenge stone') at SO 283 242 after 1.5km, near the start of some woodland on the right.

Map continues on page 68

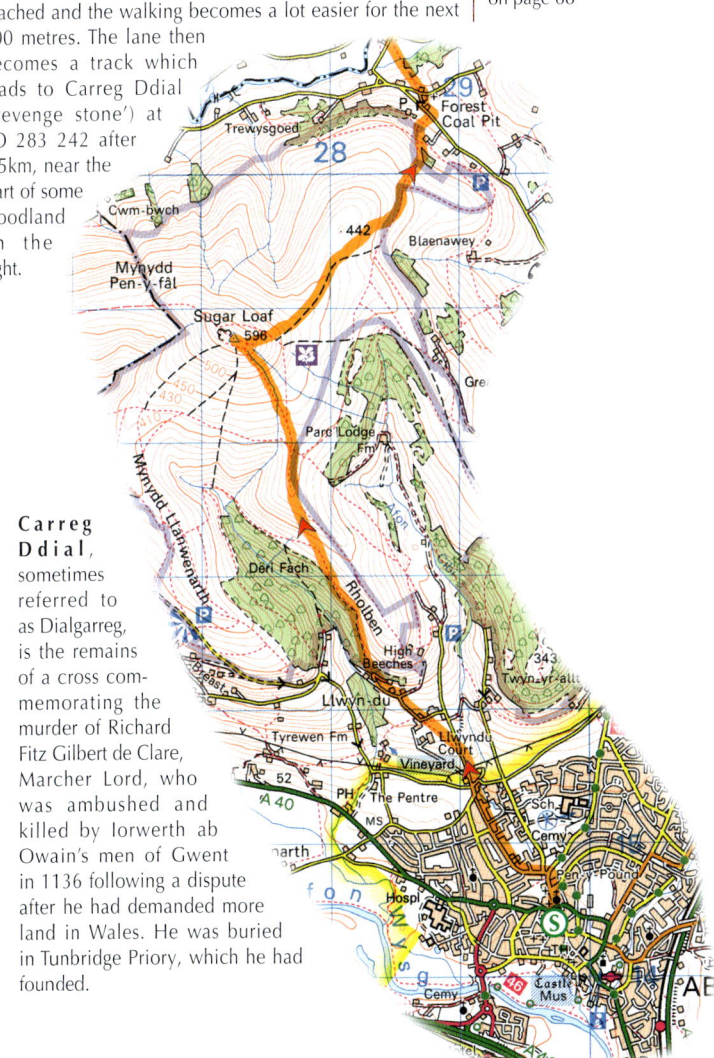

Carreg Ddial, sometimes referred to as Dialgarreg, is the remains of a cross commemorating the murder of Richard Fitz Gilbert de Clare, Marcher Lord, who was ambushed and killed by Iorwerth ab Owain's men of Gwent in 1136 following a dispute after he had demanded more land in Wales. He was buried in Tunbridge Priory, which he had founded.

Map continues
on page 69

The ridge setting provides constantly improving views: Offa's Dyke Path runs along the ridge to the east across the beautiful Vale of Ewyas, with Sugar Loaf back to the south, and the central ridge of the Black Mountains with its forested slopes to the west. (The Cambrian Way takes the ridge further west, rather than this one, on its route to Crickhowell.)

Continue N along the ridge for 1.4km to **Garn Wen** with its impressive cairn, then for another 1.5km to **Bâl Bach**.

For accommodation in Llanthony

From Bâl Bach a path NE leads down into **Llanthony** with its priory and accommodation at the Half Moon Inn (2.5km). From Llanthony it is possible to follow the road for 5.5km to Capel-y-ffin. No checkpoints will be missed, although the highest point of the ridge will have been omitted. The route takes a path going WNW for 150 metres to join a minor road then takes the right fork at SO 286 279 after a further 150 metres to follow a quiet road and cycle track on the east side of Afon Honddu crossing back over the river at Chapel Farm next

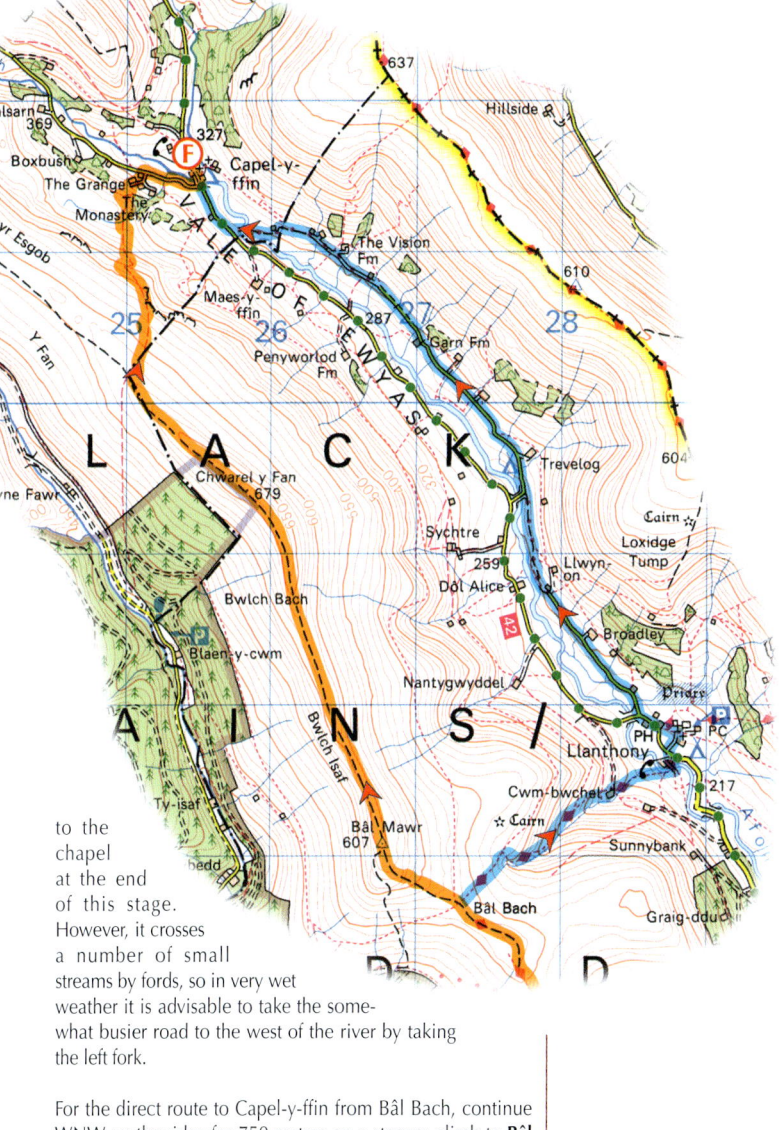

to the
chapel
at the end
of this stage.
However, it crosses
a number of small
streams by fords, so in very wet
weather it is advisable to take the somewhat busier road to the west of the river by taking
the left fork.

For the direct route to Capel-y-ffin from Bâl Bach, continue
WNW up the ridge for 750 metres on a steeper climb to **Bâl
Mawr** with its trig point at 607m (1991ft) – not quite the

2000ft required to be a true mountain but still a very good viewpoint to look back on the route so far. Continue northwards along the ridge for 2.5km to **Chwarel y Fan** ('quarry of the peak'), a true mountain at 679m (2228ft).

As its name suggests, **Chwarel y Fan** is the site of an old quarry. It doesn't have a real feeling of being a mountain, as the summit is just a small pile of stones on the highest point of the long ridge, but it does give a fine view across to the Grwyne Reservoir to the northeast, wide views of the Black Mountains all around, and a good perspective of Capel-y-ffin below.

The Grange offers B&B, meals, camping and glamping pods. There is a monastery 100 metres to the right, past the stables.

Continue NE along the ridge and look out for a large stone known as the Blacksmith's Anvil after 1.1km, where a path bears right, going N down towards Capel-y-ffin. It is quite steep in places as it runs diagonally down the hillside, with zigzags in the steepest sections. At the bottom, after 1.7km, is the Grange Trekking Centre behind some trees. ◀

Continue NE along the Grange's access road for 150 metres to its end. Turn right along a minor road leading down to the hamlet of **Capel-y-ffin**, 400 metres ahead. Turn left when you meet the road that runs from the Vale of Ewyas to Hay-on-Wye over the Gospel Pass. A tiny **chapel** lies about 70 metres N on the right-hand side of the road; this is Checkpoint 7 which, despite being at the bottom of the valley, is still 327m (1040ft) above sea level.

The tiny chapel at Capel-y-ffin marks the stage end

STAGE 5
Capel-y-ffin to Crickhowell

Start	Capel-y-ffin chapel (SO 255 315)
Finish	Bear Hotel, High Street, Crickhowell (SO 218 184)
Distance	26.5km (16½ miles)
Total ascent	950m (3110ft)
Total descent	1180m (3860ft)
Time	7–9hr
Maps	OS Explorer OL 13; OS Landranger 161
Refreshments	None close to route before Crickhowell
Public transport	Bus services to Abergavenny and Brecon from Crickhowell
Accommodation	Pengenffordd 10km (+5km); Crickhowell and Llangattock; Llangattock Mountain Bunkhouse 26.5km (+2km)

This remainder of the loop to Crickhowell features some of the finest ridges in the Black Mountains, linking a series of peaks with some short steep climbs. At Waun Fach the highest point in the Black Mountains is reached. The walking is nearly all off-road and is quite muddy in places. The views are spectacular.

Starting from the chapel in **Capel-y-ffin**, follow the road NNW for 200 metres and then take the footpath bearing left uphill from the corner of the field by a farm access road, heading NW. After 300 metres pass between some buildings and following the path for a further 200 metres as it emerges from trees and crosses the common boundary to meet another path.

Turn sharp right along this path and continue for 50 metres, then bear left along a path that goes obliquely N up the steep hillside. After 250 metres the path turns sharply left (SW); stay on it as it continues in this direction for 150 metres and then swings sharp right again as it heads N towards the top of the ridge. After 100 metres, by a cairn built on a flat rock, the slope starts to become less steep. ▶

The cairn makes a fine rest stop with views back to Capel-y-ffin and down the Vale of Ewyas.

71

The route to Twmpa provides a pleasing view of the Vale of Ewyas

Three Rivers
Pennant
419
Flynn
549
Gospel Pass
542
Rhiw Wen
690
Lord Hereford's Knob or Twmpa
385
Blaenau-isaf
327
Parc
34
Rhiw y Fan
Darren Lwyd
Pen Rhos Dirion
713
399
Tumulus
33
Rhos Dirion
Blaen-bwch
Y Das
Standing Stone
Nant Bwch
Mynydd Bychan
32
702
Twyn Talycefn
Talsarn
369
Grwyne Fawr
Boxbush
The G
Pen y Manllwyn
31
Tarren yr Esgob
Twyn Mawr
Map continues on page 74
Grwyne Fawr Reservoir
Grib
M

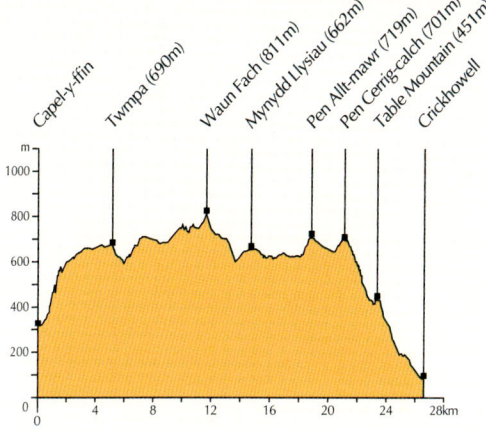

Capel-y-ffin — Twmpa (690m) — Waun Fach (811m) — Mynydd Llysiau (662m) — Pen Allt-mawr (719m) — Pen Cerrig-calch (701m) — Table Mountain (451m) — Crickhowell

Follow the path along the ridge for 2km. The walking becomes easier and the path swings NE then NNE to reach another cairn. From here continue NW for 1.7km towards the summit of Twmpa. Initially the ridge offers fine views across the Gospel Pass to Hay Bluff, but as the ridge gets broader the path moves away from the edge so views into the valley are mostly lost. However, the walking is still easy along the heather-covered ridge for the rest of the way to **Twmpa** ('hump') or Lord Hereford's Knob, which is Checkpoint 8 at 690m (2263ft) and a fine vantage point.

Twmpa offers stunning **views**. In the far distance to the west is the distinctive shape of Pen y Fan, looking temptingly close, but it's still two days' walk away along the circuitous route taken by the Cambrian Way. The extra distance, though, is more than compensated for by the magnificent scenery of the Black Mountains.

From Twmpa, follow the well-trodden path SW along the ridge for 1km as it gradually swings S towards **Rhiw y Fan**. The initial descent is quite steep with some scrambling in places, but it soon becomes easier. ▶ Bear right along the path

The steep cliffs here reveal the characteristic red sandstone that is prevalent in this area and even more so in the Brecon Beacons.

73

near the edge of the ridge, heading WSW then swinging SSW and WSW again for 1.2km to the summit of Rhos Dirion, which is higher than Twmpa at 713m (2339ft). This is the head of the Chwarel y Fan ridge that was left when turning down to Capel-y-ffin in Stage 4. Continue SW down a gentle slope for 1.1km to cross the main track from the valley of Grwyne Fawr; 130 metres later, at SO 202 323, the path splits and the main route bears left and starts to climb to S.

For accommodation in Pengenffordd

For accommodation in Pengenffordd, continue SW at the split, heading towards the western edge of the ridge for 300 metres and swinging S. Continue S for a further 700 metres with only a gentle descent, ignoring any paths to the right. The path starts to swing right, following the top of a long ridge to the W, with a gentle descent for 900 metres. Descend more

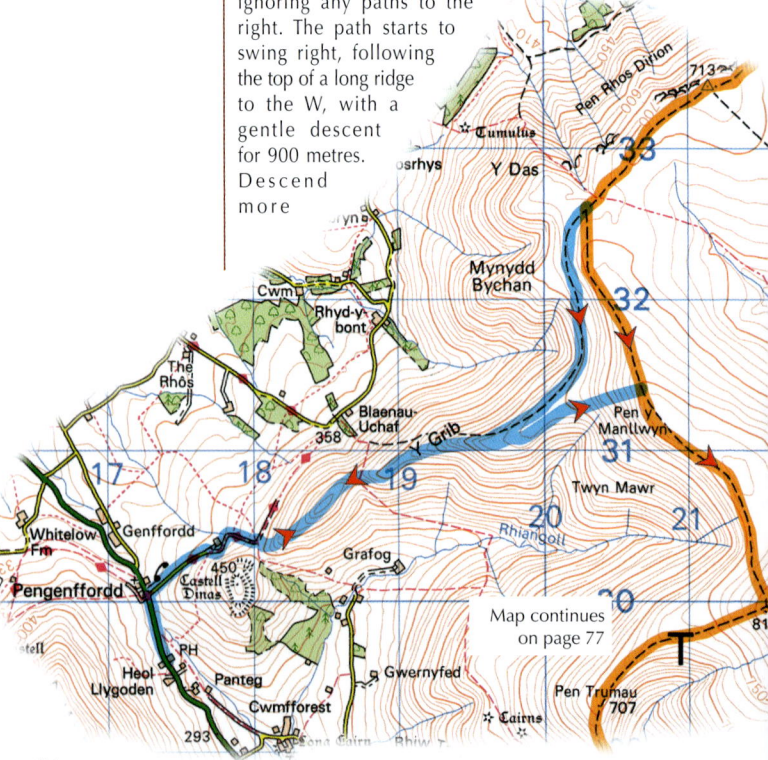

Map continues
on page 77

steeply to **Y Grib** ('the comb') and continue to follow the ridge for 1.8km as it descends WSW to the common boundary at SO 180 304. Join a track and then a minor road heading WSW for 950 metres to the hamlet of **Pengenffordd** on the A479 road. Turn left along the road and head S for 450 metres to The Dragon's Back Inn with B&B and bunkhouse.

Return to the main route by retracing your steps back past **Y Grib** to where the slope gets gentler after 3.2km at SO 196 310, then take the path forking right along the southern edge of the ridge and head straight up the hillside in an E direction to rejoin the main route at SO 207 314 after 1.1km at the northern end of Pen y Manllwyn.

Continuing on the main route from the split, the path is muddy and not very well defined, but the aim is to follow the ridge southwards. After 1.3km (at SO 207 314) the Pengenffordd alternative rejoins near **Pen y Manllwyn**. ▶ After another 1.7km the summit of **Waun Fach** ('small moor') is reached; this is Checkpoint 9 at 811m (2680ft) and the highest point in the Black Mountains. However, it is rather flat-topped.

Part of this western ridge has a lot of badly eroded peat, and the summit of **Waun Fach**, which originally had a trig point, became a large area of oozing peat bog with the concrete base of the trig point stranded in the middle. However, restoration work started in 2015, using heather brash (cut and harvested heather) to repair footpaths and help stabilise the surrounding area, resulting in great improvements.

From the summit of Waun Fach turn right, heading WSW to join the ridge towards **Pen Trumau**. ▶ Follow the ridge for 2.1km as it descends steadily, passing one cairn and swinging S to another and ignoring paths turning off to either side. Continue along the ridge for 850 metres as it swings SE to **Mynydd Llysiau** ('mountain of vegetables') with a cairn at its summit. Follow the fairly level ridge for another 600 metres, at which point it turns S and starts to descend.

There are fine views west from Pen y Manllwyn across the Rhiangoll Valley to Mynydd Troed ('foot mountain').

After 100 metres, fine views of Pen Allt-mawr, Pen Cerrig-calch and Sugar Loaf open up.

Continue for 1.4km over a few undulations to SO 213 261 where there is a rise to the left with two stones looking like headstones with inscriptions carved on them. They are, in fact, merely boundary marker stones. Stay on the path as it swings SW to the right of **Pen Twyn Glas** ('head of blue hillock'). ◄ The path then swings back S, heading up the reasonably steep hillside to reach the summit trig point of **Pen Allt-mawr** after a further 2km. This is Checkpoint 10 at 719m (2360ft).

A lesser path leads to the summit of Pen Twyn Glas for those wishing to visit.

There are magnificent **views** from here, particularly of Mynydd Troed to the northwest, which is almost completely encircled by beautiful valleys with patchworks of fields and hedgerows. To the south-east is Cwm Banw, and equally magnificent views towards Sugar Loaf and Skirrid, and to the north is the ridge that has already been traversed and other ridges that have not. One mountain that stands out is the table-topped Pen y Gadair Fawr ('head of the big chair'), which is only slightly lower than Waun Fach but more distinctive in shape.

Take care when setting off from the summit of Pen Allt-mawr as it is easy to make the mistake of taking the path straight ahead that leads along the wrong edge of the ridge. Instead, take the path going a little over to the left, heading

Wide-ranging views from Pen Cerrig-calch

SSE then S along the eastern edge of the mountain. It descends gently for 1.7km, swinging SE, but is rather stony so care is needed to avoid tripping. Continue SE for a further 700 metres on a steady ascent to the flat and stony summit and trig point of **Pen Cerrig-calch** at 701m (2300ft).

From the summit, continue SE then SSE down the mountainside for 1.9km. The stony terrain gives way to grassy slopes en route to **Table Mountain** below. Approach from the right-hand side with a bit of a scrambling to reach the summit after just 100 metres; the walk right round is only about 400 metres.

From this northern approach, very little ascent is required to reach the Iron Age fort of **Crug Hywel** from which Crickhowell takes its name. From the southern edge there are commanding views over the town and the Usk Valley. It is possible to

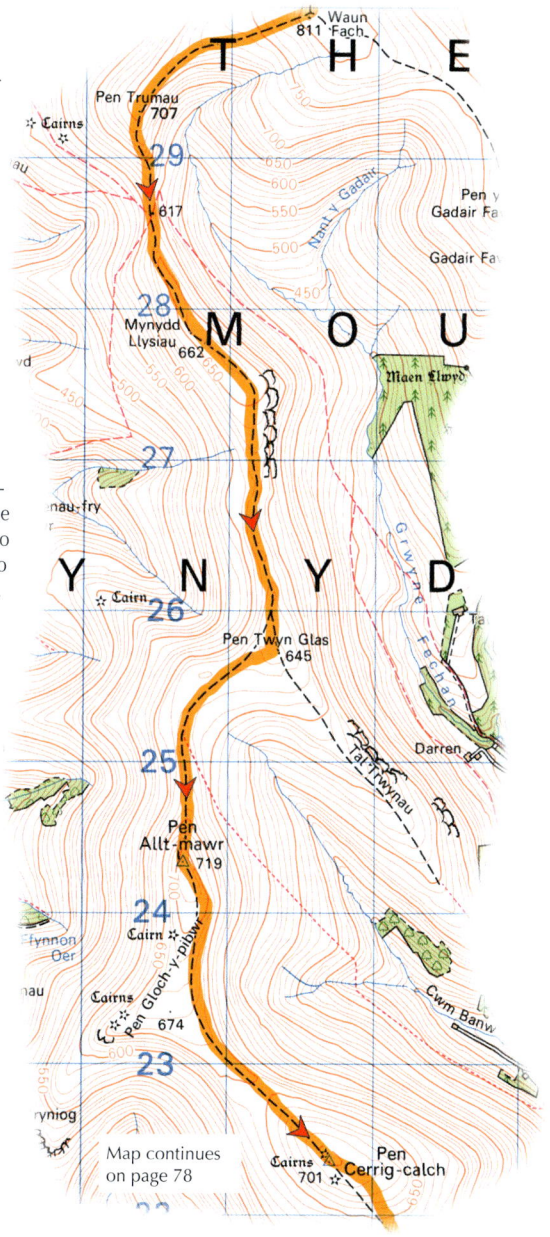

Map continues on page 78

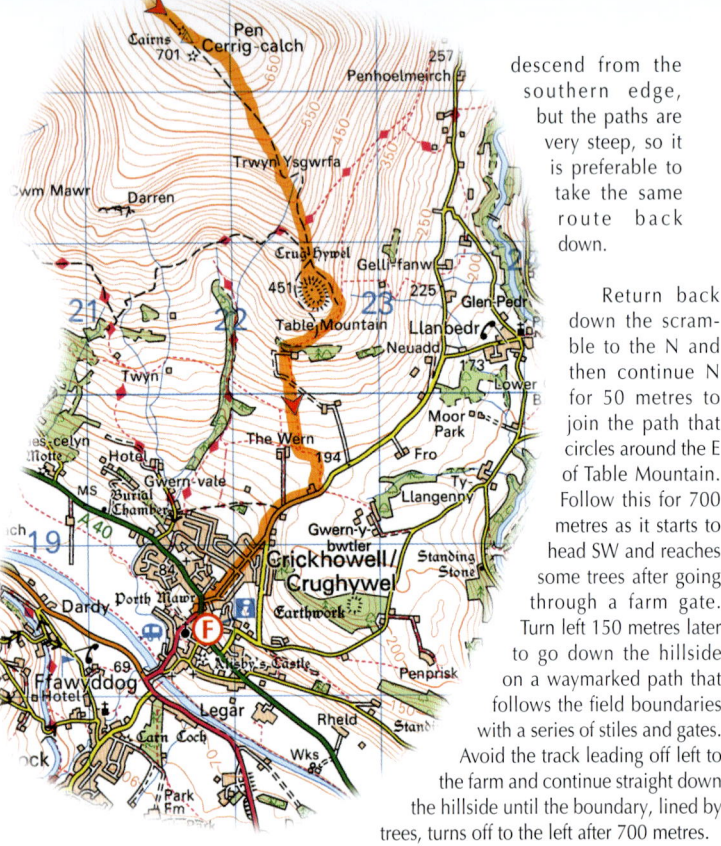

descend from the southern edge, but the paths are very steep, so it is preferable to take the same route back down.

Return back down the scramble to the N and then continue N for 50 metres to join the path that circles around the E of Table Mountain. Follow this for 700 metres as it starts to head SW and reaches some trees after going through a farm gate. Turn left 150 metres later to go down the hillside on a waymarked path that follows the field boundaries with a series of stiles and gates. Avoid the track leading off left to the farm and continue straight down the hillside until the boundary, lined by trees, turns off to the left after 700 metres.

The right of way follows the left-hand edge of the field, going E then S with more stiles. A path crosses the middle of the field but this is not a legal right of way. Pass the farm at the bottom and join the road after 350 metres. Turn right along the road, which goes WSW then curves round to the S. After 550 metres bear right at a fork in the road near to where it enters the built-up area. After a further 600 metres bear left to go S down the main A40 and follow this for 200 metres to the head of the High Street in **Crickhowell** which is the end-point of this section of the walk. The Bear Hotel, an old coaching inn dating back to 1432, stands here on the old stagecoach route from London to Holyhead and Ireland.

STAGE 6
Crickhowell to Storey Arms

Start	Bear Hotel, High Street, Crickhowell (SO 218 184)
Finish	Car park on A470 opposite Storey Arms (SN 982 203)
Distance	33.5km (21 miles)
Total ascent	1720m (5630ft)
Total descent	1370m (4490ft)
Time	9¾–12½hr
Maps	OS Explorer OL 13 and OL 12; OS Landranger 161 and 160
Refreshments	None after start until refreshment van in car park near Storey Arms
Public transport	Bus services to Abergavenny and Brecon from Crickhowell, to Merthyr Tydfil and Brecon from Storey Arms, and to Abergavenny and Brecon from Talybont-on-Usk
Accommodation	Danywenallt 16.5km (+7km); Talybont-on-Usk 16.5km (+9km); Abercynafon 16.5km (+5.5km); YHA Brecon Beacons 33.5km (+3km)

This is a hard day's walk and consideration may be given to splitting the day by leaving the trail to seek accommodation in Talybont-on-Usk. The route starts with a pleasant short walk along a canal before rising very steeply to cliffs, descending to a lonely but fast road and then heading across moorland past the Chartist Cave. From there the route descends to another road and through quarry workings before undulating to the Torpantau Pass. There then follows one of the most spectacular mountain crossings of the Cambrian Way over a series of high peaks which can be challenging in poor weather. After leaving Corn Du with a short sharp descent the path curves round to reach the main A470 road at Storey Arms.

Starting from the head of the High Street in **Crickhowell**, go SSW for 200 metres and turn right down Bridge Street at the bottom. Follow Bridge Street as it swings left then right to reach the bridge over **Afon Wysg** (River Usk) after 250 metres. Cross over the bridge where the road comes to a T-junction and take the path going across fields straight ahead. ▶

Looking back, there is a fine view of Table Mountain towering over Crickhowell.

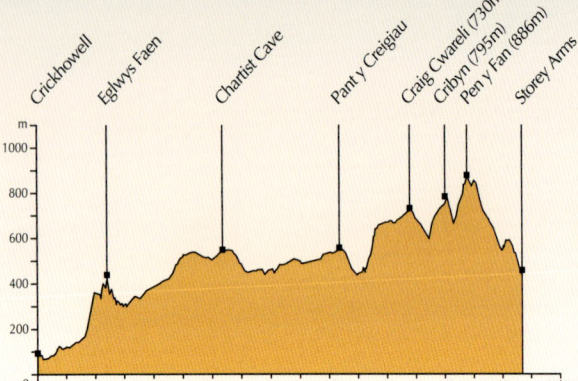

Follow the footpath SW for 300 metres to bear right at a Y-junction over a footbridge and continue alongside **St Catwg's Church**. Go through the churchyard past the church then turn right along the road and bear left after 30 metres, heading W. Follow the road as it leaves the village and climbs to meet the Monmouthshire and Brecon Canal after 350 metres. Turn left along the towpath and follow it for 600 metres as it winds its way S. This section forms part of the picturesque and popular Usk Valley Walk.

Go under the first bridge and reach a second bridge after 130 metres, then exit onto a minor road. This exit is not very obvious but is achieved by climbing stone steps protruding from the bridge after going beneath it.

Cross the canal, heading SW along the road, and continue for 300 metres to where the road turns left. Here take the track on the your right, heading SW on the route of an old tramway from the quarries. Follow this for 950 metres along the valley of Nant Onneu until you cross a stile and arrive at a crossroads with a steep slope and a wood on the left and scattered trees on the right.

Take the very steep incline of the old tramway SSW up the hillside next to the wood and follow this for 250 metres until the wood ends and there is a track along a level. Cross the track, taking another steep incline SE, this time with fewer trees, for another 250 metres until it meets the next level near **Darren Cilau**. ◄ In this short distance there has been a climb of 180m (600ft), so it is a relief to reach a level track with much easier walking ahead.

Turn left here for the Wern Watkin Bunkhouse (1.8km).

Turn right and follow the old tramway W, passing quarries and caves along the hillside, with fine views across the Usk Valley. After 800 metres the escarpment and tramway swing right and there is the entrance to the large, open cave of **Eglwys Faen** – Checkpoint 11 – up a short scramble to the left. The cave can be explored with the aid of a torch and considerable care.

Return to the tramway and continue W for 250 metres to where there is a path forking right down the hillside. Those wishing to see the entrance to Ogaf Agen Allwedd, the locked cave, should continue 200 metres further along the tramway. However, don't be tempted to continue beyond there as the path deteriorates and is increasingly difficult to follow, so a return to the fork is required.

Map continues
on page 83

To continue on the main route, go steadily down the hillside from the fork, bearing left at another waymark to reach the valley bottom after 400 metres. Along the wide

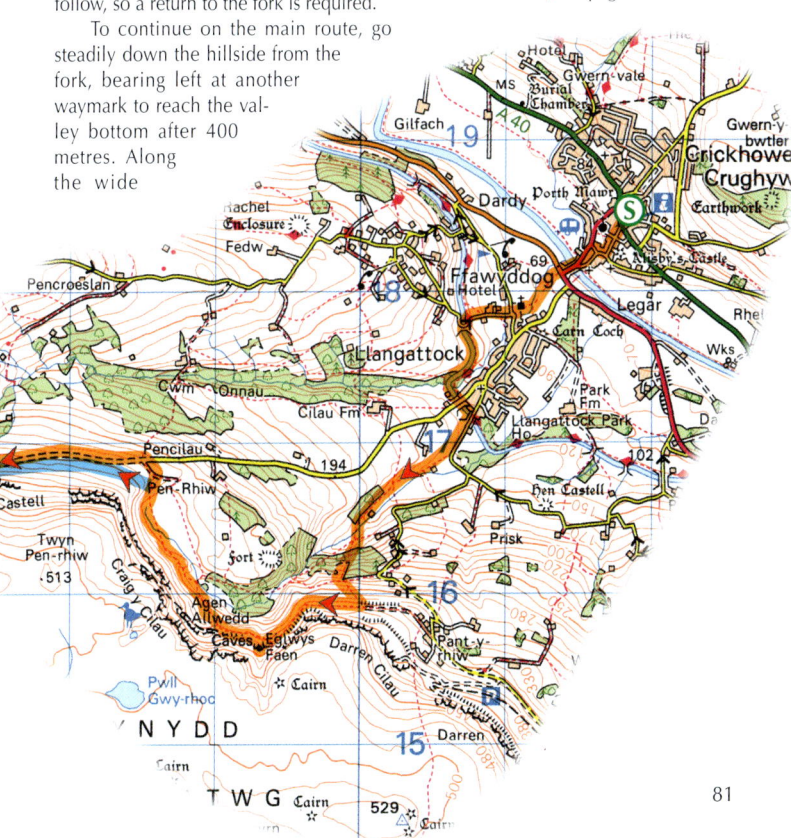

81

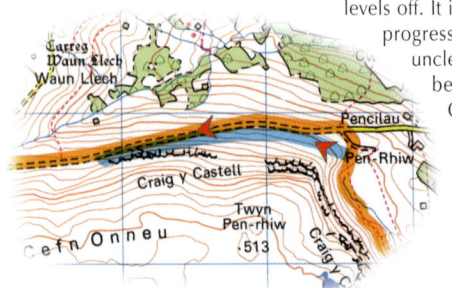

Sugar Loaf and the Craig y Ciliau National Nature Reserve with its caves and rare plants

valley floor, in this area of springs and swamps, the path is not so clearly defined but tends to keep W of the stream near the left hillside where it is dryer, rather than the line shown on OS maps which shows it going to the right of the stream.

After 700 metres the path curves right and ascends the hillside ahead for 200 metres with fine views back along the limestone cliffs of Craig y Ciliau, then it heads left again up a farm track for 130 metres, swinging from E to NE to join the Llangattock to Blaen Onnau road. Turn left along the road, heading N as it climbs steadily uphill for nearly 2.8km. There can be very fast traffic here but there are grass verges in places.

To avoid some of the road walking

It is possible to take a path that goes E up the hillside where the farm track swings right to join the road. This path heads in an easterly direction, steadily climbing up the hillside until it is about 200 metres from the road, where it levels off. It is a good path at first but gets progressively more overgrown and unclear, making it better to keep below the cliffs of Craig y Castell and meet the road after 1.6km. From then on, make use of verges where possible for the rest of the way.

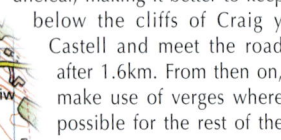

The road eventually reaches a T-junction after passing a farm building and a clump of trees. Cross the road and take the path straight ahead, leading W up onto the moor for 300 metres and then swinging SSW for a further 400 metres. At a fork in the path (beware, as faint paths can change route over time), bear right on the path that heads towards higher ground and turns W after 150 metres, heading for a **trig point** 450 metres ahead at SO 147 159. There are several paths over this heather-covered moor; if in doubt, just aim for the trig point. Continue over the open moor in a reasonably straight line, going WSW for 2.1km to reach the **Chartist Cave** at SO 128 152, the path being clearer now.

Chartism was a movement of the 1830s and 1840s that sought political rights for working-class people. On this featureless moor, finding the **Chartist Cave** used to be difficult – hence its choice by Chartist rebels for hiding weapons. Now the path is well-trodden, making the site easy to find. It is just to the right of the path and has plaques in English and Welsh explaining its use.

Map continues on page 85

Continue W along the main path for about 100 metres until it starts curving S. Take the faint path that continues straight ahead, meandering through the heather and aiming almost due W. It can be

Map continues
on page 87

quite easy to lose the path, but it is not difficult to walk across the open moor heading towards the very wide access road to the quarry. This can be seen when starting to descend from the moor and is 1.6km from the Chartist Cave. ◄

During working hours big lorries go back and forth to the quarry, throwing up clouds of limestone dust.

Turn right along the road and head NW for 500 metres, ignoring any tracks to the right until you reach an area of woodland. Take the track that goes straight on where the road bears left by a large stone and follow the edge of the woodland for 1.4km to a stile at SO 095 149. The track is an old tramway which stays level, so avoid any tracks going left up towards the quarry, which is hidden from view.

If you're planning to stay at accommodation in Abercynafon, Talybont-on-Usk or at Danywenallt Study Centre and Hostel, you will need to leave the route at this point. See the box at the end of this stage for directions.

Just before a stream at SO 095 149, bear left up the hillside, going SW for 300 metres with a farm field on the right and parts of the quarry on the left. ◄ Turn right at the end of the field and go NW for 150 metres, still following the field boundary, to meet a wide track leading to a farm gate.

The strip of land between the farm and quarry is access land but the farmland is not.

Go through the gate and head N for 150 metres, close to the fence on the right. Follow the fence as it turns W and runs along the northern edge of the quarry for 450 metres. By the end of the quarry at SO 089 150 take a faint path that veers right, going NW up the gently rising hillside. The paths are not clearly defined here but the aim is to reach the top of the ridge after 2km at around SO 071 157 by gradually swinging W and going over a lesser ridge then down a dip, crossing two tracks on the way.

The paths are clearer on the top of the ridge, going WNW for 1.6km to a trig point on **Pant y Creigiau** at SO 056 162. The ridge gradually curves N, dropping to meet the road at a junction with a forest road at SO 052 172 after 1.1km. Cross the road and take the path going up

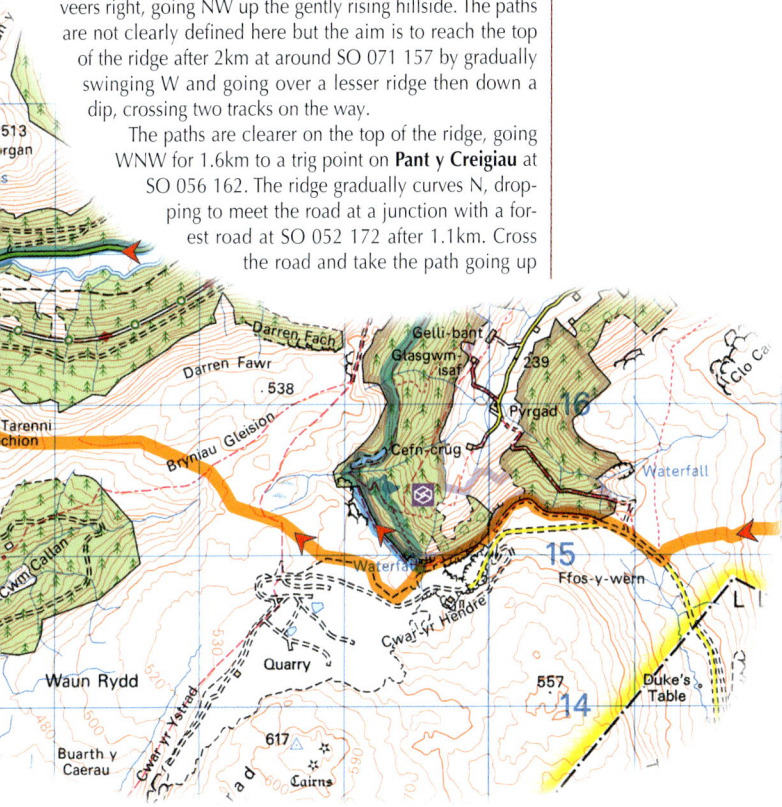

NNW and then N along the hillside for 400 metres, then head NE for 250 metres to cross the **Nant Bwrefwr** (stream) and join the main path that goes N from the Torpandau Pass car park. ▶ There are several alternative paths going in a similar direction, each joining the main path at different points.

This is a well-trodden path on the Beacons Way, so there is no mistaking the route as it climbs N to reach **Craig y Fan Ddu** ('crag of the black peak') after 600 metres. The route is much less steep for the next 1km as it follows the eastern side of the ridge to reach a stream near some

This is the point at which the Abercynafon option rejoins the main route.

This is where the alternative routes from Talybont-on-Usk and Danywenallt rejoin the main route.

crags at SO 050 192. Here take a sharp left to follow the path going SW around the hillside, still following the Beacons Way, swinging W for 400 metres and then turning more sharply NNW to join the ridge of **Craig Cwareli** at SO 042 196 after a further 1km. ◄

As the edge of the ridge is reached, the full splendour of the **Brecon Beacons** appears, with a spectacular view along the whole ridge northwards to Pen y Fan, the highest mountain in South Wales, and Corn Du, its slightly lower twin. There are steep-sided peaks with the strata of red sandstone that is characteristic of this area, and long grassy ridges sweeping over to the north creating a very dramatic appearance. The popularity of this area has caused a lot of footpath erosion, particularly around Pen y Fan. However, a major investment in pathwork by the National Trust in recent years has already started to ease the problem.

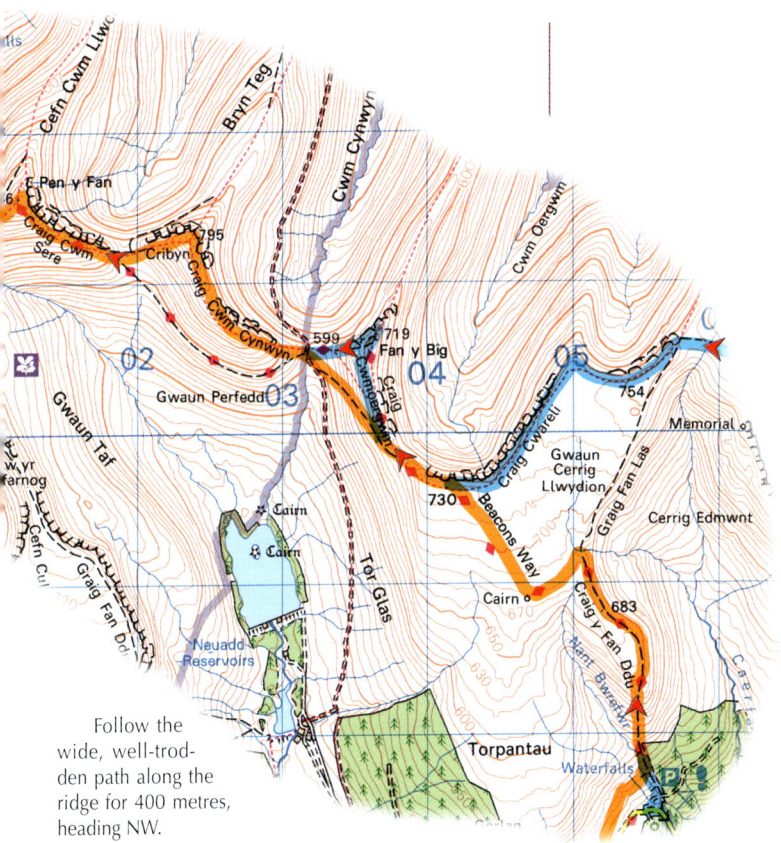

Follow the wide, well-trodden path along the ridge for 400 metres, heading NW.

To visit Fan y Big

Here there is the option, if time permits, to visit the summit of Fan y Big ('point of the peak' – but do not confuse 'Big' with its English meaning; in Welsh it means a point or a spike) for the reward of another fine viewpoint. It involves only 450 metres of extra distance with very little additional ascent. Fork right along the ridge, keeping close to the steep edge to the right, and after reaching the summit take the steep zigzag path W down to the pass of Bwlch ar y Fan to rejoin the main route.

Pen y Fan and Corn Du from Cribyn

Note that the Beacons Way takes a lower route, omitting the next peak (Cribyn). This may be preferred if time is limited.

To continue on the main route, fork left on the wider of two paths, heading NNW down the hillside for 900 metres to Bwlch ar y Fan ('pass on the peak'), where an old Roman road crosses the ridge. Bear right on this for 50 metres then turn left up the path ascending the ridge to the E. ◄ Follow the ridge as it swings N for 1.2km to the summit of **Cribyn** ('comb') at 795m (2608ft) after climbing more than 200m (600ft) from the pass. Here there are more fine views, with Pen y Fan now quite close.

Take the steep path W down from the summit for 500 metres and continue up the next ridge WNW for 850 metres to reach the summit of **Pen y Fan** ('head of the peak') after another steep climb of about 220m (670ft). The badly eroded path has been repaired with stones and steps. This is Checkpoint 12 at 886m (2906ft).

The flat summit of **Pen y Fan** is still almost completely bare because of the heavy footfall which destroys the fragile grass. This is the highest point in South Wales, offering panoramic vistas and a stunning view down to Llyn Cwm Llwch. There are closer views of this further on.

From the summit, follow the ridge down to the SW for 350 metres then upwards for 250 metres onto the flat-topped **Corn Du** ('black horn') at 873m (2865ft), the ascent comprising only about 25m. From this summit, descend steeply WNW for a short way onto the ridge and, time permitting, continue for 800 metres to the Tommy Jones **obelisk**, with bird's-eye views over Llyn Cwm Llwch below.

This **memorial** is where the body of a five-year-old boy was found after he wandered off from a farm in the valley in August 1900. He was found 29 days later high up the mountain. There is an inscription on the obelisk that tells the story. Visiting this involves a 400-metre detour from the direct route and may be omitted if time is limited.

From the obelisk, take the path SSW at right angles to the ridge. This is not very clearly defined, but just goes diagonally down the hillside for 400 metres to rejoin the main path to the Storey Arms at SN 999 214. Follow the main path WSW for 650 metres to cross the Blaen Taf Fawr stream. ▶ It may seem that it is all downhill now, after a rather strenuous walk, but there is a rise of about 50m (165ft) out of the valley before the path starts to descend again to reach the A470 road by the **Storey Arms** after another 1.4km.

This is the path used by the majority of walkers that climb Pen y Fan as it involves the least ascent.

A winter view from the Tommy Jones memorial

The Storey Arms used to be a pub but is now an outdoor centre with no facilities for the general public. However, there is normally a refreshments van parked in the car park by the main A470 road nearby, serving burgers and other snacks to hungry walkers – although opening times cannot be guaranteed. YHA Brecon Beacons or Llwyn-y-celyn ('holly bush') is 2.8km N and can be reached by following the Taff Trail to avoid the busy main road.

ACCOMMODATION OPTIONS: ABERCYNAFON, TALYBONT-ON-USK AND DANYWENALLT (see pages 92–93 for mapping)

Go over the stile at SO 095 149 and continue to follow the old tramway NW for 850 metres as it continues along the very steep hillside with rock faces on the left and the steep wooded valley of Dyffryn Crawnon Nature Reserve to the right. Parts of this old tramway used to get very wet at times, although there appear to have been some recent improvements to the drainage. If you have had to take the diversion described below, the route is rejoined here. The tramway gradually swings N and crosses Nant Ddu ('black stream'), which makes a good place for a rest. Beyond the stream, follow the tramway as it heads NE, with forest on both sides, and meanders along the hillside following the contour for 1.6km. Here the forest on the left ends and recent clear-felling on the right opens fine views into the steep valley of Dyffryn Crownon. Continue NNE for 1km as the track descends gently to meet a dip in the ridge to the left at **Pen Rhiw-calch** ('head of limestone hillside'). *From the ridge there are views over part of the Talybont Reservoir.*

Alternative route to avoid the tramway

The tramway at the start of this section is beginning to crumble where it is on the steepest part of the slope and it may have to be closed at some time. An alternative route is available: continue along the tramway for 150 metres then take a path going sharp right down the hillside through the forest. After 70 metres this turns sharply left to head NNW parallel to the tramway, dropping further down before climbing back up to rejoin the tramway at SO 091 155 after a zigzag up the hillside. This adds about 200 metres and 80m of extra descent/ascent.

For Abercynafon

Crickhowell to Abercynafon: 22km (13¾ miles); Abercynafon to Storey Arms: 15.5km (9½ miles)

To reach Abercynafon, take the track straight ahead going N down the hillside for 40 metres, then turn sharp left and go WSW down the hillside for 2km to the bottom of the valley, crossing two forest tracks and joining another one on the way.

Cross the river over a footbridge and follow the track going NW across fields for 250 metres to reach the road with **Abercynafon** Lodge just to the right. To return to the main route, follow the road W along the valley for 1.9km. Stay on the road as it crosses a bridge over the river and climbs steeply upwards, swinging N to exit the forest at the Torpantau Pass after 1.1km. Turn left then sharp right towards the **car park** and rejoin the main route after 200 metres by turning N just before the forest.

For Talybont-on-Usk
Crickhowell to Talybont-on-Usk: 25.5km (15¾ miles); Talybont-on-Usk to Storey Arms: 18.5km (11¼ miles)
From Pen Rhiw-calch, continue NE along the ridge for 100 metres and take the track that bears slightly left, going gently down the hillside – not the route of the Beacons Way, which follows the top of the ridge. After another 150 metres bear right to continue on the almost level track. This is the route of the Brinore Tramroad, which is followed for 5.2km to **Talybont-on-Usk** where it enters the village by a bridge over the canal next to the White Hart Inn and Bunkhouse. *'Brinore' is an anglicised version of Bryn Oer ('cold hill').*

To return to the main route, go back along the tramway for 700 metres from the canal bridge and turn right at SO 109 219 down a path which is part of the Usk Valley Walk. Go SW down the hillside and cross the route of an old railway to a footbridge over the river. *Look out for the bridge through the trees as it is easy to miss.* Over the river, a short turn left then right leads up the right-hand edge of the field to the road after 200 metres, coming out by **Aber Farm**. Go S along the road for 250 metres to Aber Bridge and continue S for another 300 metres to where a minor road turns right at SO 105 212. This is where the route joins the one from Danywenallt (see below), which can now be followed for the rest of the way.

For Danywenallt Study Centre and Hostel
Crickhowell to Danywenallt: 23km (14½ miles); Danywenallt to Storey Arms: 17.5km (11 miles)
Take the same route from Pen Rhiw-calch as for Talybont-on-Usk for 2.7km then bear left at SO 108 201 on a path going N down through the forest. *There are several alternative tracks through the forest; all are stony and hard on the feet.* Follow this for 500 metres to reach the Study Centre, which is 250 metres N of the dam.

To rejoin the main route, go back S for 250 metres then cross the 450-metre-wide dam. On reaching the road, turn right (do not be tempted to take a shortcut via the minor lane near here as it is not a right of way) and head NNE then N for

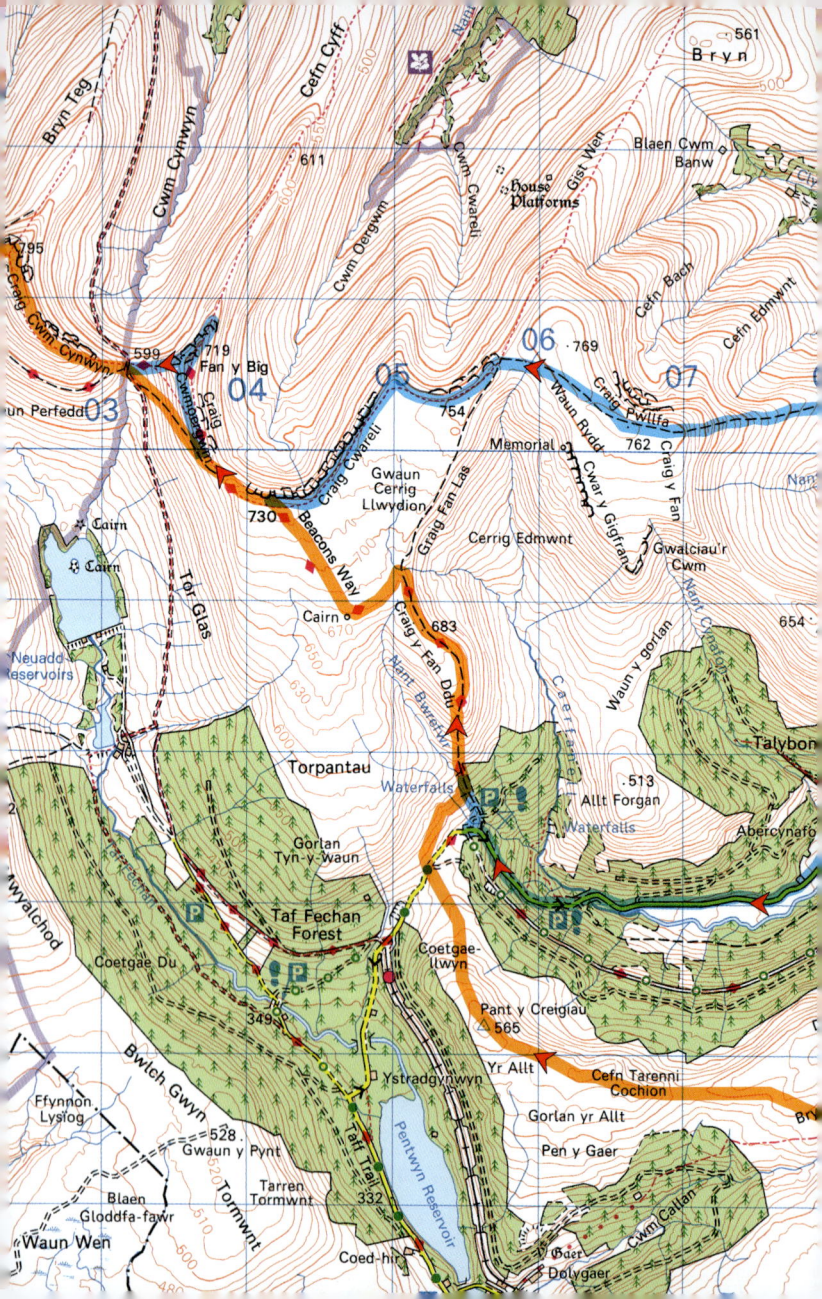

700 metres to where a minor road turns sharp left up the hillside at SO 105 212. *This is where the return route from Talybont-on-Usk joins.*

Follow this road as it starts going WSW up the hillside and doubles back SSW. After 400 metres the road narrows to a track where a farm road turns right. Continue on the track SSW for another 150 metres and stay on the track as it turns right (W) up the hillside following a stream. Go up the hillside to enter the common at SO 097 206 after 450 metres.

Continue W, climbing steeply up the end of the ridge for 1km with fine views back towards Talybont-on-Usk and Talybont Reservoir. The path levels off and the minor peak of **Twyn Du** is reached after a further 550 metres. From here, the main ridge of the Beacons can be seen ahead with a large rounded cairn at the top, although its name – Carn Pica ('pointed cairn') – suggests it once had a different shape. The path is clearly visible straight ahead and after a slight dip another steep climb leads to the cairn after 1.2km. *This is a fine vantage point and a good place for well-deserved rest.*

Continue W then WNW for 1.4km on a clear track over **Waun Rydd** ('free moor') to reach the ridge leading to Craig Cwareli ('crag of the quarries') at SO 057 206. Pen y Fan and Corn Du are now coming into sight, and a magnificent view of the whole Brecon Beacons opens up from the ridge. Follow the ridge path to the left along Bwlch y Ddwyallt, which is quite badly eroded in parts as it swings from SW to NW then turns SSW to rejoin the main route at **Craig Cwareli** after 2.1km.

Carn Pica commanding a fine view of the Usk Valley

STAGE 7
Storey Arms to Glyntawe

Start	Car park on A470 opposite Storey Arms (SN 982 203)
Finish	A4067 near Tawe Bridge, Glyntawe (SN 847 168)
Distance	19km (11¾ miles)
Total ascent	690m (2250ft)
Total descent	930m (3040ft)
Time	5–6¼hr
Maps	OS Explorer OL 12; OS Landranger 160
Refreshments	Refreshment van in car park near Storey Arms; Glyntawe
Public transport	Bus services to Merthyr Tydfil and Brecon from Storey Arms, and to Swansea and Brecon from Glyntawe
Accommodation	Glyntawe

After a day walking over some of the busiest mountain paths in South Wales, this section is much less trodden. Tracks are often faint or non-existent. It offers wild mountain scenery and solitude; only one small mountain road is crossed until approaching Glyntawe. A direct route is available for those wishing to omit Glyntawe and cut across to Bwlch Giedd (Stage 8).

REJOINING THE MAIN ROUTE FROM BRECON YH

It is not necessary to return to the Storey Arms as the main route can be rejoined on Rhos Dringarth. Go up the hostel access road NNW for 200 metres to the **A470** road. Turn left along the road and walk S for 450 metres to the middle of a large lay-by on the right. Take a track going WSW, following a stream up the hillside. After 250 metres cross over a wall then turn left and continue up the hillside, going SSE for 130 metres. Follow the path for another 300 metres as it swings SW towards the ridge ahead and follows the fence up the steep slope. *There are signs at the bottom warning of steep cliffs ahead.* At SN 968 218 there is a choice of two routes.

Cambrian Way route
The Cambrian Way route involves a lot of walking over open moorland with only faint footpaths and requires greater navigational skills, especially in poor

visibility. Cross the fence at SN 968 218 and climb SW over the broad ridge for 600 metres to where it levels off, avoiding any paths going S. Cross a path that follows the ridge and drop into the valley of **Nant y Gwair**, following it SW downwards until it meets the main route after 1.5km at around SN 953 203. There are a few faint paths that can be followed here and there but the aim is to follow the stream to where a number of small streams converge, and the main stream has steeper sides, craggier on the N side. Head W along the main route on a moderately clear path.

Beacons Way option

This route is more well-trodden and has clearer footpaths for much of the way, although it is about 700 metres longer. From SN 968 218 continue up the steep ridge of **Craig Cerrig-gleisiad** for 750 metres to its peak (there are paths on either side of the fence), then continue downwards for 300 metres to reach a dip after gradually swinging round N, still following the fence. Turn left and head W then SW then S onto the ridge of Fan Dringarth to meet the main route at SN 943 203 after 2.7km.

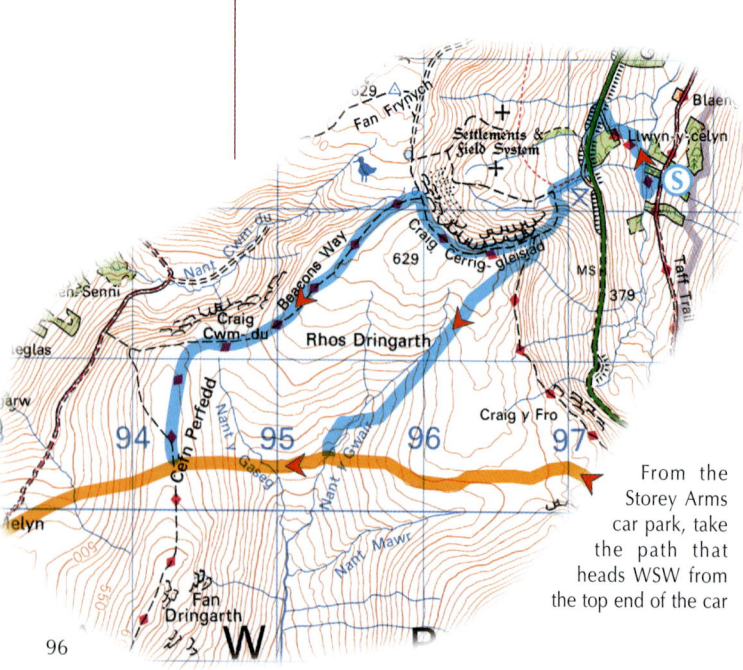

From the Storey Arms car park, take the path that heads WSW from the top end of the car

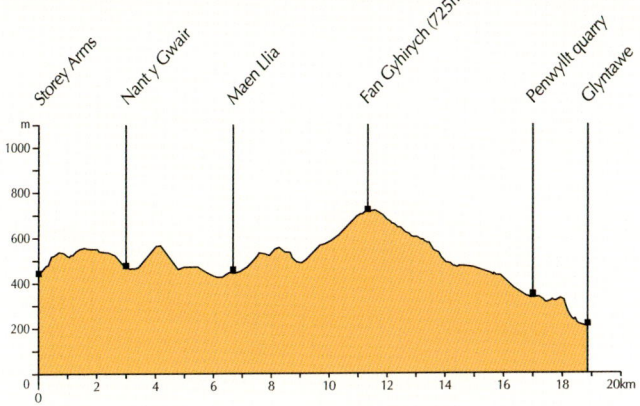

park, following the route of the Beacons Way for 350 metres until it bears right along the hillside to follow a contour. Here keep straight on, continuing to climb diagonally upwards, heading almost due W for 550 metres. The faint path then dips to cross the Nant y Gerdinen (stream) after 250 metres.

Head ENE, aiming for the lowest part of the ridge 500 metres ahead. There are some faint paths, but it is not too difficult to cross the open moorland where necessary. Cross a path running N to S and continue W for 1.3km down towards **Nant y Gwair** where a few other smaller streams and a path join and there are small crags beside the main stream. (This is where the Brecon YH option joins, at SN 953 203.)

Continue heading almost due W along a path that crosses the **Nant y Gaseg** after 500 metres, then head straight up the hillside ahead onto the northern ridge of Fan Dringarth at SN 943 203 after another 600 metres. (This is where the Beacons Way option joins.) There may be faint paths in places, but much is just open moorland. The exact point on the ridge is not important as the route beyond the ridge is also over open moorland. ▶

Head W, gradually swinging WSW straight down the open hillside to cross the Nant Ystwyth after 700 metres. There are several paths going across the hillside but only faint paths going down. Head WSW for another 700 metres to the old Roman road of Sarn Helen via the gentle slopes

To the S, Fan Dringarth summit can be reached in 1.1km, and Fan Llia is a further 700 metres. Go WNW down the steep hillside to rejoin the main route.

97

Map continues
on page 101

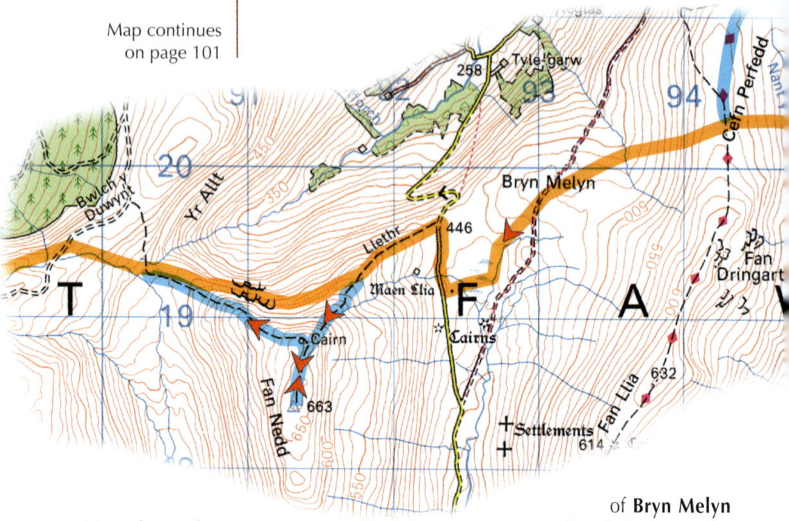

of **Bryn Melyn**
('yellow hill'), aiming to
cross Sarn Helen at SN 930 198 or thereabouts. By now the
standing stone of Maen Llia should be visible across the

*Maen Llia standing
stone and
information board*

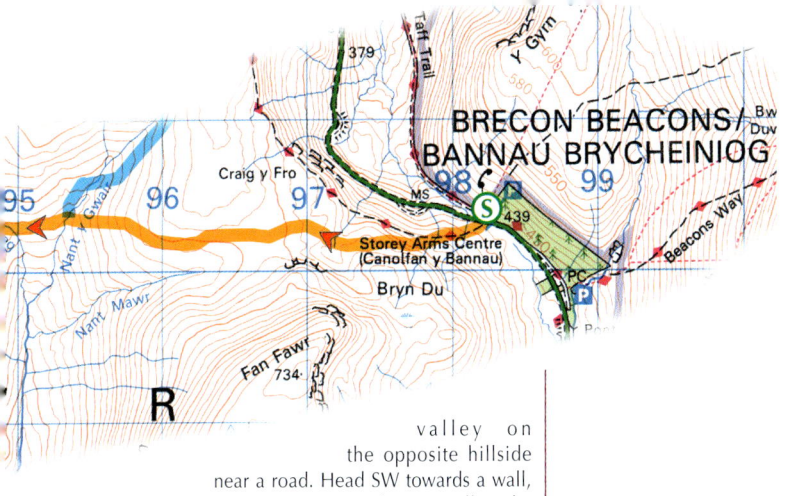

valley on the opposite hillside near a road. Head SW towards a wall, broken in places, about 450 metres to the SW. Follow the wall S as it runs beside a stream for 200 metres, then take the path W for 300 metres to reach **Maen Llia**, crossing a stream on the way.

> The exact purpose of **Maen Llia** is uncertain but it is thought to date back 4000 years to the Bronze Age, and to have been used to mark a boundary or a site of some other special significance. It is made of an unusual form of Old Red Sandstone called calcrete that would have been brought from some distance away. A legend says that the stone walks to the river to drink on Midsummer's Eve; this probably relates to its shadow.

A path leads W to the minor road, which has an information board in the shape of the stone itself. ▶ From the standing stone, go N along the road for 450 metres to its highest point, then turn sharp left to follow a path along the left side of the wall, heading WSW for 650 metres.

To visit Fan Nedd

To make a detour onto Fan Nedd, carry straight on up the ridge to a big **cairn**, passing a large area of cotton grass on the lower slope. The **summit** is 400 metres further S over the reasonably flat top. Return to the cairn and take the path WNW to rejoin the main route 1.7km further on.

If lost in mist, just keep heading W, avoiding any steep descents to the N until you reach the road where you should be able to regain your bearings.

For the main route, continue to follow the wall as it skirts W along the hillside for 1.5km to another wall, where the path from Fan Nedd rejoins. Go through a gap in the wall on a lesser path heading WNW up the hillside and following a stream on the left for 650 metres, then go over a stile onto a very wide track. Cross the track and follow a small track WSW up the ridge for 1.7km to the summit trig point of **Fan Gyhirych**, which is Checkpoint 13A at 725m (2379ft) – one of the two alternative checkpoints on this part of the way. (Checkpoint 13B in Ystradfellte is only retained for historical reasons. Ystradfellte once had a hostel but now has only one B&B, so the alternative route has been dropped.)

From here it is possible to take a direct route to Bwlch Giedd (Stage 8) if you don't need to visit Glyntawe. See the end of this stage for directions.

From the summit of Fan Gyhirych, head due S along the ridge for 400 metres following a faint path that takes a gentler slope down the mountain and swings SE for 200 metres to join a clear track by a stream.

Heading towards Fan Gyhirych (photo: Oliver Wicks)

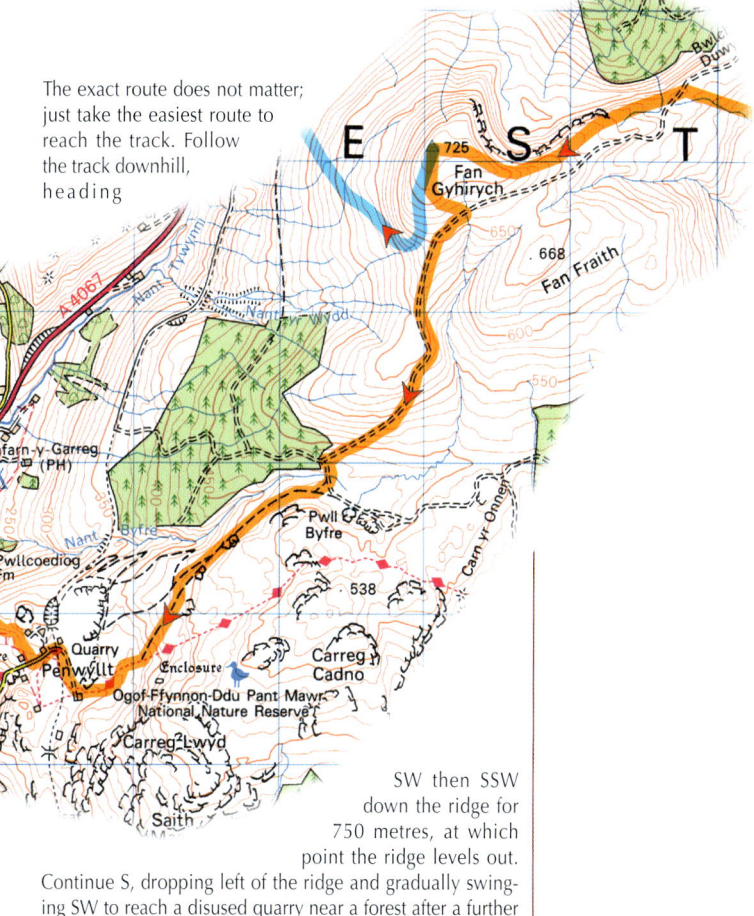

The exact route does not matter; just take the easiest route to reach the track. Follow the track downhill, heading

SW then SSW down the ridge for 750 metres, at which point the ridge levels out. Continue S, dropping left of the ridge and gradually swinging SW to reach a disused quarry near a forest after a further 1.3km.

Turn sharp left onto another clear track and head SE then S for 120 metres to cross a stream. Bear right shortly after the stream onto a path and go SW for 100 metres to join a wider track heading W, and follow this along the valley side as it swings SW for 1.1km.

Where the track splits at SN 863 162, bear left and head S for 150 metres to buildings at the top of an incline from an old tramway, then continue SSW down the incline for 450 metres. Look out for a track bearing right: the route

The buildings belong to the South Wales Caving Club. There are numerous shake holes, potholes and caves in the area.

of the Beacons Way. Follow this SW for 550 metres until it reaches the access road to the right of a row of buildings. ◄

Turn right along the road and continue for 350 metres, going N past the disused **Penwyllt quarry** on the right to where the road becomes a minor road. Follow this WSW for 200 metres to where a footpath goes off to the right alongside a wall.

If seeking accommodation to the south of Glyntawe, continue along the road and follow the Beacons Way as it loops round via Rhongyr before turning back N to Glyntawe. Otherwise, follow the footpath for 350 metres as it winds along, passing crags on the right, to enter a reasonably level grassy field. After a further 150 metres the path turns N down the steep hillside with a fine view over the Tawe Valley ahead. Continue for another 450 metres to join a minor road by a farm. Follow the road as it swings NW downhill for 500 metres, passing a group of houses to reach the A4067 road near Tawe Bridge, the end of the stage, at the northern end of **Glyntawe**.

1km SSW from here along the A4067, the river Llynfell emerges from the mountain as you approach the entrance to nearby **Dan-yr-Ogof caves** which were discovered in 1912. With the adjoining dinosaur park and dry ski run, they are a major tourist attraction.

Close by is the dramatic gothic **Craig y nos Castle**, home of the opera singer Adelina Patti, built in the mid-19th century. It provides B&B and refreshment.

Heading across the open countryside towards Glyntawe (photo: Oliver Wicks)

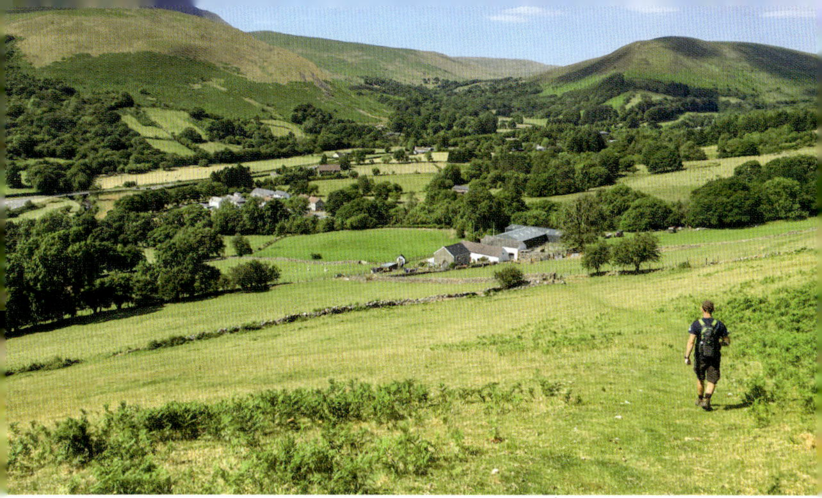

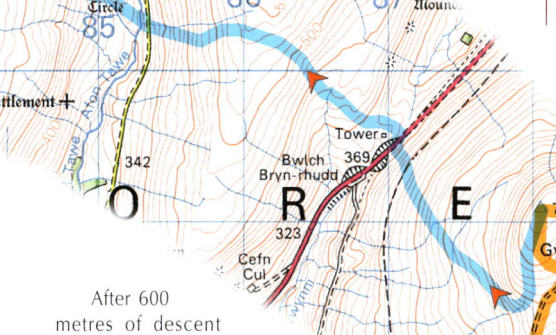

Direct route omitting Glyntawe

For those not seeking accommodation in Glyntawe there is a more direct route which rejoins the main route at Bwlch Giedd near Llyn y Fan Fawr. From the summit of Fan Gyhirych head SSW along the steep edge on the mountain, bearing right as much as possible while avoiding the steep edge.

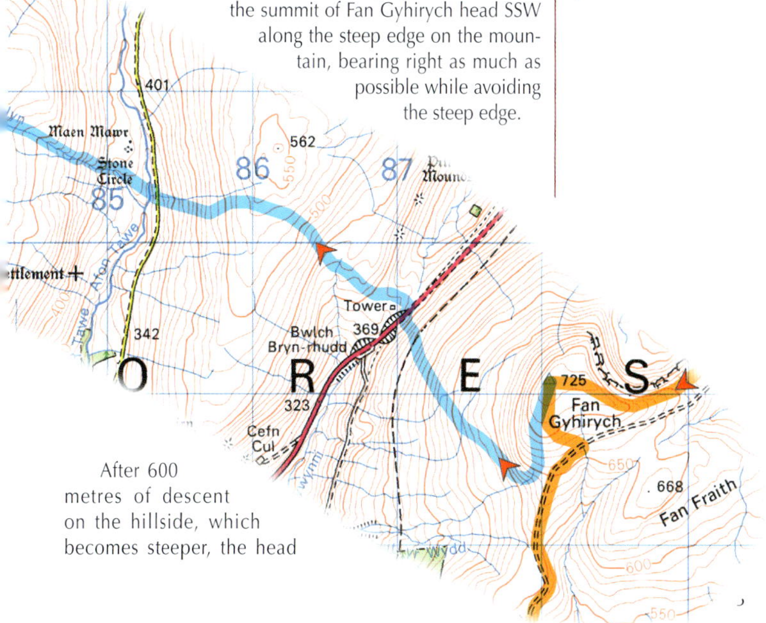

After 600 metres of descent on the hillside, which becomes steeper, the head of a stream can be seen. Start swinging round to the right towards a boundary marker stone at SN 878 184, 150 metres away. Follow the line of several marker stones going NNW to the A4067 road 1.3km ahead. ◄ Nearer the road, the Cray Tower comes into sight, giving further indication of where to aim for, and there is a path down the steeper slope to the road opposite the tower. Oddly, this is marked as '**Tower**' on the 1:50,000 map, but not marked at all on the 1:25,000 map.

Turn right and head NE along the road for 60 metres, then cross the road and take the wide track going NNW for 60 metres up the hillside. Here a path detours 100 metres to the left for those wishing to visit the tower. ◄

Continue up the hillside on the wide track, heading NW for 650 metres. The way becomes indistinct after a while but eventually crosses the Nant-y-moch stream then follows a smaller stream through a gap in a wall. Continue NW beside another wall to its end 350 metres further on, and continue WNW for another 300 metres to the top of the ridge at around SN 860 202. Follow a faint path almost due W for 700 metres, passing some old fence posts and going to the right of a circular sheep pen to reach a ladder stile onto the road.

Turn right and walk for about 50 metres up the road to the N, then turn left along a path to cross **Afon Tawe** at SN 853 203. ◄ On the other side, head NW along a path up the hillside for 250 metres to join **Nant y Llyn** ('stream of the lake'), which is followed WNW for 1.8km then NNW and WNW again for 600 metres up to **Llyn y Fan Fawr** ('lake of the big peak'), passing several waterfalls on the way.

Near the lake, turn left and walk for 300 metres along a clear track going WSW past the bottom of the lake and up the hillside. It becomes steeper and bears right for 200 metres as it nears **Bwlch Giedd**, where it joins the main route of Stage 8 after bearing left for the last 80 metres.

Avoid the many tracks along the hillside as they are mainly sheep tracks going in the wrong direction.

The Tower is a ventilation shaft for an underground culvert supplying water from the Cray Reservoir, which is 1.4km NE.

The river is usually fordable here, but if not, go further N to find a better crossing.

STAGE 8
Glyntawe to Llandovery

Start	A4067 by Tawe Bridge, Glyntawe (SN 847 168)
Finish	Market Square, Llandovery (SN 768 344)
Distance	29.5km (18½ miles)
Total ascent	1360m (4460ft)
Total descent	1500m (4930ft)
Time	8¼–10¾hr
Maps	OS Explorer OL 12; OS Landranger 160
Refreshments	Myddfai Community Hall café
Public transport	Bus services to Swansea and Brecon from Glyntawe, and to various locations from Llandovery; train service to Swansea and Shrewsbury from Llandovery
Accommodation	YHA Llanddeusant 13.5km; Llandovery

This walk through the Carmarthen Vans – 'van' is the anglicised spelling of 'fan' (peak) in Welsh – offers the mountain connoisseur wild mountain scenery, peace and solitude the like of which is hard to find. Footpaths are fairly clearly defined and there are a number of good landmarks. There are steep ascents and descents at Llyn y Fan Fawr and Fach, both iconic lakes. After Llanddeusant the rugged landscape gives way to the rolling hills and valleys that are typical of Mid Wales.

From **Glyntawe**, follow the A4067 road near Tawe Bridge NNE for 400 metres to the **Tafern-y-Garreg pub** and bear left along the footpath heading NNW just before the car park opposite the pub. After 100 metres cross a footbridge over Afon Tawe and follow the riverbank to the right as it swings from NE to N for 200 metres. Turn left, going to the right of some walled areas after 100 metres, and take the left-hand Beacons Way trail to start a steep ascent of the hillside due W.

After 200 metres the path swings NNW and climbs onto the ridge for 800 metres, then the slope becomes gentler. There are a few other paths up the hillside, but the aim is to make for the ridge. Continue climbing steadily upwards for 1.4km at which point the path starts to run along the E

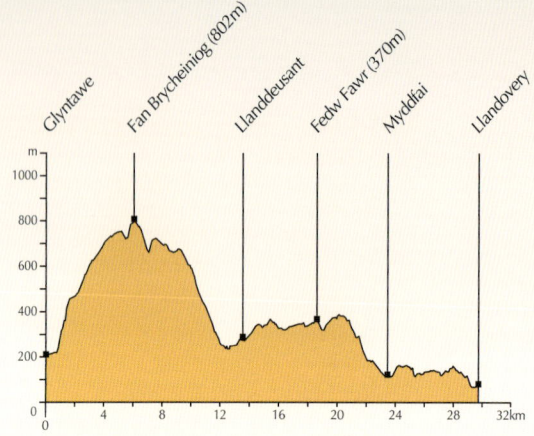

edge of the ridge giving good views down into and across the valley. Continue for another 1.9km to the summit of the aptly named **Fan Hir** ('long peak'). From here Llyn y Fan Fawr ('lake of the big peak') comes into view and the path starts descends for 500 metres to **Bwlch Giedd**, where the direct route from Fan Gyhirych in Stage 7 rejoins.

Climb NNW up the ridge ahead to reach the trig point at the summit of **Fan Brycheiniog** ('Brecknock peak') after 600 metres. This is Checkpoint 14 at 802m (2630ft) – the highest

Looking back towards Glyntawe from Fan Hir

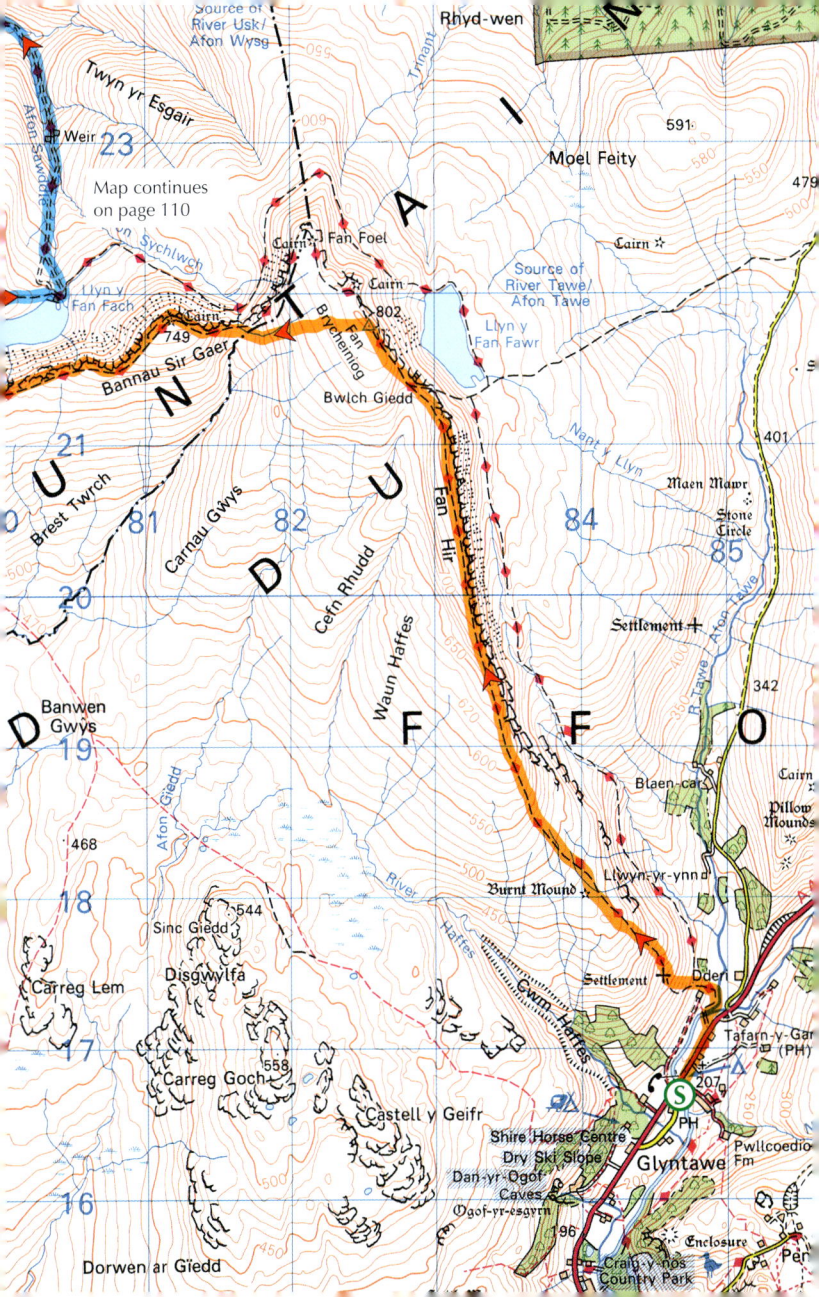

Map continues
on page 110

Rhyd-wen

Twyn yr Esgair

Afon Sawdde

Weir 23

591

Moel Feity

580

479

500

Source of
River Usk/
Afon Wysg

Source of
River Tawe/
Afon Tawe

Llyn y
Fan Fawr

Cairn

Cairn

Fan Foel

Cairn

Cairn

802

Fan Brycheiniog

Llyn y
Fan Fach

Cairn

749

Bannau Sir Gaer

Bwlch Giedd

Nant y Llyn

401

Maen Mawr

Stone
Circle

85

Brest Twrch

81

Carnau Gwys

82

Cefn Rhudd

Fan Hir

84

Settlement

342

R Tawe

Afon Tawe

Waun Haffes

F

F

O

Blaen-car

Cairn

Pillow
Mounds

Banwen
Gwys

19

Afon Giedd

D

468

Llwyn-yr-ynn

Burnt Mound

18

Sinc Giedd

544

River Haffes

Disgwylfa

Settlement

Dderi

Carreg Lem

17

Carreg Goch

558

Castell y Geifr

Cwm Haffes

Tafarn-y-Gar
(PH)

207

S

PH

Pwllcoedio
Fm

Dorwen ar Giedd

Shire Horse Centre
Dry Ski Slope
Dan-yr-Ogof
Caves
Ogof-yr-esgyrn

196

Glyntawe

Craig-y-nos
Country Park

Enclosure

Per

20

21

U

N

T

A

I

N

D

U

F

D

20

Sychlwch

If time permits there are better views to be had by following the Beacons Way around Fan Foel to the N, but this adds 700 metres.

point in the Bannau Brycheiniog ('Brecknock peaks'). There is a large circular cairn giving shelter from the wind. Turn left at the trig point and head W for 900 metres to the pass of Bwlch Blean-twrch. ◀

Head up the steep slope ahead to the summit of Picws Du, 500 metres W with a **cairn**. At 749m (2457ft) this is the second highest point in the Bannau Brycheiniog with views down its very steep craggy hillside overlooking Llyn y Fan Fach ('lake of the small peak').

According to folklore, a young man met a beautiful girl by **Llyn y Fan Fach**. She agreed to marry him on the condition that if he were to strike her three times she would return to the lake. They lived happily and had three children, but over the years he admonished her with three minor taps and she disappeared into the lake, taking all their cattle with her.

Continue to follow the ridge as it descends for 1.3km then rises a little and drops again, curving around the head of the lake for a further 700 metres and giving stunning bird's-eye views of the lake throughout. Reach a fork in the path after some rocks on the left at SN 797 219, where there is the option to take a low-level route to Llanddeusant.

Llyn y Fan Fach from Picws Du

Low-level option

The low-level route offers shelter in bad weather, although it does involve more road walking. At the fork, take the path E for 700 metres down to the dam of Llyn y Fan Fach where there is an old waterworks hut offering shelter. Follow the access road N then ENE for 4.6km towards **Llanddeusant**.

The main route continues on the Beacons Way along the top of the ridge: descend steadily NNE for 350 metres, and stay on the path as it swings round NNW and goes in an almost straight line down the grassy hillside for a further 1.5km. Halfway down is the head of the valley of Garwnant ('rough stream'); the path keeps to the right of this until it reaches the bottom of the common.

There are a number of paths near the bottom of the common but keep close to the stream and avoid tracks off to the right. For the last 200 metres of the common, head closer to the stream and enter woodland, going N for another 200 metres to the bottom of the hill to meet Afon Sawddle, crossing the Garwnant on the way. Turn left and go WNW beside the river for 150 metres to reach a road that turns right and crosses the river. This may be followed to Llanddeusant, but the route avoids some road walking by continuing along the farm road S of the river for 350 metres, heading W.

Looking back at the majestic Bannau Sir Gaer (Carmarthen Vans) en route to Llanddeusant (photo: Oliver Wicks)

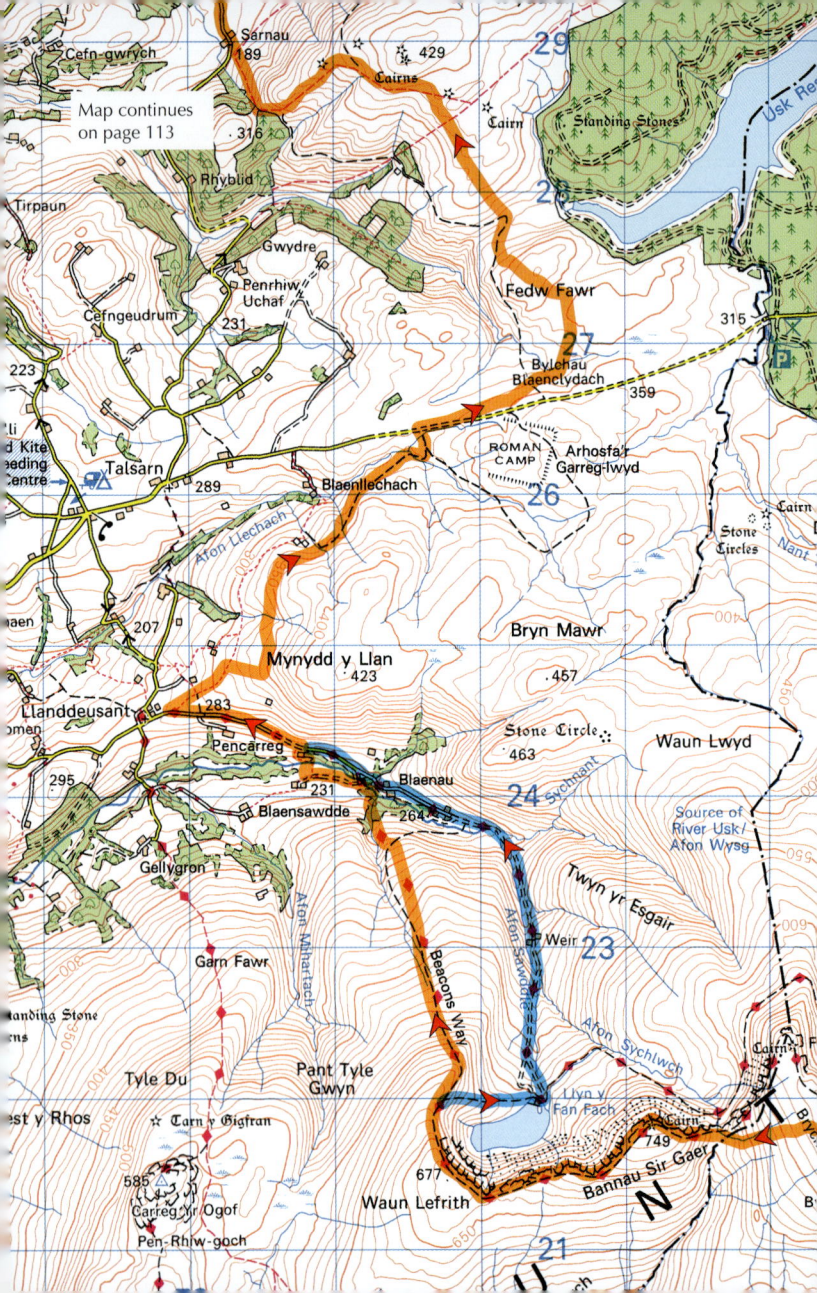

Turn right at the farm along a path going N through woodland and continue for 100 metres to cross the river over a footbridge. Turn left going WNW then N up the hillside to join the road after 150 metres. Follow the road W as it climbs steadily uphill then starts a gradual descent towards **Llanddeusant**. After 1km, about 150 metres before reaching the village, look out for a very sharp right turn along a lane heading NE. (Ignore earlier right turns which are not rights of way.) ▸

YHA Llanddeusant (self-catering with no shop) is in the village just past the church.

Follow the lane as it climbs gently for 500 metres. Cross one lane, then turn right along a wide lane by a ford over a small stream. Follow this lane up E for 250 metres to cross the common boundary, then follow the boundary N for 650 metres, crossing two small streams on the way. Continue to follow the boundary as it swings NNE then ENE round the hillside for another 650 metres, crossing two more streams. The boundary then turns off downhill towards **Blaenllechach** beside the second stream but the path (which you follow) heads NNE then ENE along the hillside for 750 metres to reach another stream with a ford. Cross the stream and bear right, going E for 100 metres, then turn left up the hillside and continue for 250 metres to reach the road at SN 796 264. ▸

After heavy rain it may be necessary to cross further upstream; the road can be joined further E.

Turn right and follow the road E for 200 metres, then take a path on the left that starts heading over the open common close to the road. There a few other paths going in the same general direction, but the aim is to gradually swing N away from the road, going a little way down the valley to cross Afon Clydach at SN 805 268 after 850 metres. ▸

Afon Clydach is just a small stream near the river's source at this point.

Follow the grassy path NNE, heading upwards and gradually turning N to a dip in the ridge 500 metres ahead. From here go NW for 300 metres, following marker posts that lead to the summit of **Fedw Fawr** with views of the Usk Reservoir to the right. The path is clearer here and continues down (NW) for 300 metres to join a green lane which heads NNE for 200 metres into a dip. The track turns NNW up the next hill, keeping to the left of the ridge, then runs along the hillside staying at roughly the same height, eventually reaching some disused pits at SN 792 288 after 1.5km.

A number of paths lead ahead but take the one that bears left, going downhill for 150 metres to cross the common boundary. Then head SW for 500 metres, passing Pen Caenewydd and going down into the valley where the route turns W for 200 metres and then NNW for 500 metres to join a minor road at **Sarnau**. Follow the road NW for 1.6km towards the village of **Myddfai**, going N then WNW and passing a sewage works on the right.

Opposite Myddfai churchyard there is a community hall with café and gift shop.

Turn right at the T-junction and go N through the village for 100 metres then turn left by the **church**. ◀ Take the more major road that forks right after 50 metres, going N then NNE, and follow it for 900 metres to a T-junction at **Myrtle Hill**. Here you will start to see the Heart of Wales Line Trail waymarks, which are linked to the train line that runs across Wales from Swansea to Shrewsbury.

Cross the road and follow the track NW, passing farm buildings on the left then going along the northern edge of two fields downhill to enter a wooded area by a stream after 400 metres. Go NW for 150 metres, cross a farm road and continue WNW for 150 metres down the left side of a field to reach a footbridge at the bottom. Cross the bridge and climb the path W for 50 metres to meet a farm track. Go left here and then right to take the track heading N for 250 metres to **Pantygaseg Farm**. Follow the track through the farmyard and go through a gate to follow the left edge of a field for 150 metres. Cross over a stile to follow the other side of the boundary and enter woodland after 150 metres, still heading N.

On exiting the woodland after 200 metres, join a wide track and walk along it for a further 200 metres, then follow it round to the left for 70 metres. Here the wide track turns sharp right, but this is not a right of way, so look out for a waymarked path to the left. The path runs along the bottom of a field, going NE beside a track for 100 metres then sharp left up the hillside for 130 metres to meet another farm track.

Turn right and follow this track N for 400 metres, going steadily downhill to meet another wide track just after swinging right. Turn right along this track and look out for a track forking left through the trees after about 30 metres. Take this track and head E for 100 metres, then ENE for 500 metres to SN 768 328 and cross a stile. The track continues straight on, but look out for a path that forks left up the grassy hillside through some trees and bushes and follow this NNE for 200 metres to where it meets a farm lane.

Turn left along the lane and go WNW uphill for 100 metres. The lane swings right towards the old buildings of **Cefn-yr-allt-uchaf Farm**; take the waymarked path forking

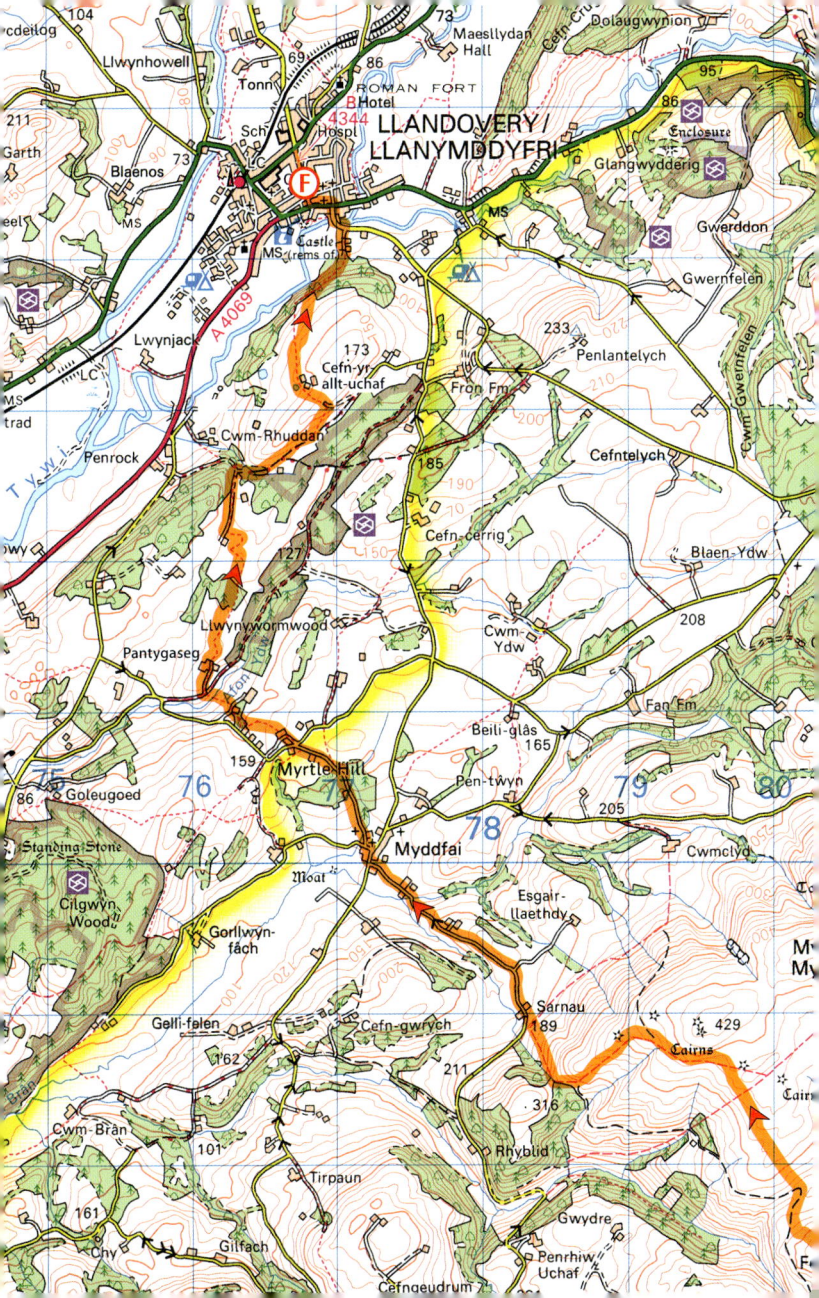

left into a field, heading WNW for another 100 metres then NNW past a pond and into another field on the hillside. The path isn't very clear but just head N to a gap between the woodland and the boundary a little way down the hillside 200 metres away. Again there is little or no visible footpath, but the right of way follows the boundary, heading NNE for 100 metres then N across to the far corner of the field 300 metres away down the hillside where a gate leads into woodland.

Follow the track going down NE through the woodland for 250 metres to join a forest track. Follow this for 20 metres, then keep right where it forks, heading NNE for 70 metres then N for 200 metres, exiting the forest and passing through Bronallt Farm to meet a road. Turn left and then swing N over Waterloo Bridge to meet the main A40 Brecon Road in **Llandovery** after 200 metres. Turn left and walk for 150 metres with Castle Street to the left and the Market Square on the right – the end of this stage.

Market Square in the historic town of Llandovery, the end of this stage

STAGE 9

Llandovery to
Tŷ'n-y-cornel Hostel

Start	Market Square, Llandovery (SN 768 344)
Finish	Tŷ'n-y-cornel Hostel (SN 750 535)
Distance	26km (16 miles)
Total ascent	870m (2850ft)
Total descent	620m (2030ft)
Time	6¾–8½hr
Maps	OS Explorer OL 12 and 187; OS Landranger 160 and 147
Refreshments	Rhandirmwyn and Towy Bridge Inn
Public transport	Rail and bus links at Llandovery
Accommodation	Llanerchindda 7.5km (+3km); Rhandirmwyn 11.5km; Tŷ'n-y-cornel Hostel

Much of this section is on minor roads with linking paths and tracks. The Doethie Valley, which the trail follows north of Llandovery, is very picturesque. Few other walkers are likely to be met and Ty'n-y-cornel ('house in the corner') Hostel is said to be the most remote in Wales. Here the weary walker can rest on the carved bench outside dedicated to Tony Drake, the creator of the Cambrian Way. Alternatively, a direct option to Nantymaen via Soar y Mynydd, omitting both the hostel and the more difficult terrain encountered at the start of Stage 10, can be taken towards the end of the route.

From Market Square in **Llandovery**, head N along the B4344 (Stone Street) for 400 metres to reach a T-junction at the A483 (New Road). Bear right along the A483 going past the fire station and continue for 200 metres, passing the hospital on the left. Take the minor road that forks left, going NNE and past **Llanfair Church** to rejoin the A483 after 400 metres. (This avoids a very bad part of the main road with no pavement or verges.) Follow the A483 for 150 metres to where a minor road forks left, and take this road to cross the railway line and head N uphill. ▶

There is little traffic on this road and some open views to the east between trees and hedges.

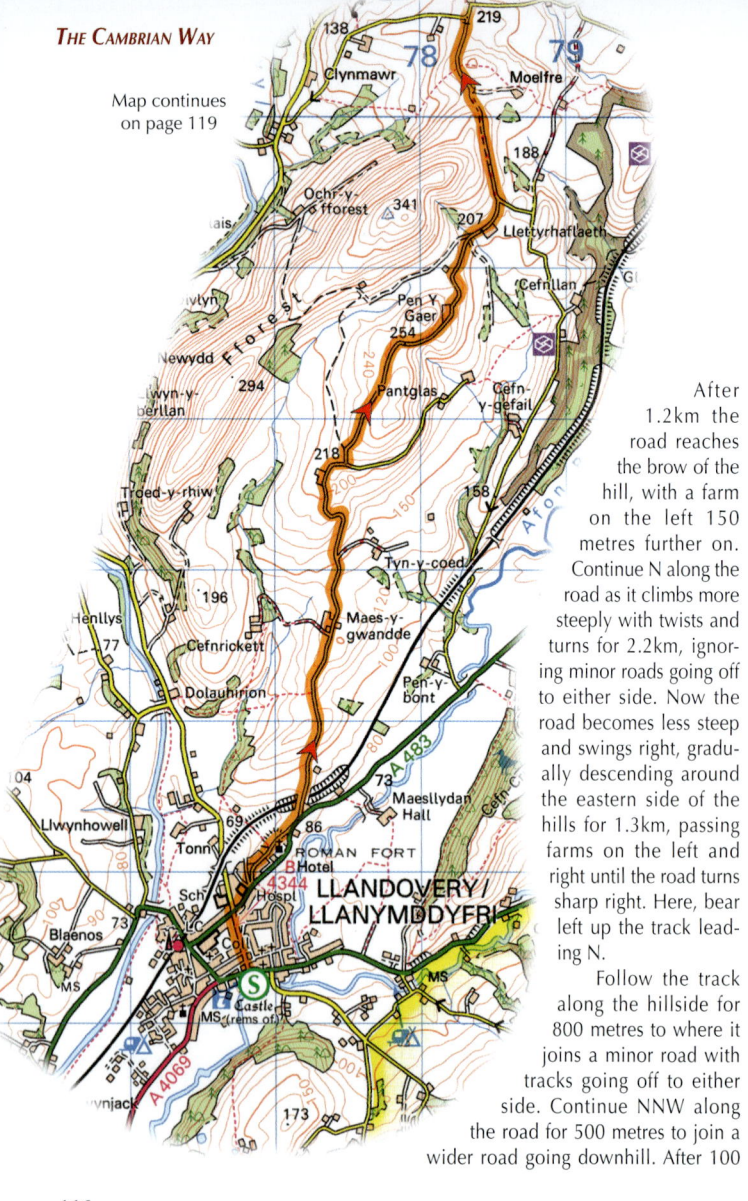

Map continues
on page 119

After 1.2km the road reaches the brow of the hill, with a farm on the left 150 metres further on. Continue N along the road as it climbs more steeply with twists and turns for 2.2km, ignoring minor roads going off to either side. Now the road becomes less steep and swings right, gradually descending around the eastern side of the hills for 1.3km, passing farms on the left and right until the road turns sharp right. Here, bear left up the track leading N.

Follow the track along the hillside for 800 metres to where it joins a minor road with tracks going off to either side. Continue NNW along the road for 500 metres to join a wider road going downhill. After 100

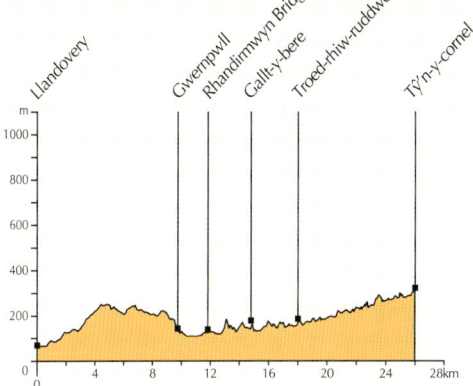

metres, where the wider road turns sharp right, go straight ahead along a BOAT (byway open to all traffic) with cottages on either side – Pendrainllwyn. ▶ Follow the BOAT for 1.2km, still heading roughly N until it joins a bend in a road.

Take the road straight ahead and follow it for 500 metres as it descends more steeply, swinging first left then right before meeting a wider road that curves around the hillside. Cross this road and look for another BOAT that drops steeply down the hillside among the trees and can easily be missed. (This BOAT was wrongly classified for a long time and was

Turn right along the road and continue for 3km to reach Llanerchindda Farm B&B.

Afon Tywi (River Towy) at Llandovery (photo: Oliver Wicks)

not waymarked at all until the local authority was made aware of this and corrected the problem in 2016.)

The route goes steeply downhill, then obliquely to the left until almost at the bottom of the hill, where it turns right down to a gate. Do not take the track to the left, which appears to go towards the river, as this turns off in the opposite direction. Go through the gate and across the field along the right of way on the left-hand side – which can become boggy, in which case it may be better to skirt around this. After 300 metres the path turns left then right behind some buildings at **Gwernpwll** ('swamp pool').

> **Gwernpwll** used to be a farm but is now used as part of Coleg Elidyr, a college for young adults with learning difficulties. Because of the confusion about the status of the track, walkers were sometimes turned away in the past, but the route is now properly waymarked with the college aware of its status.

After passing to the north of the first building, go to the south of the next group of buildings and look for a waymarked track partly obscured by trees that goes N downhill past the end of the buildings. After a short descent take the path through the farm gate on the left, heading W for 130 metres to the opposite corner of the field where a stile gives access to the riverside path of **Afon Towy**. Turn right by the river and head N for 500 metres to where a track turns off by the sewage works. ◄

This track can cut off a corner for those visiting Rhandirmwyn. It joins the road towards the village near the church.

> At Rhandirmwyn ('land of minerals') there are disused **lead mines** which were the most extensive in South Wales and included two underground canals. They were owned by the Cawdor Estate and some of the profits were used to create a series of ornamental lakes in Pembrokeshire including the Bosherston lily ponds. Miners used to walk over the hills from valleys such as the Doethie to work at Rhandirmwyn. The mining dates back to Roman times and over 400 people were employed in the 1700s and 1800s, but the mines finally closed in 1932.

Continue along the riverbank for 400 metres, going past the **caravan and camping site** to the point just before the road

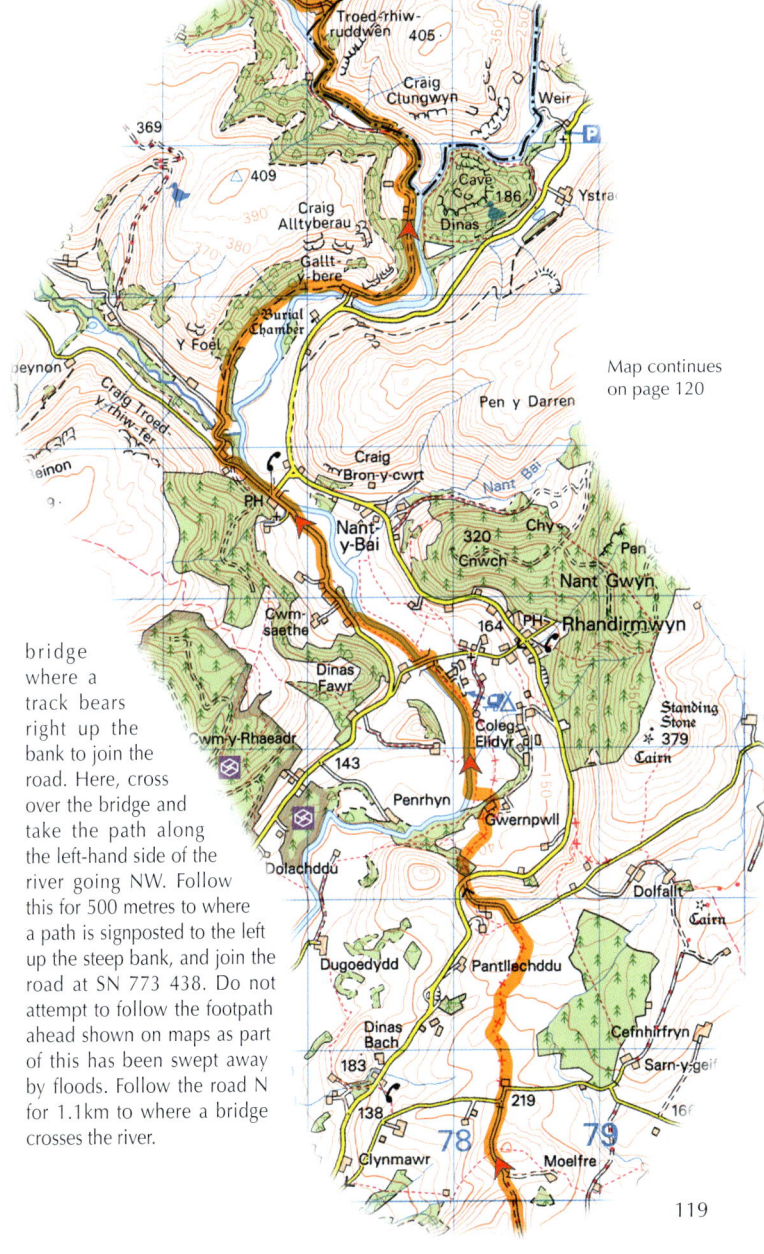

bridge where a track bears right up the bank to join the road. Here, cross over the bridge and take the path along the left-hand side of the river going NW. Follow this for 500 metres to where a path is signposted to the left up the steep bank, and join the road at SN 773 438. Do not attempt to follow the footpath ahead shown on maps as part of this has been swept away by floods. Follow the road N for 1.1km to where a bridge crosses the river.

Map continues on page 120

There is some confusion here in that this bridge was always known as **Towy Bridge**, with the pub nearby called the Towy Bridge Inn. However, recent OS maps call this **Rhandirmwyn Bridge** even though it might be assumed that the previous bridge nearer the village would take that name.

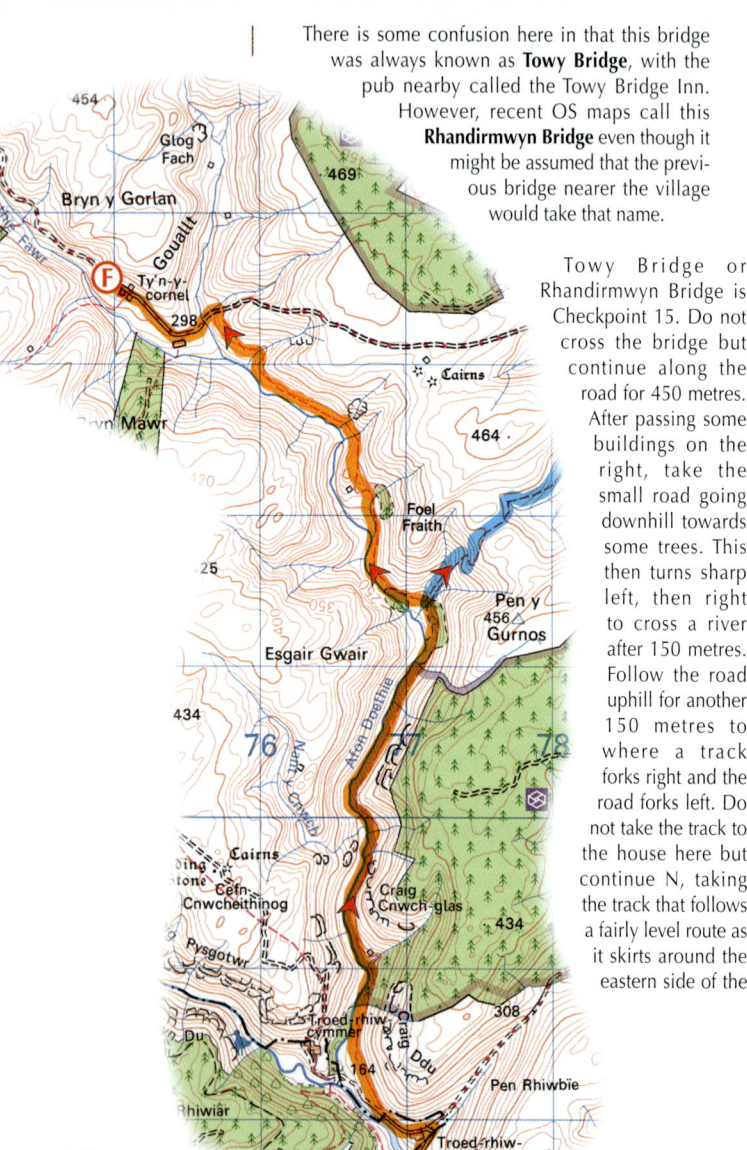

Towy Bridge or Rhandirmwyn Bridge is Checkpoint 15. Do not cross the bridge but continue along the road for 450 metres. After passing some buildings on the right, take the small road going downhill towards some trees. This then turns sharp left, then right to cross a river after 150 metres. Follow the road uphill for another 150 metres to where a track forks right and the road forks left. Do not take the track to the house here but continue N, taking the track that follows a fairly level route as it skirts around the eastern side of the hill overlooking the river – although the views are mainly obscured by trees.

After 400 metres be careful to take the track on the left, avoiding the one going down to the riverside. Follow the track for another 800 metres as it gradually curves round towards the NE. This track sometimes gets overgrown by nettles, but it is generally possible to get through with care. After emerging from the trees, the track becomes a road near **Gallt-y-bere Farm**. Continue past the farm, following the road along the hillside for 1.7km as it winds around tracing the course of the river on its western side. Where the river goes N near the end of this stretch, the Gwenffwrd-Dinas Nature Reserve can be seen on the other side. ▶

Follow the road as it turns right to cross the river at SN 776 471 and continue to follow it as it runs close to the right-hand side of the river, for 850 metres. Here it leaves the riverbank and heads up the hillside to the NE then turns sharp left to reach **Troed-rhiw-ruddwen Farm** after 450 metres. Go through the farm and two gates and look out for a signposted track forking to the right up the hillside after 300 metres, heading NNW. Follow this for 1km to SN 767 490 as it levels

There is a good view of some waterfalls at SN 777 466 – seen better by a short detour from the road. A good place for a rest break.

The Doethie Valley is a scenic highlight of the stage (photo: Oliver Wicks)

out gradually, getting closer to the river, and swings NNW as it approaches the Nant Cnwch-glas stream.

Take the riverside path NNW rather than following the right of way that does a loop round to the right. (This is access land so there is no problem with right of way.) Follow the path as it runs alongside the river for 2.7km, passing through a gated forestry area and some scattered trees towards the end as it climbs to SN 772 514. ◄

This part of the route is where the Doethie Valley shows its greatest beauty, which continues for some way to come.

Soar y Mynydd option

At SN 772 514 there is a steep hillside ahead, with a track turning off to the right by the Nant Lluest-fach stream, leading past Nant-llwyd to join a mountain road at Soar y Mynydd where the Calvinist Methodist chapel claims to be the most remote chapel in Wales. This is an alternative connection to Stage 10 for those who are not staying at the hostel and prefer road walking to avoid some of the more difficult terrain on the main route to Nantymaen. The path climbs steeply up the hillside with a zigzag near the top, becoming a clearer track as it approaches **Nant-llwyd Farm**, which it reaches after 1.9km. Past the farm, take the track that forks uphill to the left of the main access road. The track swings round the hillside towards the N, then NW, crossing the access road on the way and reaching the chapel at **Soar y Mynydd** after another 1.2km. From there a road bridge leads to the mountain road, which is followed N to rejoin the main route on Stage 10 at the **Nantymaen** road junction at SN 762 576 after 5.6km.

To continue to the hostel from SN 772 514, cross a stream and head E along the hillside towards the river, onto the path following its course again for 750 metres. Where the river turns NW, the path goes N and straight ahead. After a further 300 metres the right of way loops around by some old buildings to the left, but take a path NW avoiding this loop, picking up the right of way after 100 metres at which point it goes N again. Cross a stream after 300 metres, then another after 100 metres.

Now heading WNW, follow the path for 700 metres, turning N to cross the Nant y Benglog stream after a futher 100 metres. Go W and follow the hillside, then swing N to meet a wide track after 450 metres. This is the main access track to Tŷ'n-y-cornel Hostel from Soar y Mynydd. Go SW downhill towards the ford for 150 metres and take the footbridge over

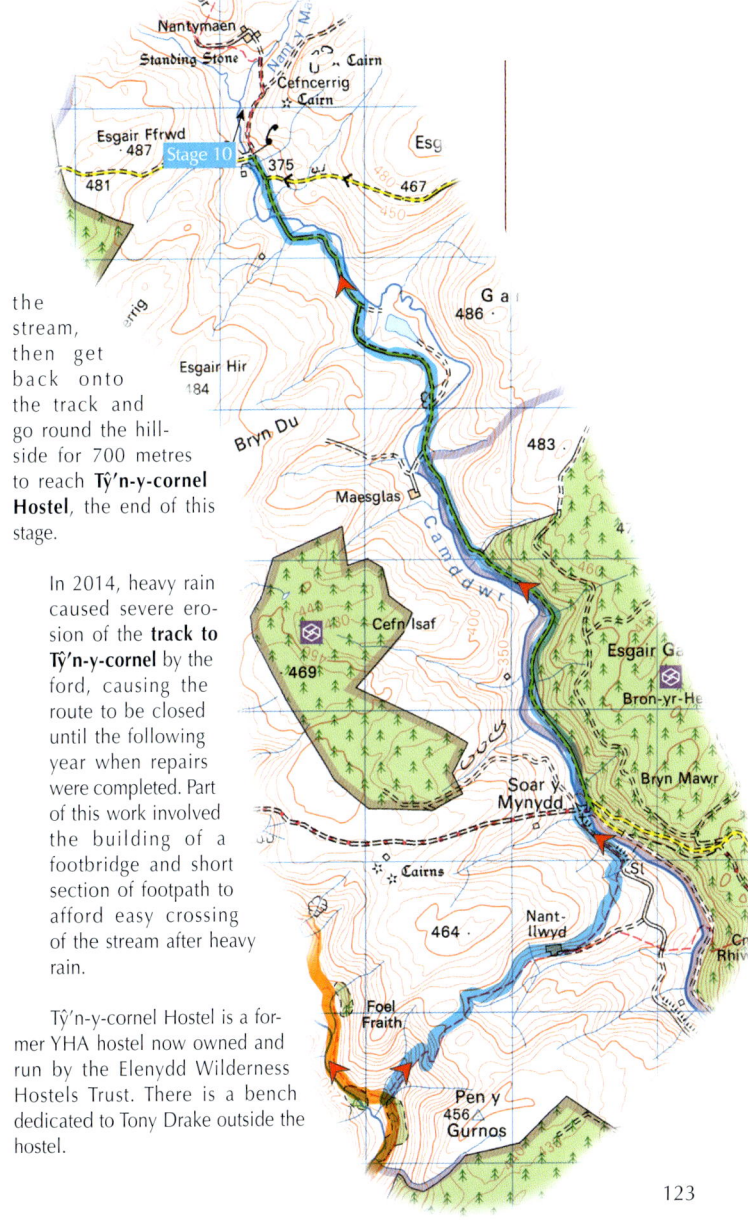

the stream, then get back onto the track and go round the hillside for 700 metres to reach **Tŷ'n-y-cornel Hostel**, the end of this stage.

In 2014, heavy rain caused severe erosion of the **track to Tŷ'n-y-cornel** by the ford, causing the route to be closed until the following year when repairs were completed. Part of this work involved the building of a footbridge and short section of footpath to afford easy crossing of the stream after heavy rain.

Tŷ'n-y-cornel Hostel is a former YHA hostel now owned and run by the Elenydd Wilderness Hostels Trust. There is a bench dedicated to Tony Drake outside the hostel.

STAGE 10
Tŷ'n-y-cornel Hostel to Claerddu

Start	Tŷ'n-y-cornel Hostel (SN 750 535)
Finish	Minor road near Claerddu Bothy (SN 791 683)
Distance	23.5km (14½ miles)
Total ascent	820m (2700ft)
Total descent	690m (2250ft)
Time	6¼–7¾hr
Maps	OS Explorer 187 and 213; OS Landranger 147
Refreshments	Strata Florida Abbey
Public transport	Nearest bus service at Pontrhydfendigaid
Accommodation	Tregaron 9km (+8km); Pontrhydfendigaid 16km (+1.5km); Claerddu Bothy 23.5km (+0.5km)

This section gives the lover of wilderness an opportunity to traverse some very wild and remote areas where paths are often faint or non-existent. A considerable amount of peat bog has to be negotiated in addition to stream crossings. Garn Gron gives good views back to the Brecon Beacons and ahead to Pumlumon. A detour to Pontrhydfendigaid is available for accommodation, but the direct route is on road and clear tracks to Claerddu Bothy.

From **Tŷ'n-y-cornel Hostel**, follow the track NW alongside the Doethïe Fawr (river) for 1.2km. Just before the main track swings round left, take the first track going up the hillside straight ahead. (There is a smaller track a little further on, but this can be boggy, whereas the first one stays dryer.) Follow the track as it winds its way steadily up the hillside, getting closer to the forest on the left, ignoring the track that drops to the left.

After 600 metres the track starts to turn NNE, getting further away from the forest and higher up until it becomes indistinct after a further 300 metres. The area ahead can become very boggy, especially closer to the forest, so keep to the higher ground heading for a low ridge that is about 200 metres from the forest. There may be a faint track that can be followed, otherwise walk over the rough ground, which is

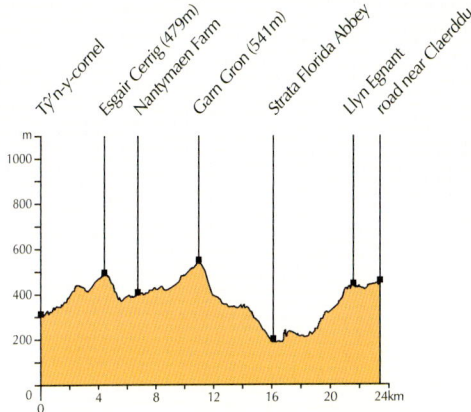

Map continues
on page 126

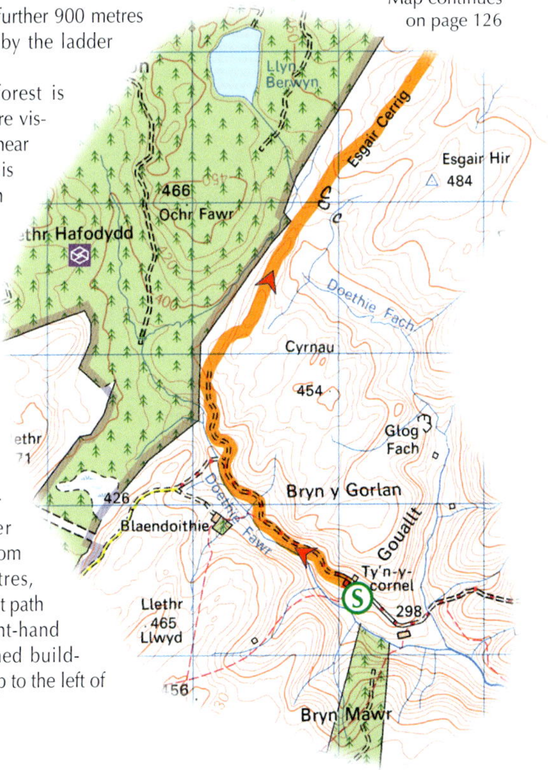

not too difficult. After a further 900 metres cross a low wire fence by the ladder stile near the forestry.

At this point the forest is much closer and the more visible path goes left down near the edge of the forest; this may be reasonable in very dry weather, but generally it is better to aim for the next low ridge, keeping about 100–200 metres from the forest, picking up whatever faint paths there are in places.

Continue NNE, heading for the higher ground of **Esgair Cerrig** until you reach another low wire fence after 1.5km. Descend NNE from the ridge for 800 metres, picking up a more distinct path that leads down its right-hand side towards some ruined buildings and enclosures. Keep to the left of

The telephone box marked here on maps was removed after being vandalised some years previously.

Map continues on page 130

these to cross a small stream and join the road at SN 761 576. (Do not go too far east, as the stream is much wider there having been joined by two others.)

Turn right along the road, which crosses the larger stream, with waterfalls visible 100 metres to the N. After 130 metres, where the road turns SSE, take the track going N towards Nantymaen Farm. ◀ Follow the wide track for 500 metres as it climbs steadily, then bear left on the track going downhill towards **Nantymaen Farm**. After 200 metres the track crosses a stream; take the waymarked diversion first going left by the stream for 50 metres, then NW across fields for 200 metres, then W parallel to the farm track, which it eventually joins after another 100 metres. Take the waymarked field gate here and head NW

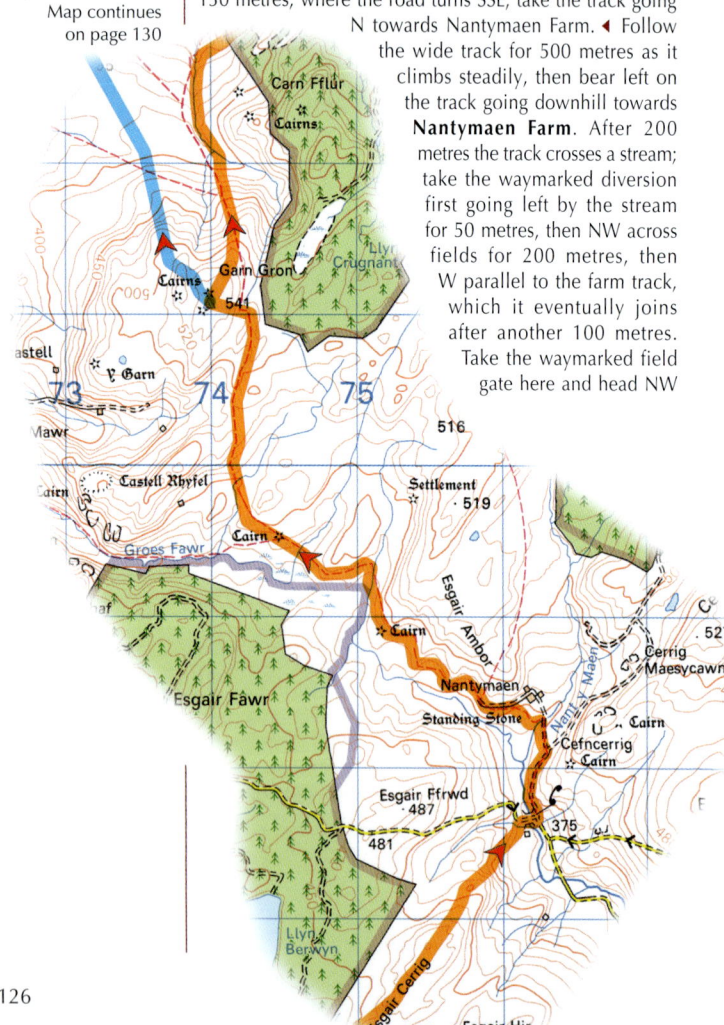

for 1.4km, staying on the dryer part of the hillside as the way follows the stream.

Cross the ford of the Camddwr stream and head N for 150 metres, then turn sharp left and walk for 300 metres before heading NW for 400 metres. ▶ Otherwise, continue NW for another 600 metres, gradually swinging NNW. Some tracks are indistinct but just about visible, avoiding the boggy areas in the valley bottom. Here the route crosses another small stream and joins a track coming from the SW.

A cairn at SN 744 595 marks where a faint path turns off left to eventually join the road to Tregaron (8km W) for those seeking accommodation.

Head N for 1km to SN 743 610, which is about 50 metres W of the corner of the forest. The summit of Garn Gron is 270 metres WNW of here but has been hidden by another hill for some time. There is no clear path to the summit, so just head W up the hillside until the summit trig point and cairn come into sight. **Garn Gron** is Checkpoint 16 at 541m (1776ft) and offers fine long-distance views of Pumlumon to the north and the Brecon Beacons to the south on a clear day. ▶

Pumlumon (anglicised as Plynlimon) means 'five peaks'.

From Garn Gron there is a choice of routes, depending on whether you are seeking accommodation in Pontrhydfendigaid or continuing on the Cambrian Way to Claerddu Bothy. For the route to Pontrhydfendigaid, see the box.

FOR ACCOMMODATION IN PONTRHYDFENDIGAID

There are two options to get to Pontrhydfendigaid ('bridge of the ford of the blessed ones'). The shortest is the direct route from Garn Gron involving about 3km of walking over rough, boggy moorland with few clear paths, then clearer paths into the village; a total of 6km. The other continues to Strata Florida Abbey along the main route, with 2km of rough walking then forest paths to the abbey and good riverside footpaths into the village, totalling around 7km.

Direct route from Garn Gron

From the summit of Garn Gron, head NNW over rough ground for 1.8km, heading just right of **Bryngwyn Bach** ('little white hill') around SN 731 628. Then head N down the hillside, aiming to reach the boundary of the common at SN 732 631 after 500 metres and passing some ruins. There are clearer paths here as you head N for 700 metres to reach a footbridge over **Afon Flur** at SN 730 639, leading to a minor road.

Turn left along the road and head NNW for 100 metres, then fork right and go NE on the farm road, then N for 200 metres to Gilfach-y-dwn-fach Farm. Past the farm, follow the track going left (NW) down the hillside, then N for 450 metres to

Gilfachydwn Fawr. About 150 metres N of this farm, cross a lane and head across the field to its far right-hand corner 150 metres away. Go through the gate into the corner of the next field and head again for the far right-hand corner 300 metres away, near a wood. *The map shows a rather zigzag route, but on the ground this may not be visible.* Cross over a stile into the next field, where the path again heads for a stile at the far-right corner, this time heading NNW for 200 metres. There was a large tree overhanging the stile and it was broken at the time of writing, but hopefully this has now been resolved.

Follow the right-hand boundary of the next two fields for 350 metres, then enter the **caravan park** and follow its right-hand boundary NNW for 150 metres. A row of caravans blocks the right of way in places, so go along the road to the left of them. Beyond the caravan park, continue NNW along the right-hand boundary of the field for 150 metres to meet the main road into Pontrhydfendigaid at SN 728 660. Turn right along the road and continue for 500 metres to the bridge over Afon Teifi in the middle of **Pontrhydfendigaid**.

From Strata Florida Abbey

From the road junction just north of **Strata Florida Abbey**, take the path heading N and follow it for 50 metres to cross Afon Teifi over a footbridge. Fork left, head NW for 150 metres and follow the riverside path NNW for a further 1.3km until it joins a farm access road. Follow this NW for 150 metres; it becomes a minor road – Mill Street – and 200 metres later meets the B4340 road in the middle of **Pontrhydfendigaid**. Turn left along the B4340 and continue for 100 metres to the bridge over Afon Teifi, with the Red Lion pub and the village shop nearby.

Rejoining the main route

From the bridge over Afon Teifi in **Pontrhydfendigaid**, go N for 100 metres then turn sharp right along Mill Street and head ESE for 370 metres. Where the lane swings left by a line of trees, take the path that continues ESE and continue for 100 metres to the riverside, then follow the meandering river E for 1.3km. The path bears SE to cross a small tributary of Afon Teifi, then S to cross the river itself, reaching the road at **Strata Florida Abbey** after a further 200 metres. (This is the reverse of the route from Strata Florida to Pontrhydfendigaid described in the paragraph above.)

The forest to the right is 200 metres away at first, increasing to 400 metres where the streams join.

From Garn Gron, head NNE from the summit down the ridge. There is no clear path down here, but after about 300 metres head N towards the junction of two streams 700 metres ahead. ◄ Follow the stream N for 700 metres until you're becoming level with the start of some enclosures to the left, then swing right and head ENE to enter the forest via a gate at SN 741 628 after 250 metres. There is a Cambrian Way waymark sign made by Tony Drake at the entrance and two more at strategic points through the forest.

Follow the track as it swings to the N for 750 metres before meeting a wide forest track. For the next 700 metres the two tracks run side by side, then the route forks left on the narrow track with another waymark (partially hidden). From here keep heading N for another 750 metres. The track emerges from the forest along a farm lane, and after 100 metres the right of way goes NE for 200 metres, heading diagonally left across a field to the opposite corner. If crops are growing and there is no visible path, follow the left edge of the field.

Cross a stream and follow the left side of the boundary for 300 metres, ignoring a stile, then enter more woodland and continue for another 300 metres. At the bottom of the hill, the woodland ends and a minor road is joined after going N for 200 metres, at **Strata Florida Abbey**.

Strata Florida Abbey is a former Cistercian abbey, founded in 1164, and was an important centre in the medieval period. In 1401 it was taken by King Henry IV and used as a military base against Welsh

The ruins of Strata Florida Abbey

rebel forces led by Owain Glyndŵr. After the rebellion it was returned to the monks, but it was dissolved by Henry VIII in 1539. The ruins are now preserved and are open to the public for a fee. The shop at the Abbey will refill water bottles.

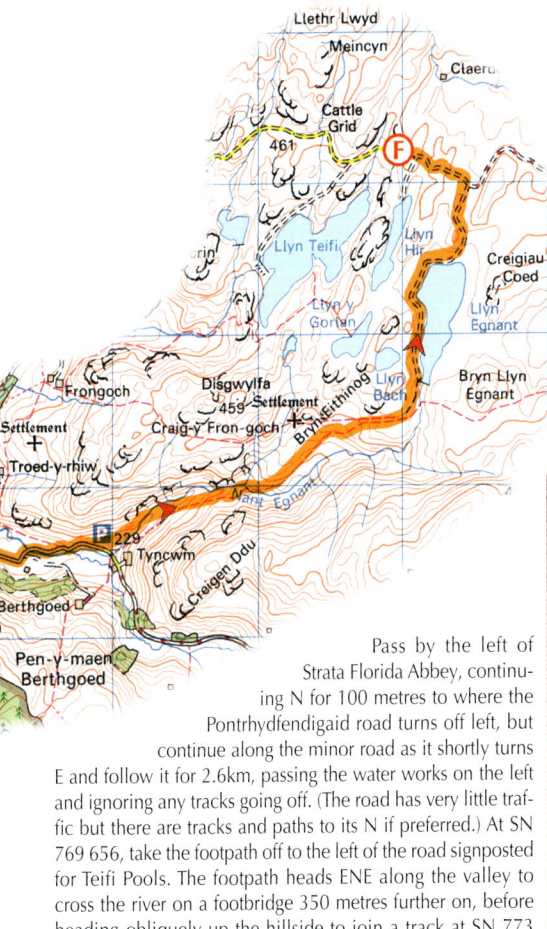

Pass by the left of Strata Florida Abbey, continuing N for 100 metres to where the Pontrhydfendigaid road turns off left, but continue along the minor road as it shortly turns E and follow it for 2.6km, passing the water works on the left and ignoring any tracks going off. (The road has very little traffic but there are tracks and paths to its N if preferred.) At SN 769 656, take the footpath off to the left of the road signposted for Teifi Pools. The footpath heads ENE along the valley to cross the river on a footbridge 350 metres further on, before heading obliquely up the hillside to join a track at SN 773 658, NW of a farm. ▶ Here the track climbs the Nant Egnant valley with the stream cascading down to the left in a series of cataracts.

Follow the track, climbing ENE for 650 metres to where it crosses Nant Egnant at a ford. (If the water is too deep at the ford, there are other crossing points and a makeshift footbridge further upstream.) Continue to climb steadily for another 1.2km. The track levels off and curves left round the hillside, bringing the dam of **Llyn Egnant** into sight. Do not take the track that bears right to cross the stream but head N

This is roughly the halfway point of the Cambrian Way on the main route.

to the left side of the dam 300 metres ahead, at which point the grassy track joins a road.

Although accessible by road, this area is very tranquil, with a series of moorland lakes, reservoirs and wild hills to add to the beauty of the **wilderness**. There are often a few anglers around, but they are there for the peace and quiet and rarely even acknowledge walkers as they pass by.

Head N on the road for 1.6km, first alongside the lake, then up to a T-junction with another minor road. Turn left and follow the road for 500 metres as it meanders W, going up and down over ridges and giving fine views of **Llyn Hir** ('long lake') and **Llyn Teifi** to the left. At SN 791 682, just past a track on the left to Llyn Hir, look out for a track turning right. The stage ends at this point.

This road provides a pick-up point for vehicles from Pontrhydfendigaid for those not using the bothy. Claerddu Bothy is 500 metres further N along the valley. The track is not very good at first but improves after 250 metres. The bothy is an old farmhouse renovated by the Elan Valley Trust as a camping barn with two sleeping platforms, a simple kitchen with bottled gas and outside toilet but no bedding. It is maintained to a high standard.

STAGE 11
Claerddu to Ponterwyd

Start	Minor road near Claerddu Bothy (SN 791 683)
Finish	A44 bridge over Afon Rheidol, Ponterwyd (SN 749 808)
Distance	24km (14¾ miles)
Total ascent	910m (2970ft)
Total descent	1140m (3740ft)
Time	6½–8¼hr
Maps	OS Explorer 213; OS Landranger 147 and 135
Refreshments	Devil's Bridge
Public transport	Bus services to Aberystwyth, Pontrhydfendigaid and Tregaron from Devil's Bridge, and to Llanidloes and Aberystwyth from Ponterwyd
Accommodation	Cwmystwyth 8km; Devil's Bridge 16km; Ponterwyd

The wild and remote walking continues as a large expanse of peat bog is crossed before the route follows a track down to Cwmystwyth. After a short ascent, forestry tracks lead to a stone road dropping gently to Devil's Bridge, after which the Rheidol railway is crossed and re-crossed as the Cambrian Way negotiates the steep gorge of Cwm Rheidol. Country roads and farm tracks then lead to Ponterwyd.

From the road near Claerddu at SN 791 682 (unless you are already at the bothy), take the track going N, just W of

Claerddu Bothy (photo: Rebecca Brough)

133

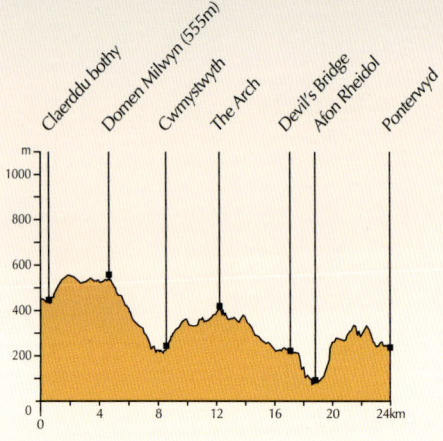

the track at the top of Llyn Hir. It is rather faint at first, but after 250 metres it becomes very clear for the remaining 250 metres to the bothy. Walk over the clapper bridge beside the ford to reach the **bothy**.

Continue along the track, heading NE for 200 metres to where the track crosses a stream and turns left. Here, head N up the hillside to the right of the stream, Nant y Ffynnon, then follow the ridge NNE, heading for the highest point on the ridge 1.2km ahead – Carreg naw llyn ('stone of nine lakes'). ◀ Keep heading NNE along the ridge for a further 1.5km, with Llyn Fyrddon Fawr coming into view. The ridge dips where a stream crosses, then rises again onto Bryn Poeth ('hot hill').

The next objective is Domen Milwyn, the prominent peak 900 metres ahead. If it has been very dry, it is easy just to head across rough ground to reach it, but after wet weather the ground can be very boggy, so the direct route is best avoided by skirting round the base of the hillside until you're beyond the highest point of the valley and then heading across. In which case, keep heading N, avoiding the lower ground to the right, passing the highest point of the valley and starting to descend into another valley ahead. Keep to the left of this valley and cross a small stream, Nant y Domen, near the rocks of Carreg Ddiddos at SN 804 715 after 500 metres. Then take a faint path that swings round to the right, crossing the stream again before climbing W

This is a fine vantage point with Llyn Fyrddon Fach to the left, Llyn Du to the right and Teifi Pools back south.

and following the higher ground to reach the southern end of Domen Milwyn after a further 500 metres. Approach the peak along its eastern side, then turn left to reach the summit after 250 metres. **Domen Milwyn** is Checkpoint 17 at 555m (1820ft). ▶

The view from the summit is even more wild and remote than that from Garn Gron.

Descend from the summit on its eastern side then head slightly W of N, gradually descending the hillside for 500 metres, then head NW for 150 metres to cross Nant Milwyn (stream) at around SN 807 725. (There are faint paths, but it is not critical where the stream is crossed as there are a few stiles further W that can be used.) Head W to join a track along the hillside that initially runs about 100 metres north of the fence. Follow the track for 1.5km, going W and gradually turning NW past the ruins of a cottage on the right to a junction of tracks near the ruins of **Esgair Milwyn Farm**.

Map continues on page 137

Turn left down the hill then go round the right-hand side of the ruins and left down the hillside, heading E to cross a lane 200 metres further down. Across the lane, bear right down the field to join another lane amid trees after 100 metres. There may be no path to follow across the field, but pass by the left of a clump of trees near the bottom. Go right (NNW) along the lane, passing **Tynewydd Farm** after 150 metres. Do not continue along the lane but follow a path straight ahead and descend along the left of a field for 200 metres, then go through some trees to a metal road bridge, where Nant Milwyn joins **Afon Ystwyth** by waterfalls.

Cross the bridge and follow the road up a steep hill for 200 metres, then turn left at the junction with a wider road and follow it for 600 metres as it goes NW to Pentre Farm, then WNW to the old chapel and a group of houses in the middle of **Cwmystwyth**. Turn right up a track opposite the chapel by a house called Y Fron, heading N to the left of the Nant Cae-glas stream which is in a steep valley below. Keep following the stream upwards for 500 metres, keeping to the top of the valley and ignoring a footpath halfway down leading to the first footbridge.

The faint track continues upwards towards the farmhouse of Ty'n-y-rhŷd, passing a waterfall on the opposite side of the valley – this can be quite spectacular after heavy rain. About 150 metres before the farmhouse another footbridge crosses the stream, which by now is not very wide. Cross this footbridge and then climb a set of steps to a reasonably level track and follow alongside the stream to a farm gate.

Through the gate, cross back to the left of the stream – which is narrow enough to step across at this point

Arch at Coed yr Arch (photo: Oliver Wicks)

– and walk past the farm, heading out onto open grassland with a marker post pointing NW up the hillside. The path gradually gets steeper as it approaches the road 500 metres ahead, crossing over a stile on its way.

Turn right along the road and walk for 250 metres, then enter the forest on the left where the road turns sharp right. Follow the forest track as it heads NW then WNW for 600 metres and climbs over a rise, crossing a wide track on the way. At the next wide track, take a short left and right to get onto the track going W to **Gelmast Farm**, which is in a clearing in the forest. Pass to the left of the farm after 250 metres and follow the track W along the hillside until it enters the forest again after 500 metres. After another 300 metres the track bears left

Map continues on page 139

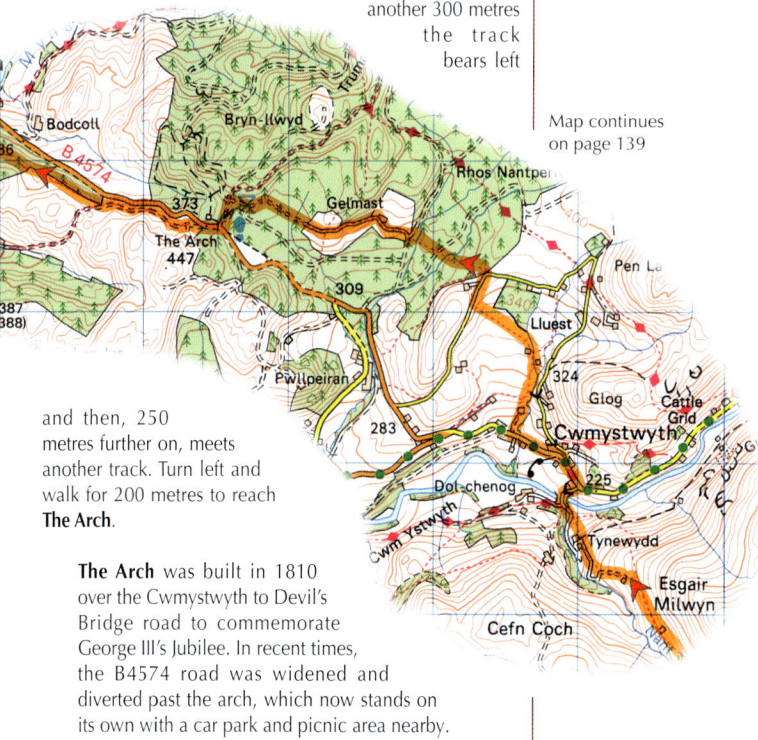

and then, 250 metres further on, meets another track. Turn left and walk for 200 metres to reach **The Arch**.

The Arch was built in 1810 over the Cwmystwyth to Devil's Bridge road to commemorate George III's Jubilee. In recent times, the B4574 road was widened and diverted past the arch, which now stands on its own with a car park and picnic area nearby.

Turn right and head W along the road for 100 metres, then take the track that forks left, following it for 75 metres. This follows the main road at a higher level, offering fine, open views across the valley, improved by recent clear-felling. At a fork in the track, keep right and continue for a further 1.6km of reasonably level walking, avoiding any tracks to left or right, to exit the forest.

Continue W along the moorland track to meet a bend on the B4343 road towards Devil's Bridge after 1.1km. Go straight ahead (WNW) on the road for 100 metres to where it bears right, and NW for 150 metres to a school on the right. Turn sharp right past the buildings on a lane going E and walk for 100 metres then NE for another 100 metres to a line of trees. Leave the lane at a waymark, bearing left down the hillside for 450 metres. ◄ Cross a stile on the right onto a track and head down to the A4120 road in **Devil's Bridge**.

For Nant Syddion Bothy (5.3km) continue E along the lane, passing above and S of Rhos-tyddyn.

Where the route enters **Devil's Bridge**, immediately opposite is the terminus of the Vale of Rheidol Railway, with a café which is open whenever the railway is running – see www.rheidolrailway.co.uk. The bridge itself over Afon Mynach is 300 metres east, near the Hafod Hotel. It is in three tiers as it is built on top of two earlier bridges. The famous Devil's Bridge Falls (Rhaeadrau Pontarfynach) can be visited for a fee, with a coin-operated turnstile when not manned – see http://devilsbridgefalls.co.uk.

Go left up the main road, heading W for 250 metres through the village. The road swings NW for 200 metres; look out for a path going N beyond the houses where the main road swings left. Follow this waymarked trail for 500 metres as it swings round the hillside and heads NW and descends to the railway line. Cross the level crossing through the gate and follow the path running alongside the railway line NW for 200 metres as it swings N, then continue along the path as it descends steeply through the Coed Rheidol Nature Reserve forest for 300 metres, gradually swinging round W and then NW to reach the bridge **Pontbren Pwlca** after 700 metres. ◄ This is Checkpoint 18.

This is only named on detailed local maps (Pontbren means Wooden Bridge).

After crossing the bridge, turn right and follow the lower road, going ESE beside **Afon Rheidol** for 500 metres, passing some waterfalls. The road then becomes a track and starts climbing and swinging ESE, departing from the river through woodland. After 300 metres a track turns off sharp left, going N. Follow this up the steep slope, ignoring any tracks going off to the left. It swings round to the right and levels off after 600 metres before reaching a T-junction. Turn left along the track, going N to Penrhiw Farm then left and right to the hamlet of **Ystumtuen** after 550 metres. Here, bear right along the road and go downhill to the NE, then uphill, passing some buildings on the left after 400 metres.

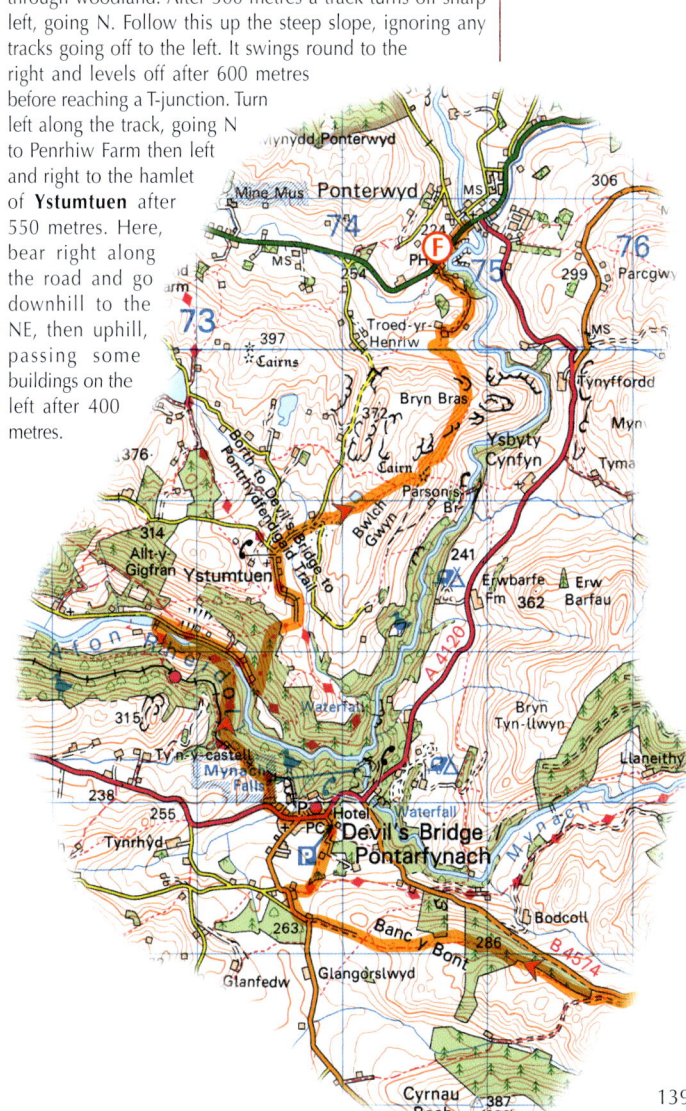

Fork right from the road up a track heading E through an area of disused lead mines. (Do not confuse this with the minor road turning sharp right 50 metres earlier.) After 100 metres, from the top of the hill a small tarn can be seen ahead at the foot of Bryn Bras. Take the waymarked path that passes to the right of it, heading ENE and up the valley, crossing a stile on your left on the ascent. After 450 metres the path starts to descend and after a further 200 metres it reaches a junction.

Do not take the path ahead, which continues downhill to Parson's Bridge. Instead take the path to the left, which heads N to cross a stile in the fence and then a stream, where it swings right and descends beside the stream's left bank. After 250 metres the path turns left, gradually ascending the craggy, heather-covered hillside and heading NNE. The path is not very clear in places, but a series of marker posts guide the way. ◄

There are good views east across the steep-sided Rheidol Valley from here.

After a further 450 metres the path reaches the top of the ridge and curves left round the hillside, descending into the valley bottom in another 450 metres. Near the bottom it turns sharp right to cross the stream, then left up to Bryn-brâs Farm. At the farm, turn right along the access track, which heads E then curves round the hillside until it is heading NW where it joins the **A44** road at the George Borrow Hotel after 650 metres. **Ponterwyd** village centre is 400 metres NE along the main road, with a filling station and shop on the way.

Ponterwyd and Pumlumon from Bryn Bras

STAGE 12
Ponterwyd to Dylife

Start	A44 bridge over Afon Rheidol, Ponterwyd (SN 749 808)
Finish	Minor road near Star Inn, Dylife (SN 861 940)
Distance	23.5km (14½ miles)
Total ascent	920m (3030ft)
Total descent	780m (2550ft)
Time	6½–8¼hr
Maps	OS Explorer 213, 214 (for 3km only) and 215; OS Landranger 147 and 135
Refreshments	None on route
Public transport	Bus services to Llanidloes and Aberystwyth from Ponterwyd
Accommodation	Dylife

The Cambrian Way now ascends Pumlumon, one of the wildest and most remote mountain areas in Wales. It provides a watershed between the east and west of the country and the sources of the Rivers Wye, Severn and Rheidol. There are 13km (8 miles) over 600m (1970ft), and in bad weather – especially mist – very careful navigation is necessary. There are fences and large boundary markers to follow but the former can lead the walker astray in places. The route drops to Bugeilyn lake, from which easier tracks lead to Dylife, once a thriving lead mining village, and its welcoming Star Inn.

From the bridge in **Ponterwyd** take the A44 NE for 80 metres, then turn right along the A4120 and continue for 250 metres to where the road turns to the right. Take the track that turns off left on the bend, heading ENE with a row of trees on the right. After 250 metres, where the trees end, bear a little to the right and follow a path across a field which then bears left up the hillside ahead. The path gets closer to the road, which is higher up to the right, until it emerges onto the **B4343** after 600 metres. Follow this road E for 1.4km as it gradually descends to join the A44. Fortunately, this road is fairly quiet and there is only another 400 metres to walk along the busy A44, heading E to **Dyffryn Castell** ('castle valley').

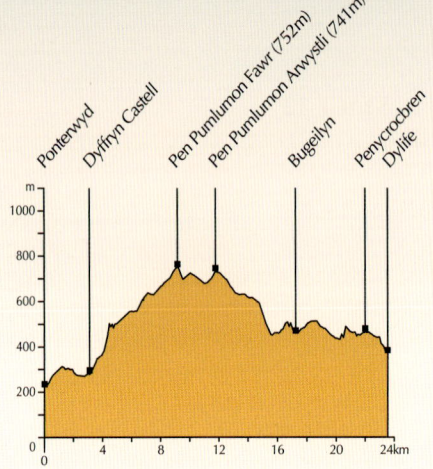

Dyffryn Castell Hotel was built over 400 years ago and used to be a staging post for travellers to Aberystwyth. Modern transport made this unnecessary, but it continued to attract visitors in declining numbers until it closed around 2008. Renovation work was started but not completed, and it has been on the market ever since. It is unlikely to reopen as an inn and is more likely to be converted to other uses.

Just past the hotel buildings, take a path going N up the hillside to the left of a line of trees, with the stream down to the left, and continue for 250 metres before bearing NNE for 400 metres. After levelling off, the path starts a steeper ascent diagonally up the hillside, still heading NNE. It is rather faint and doesn't follow the line shown on OS maps.

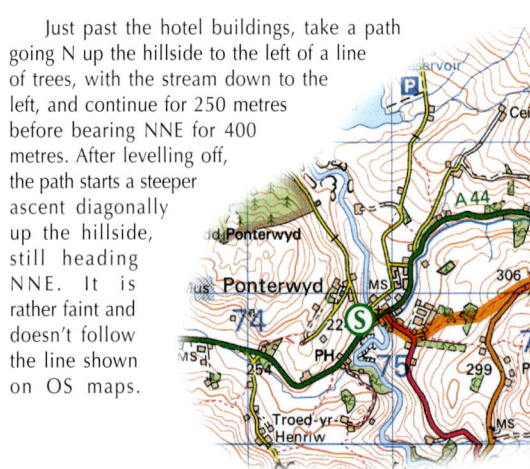

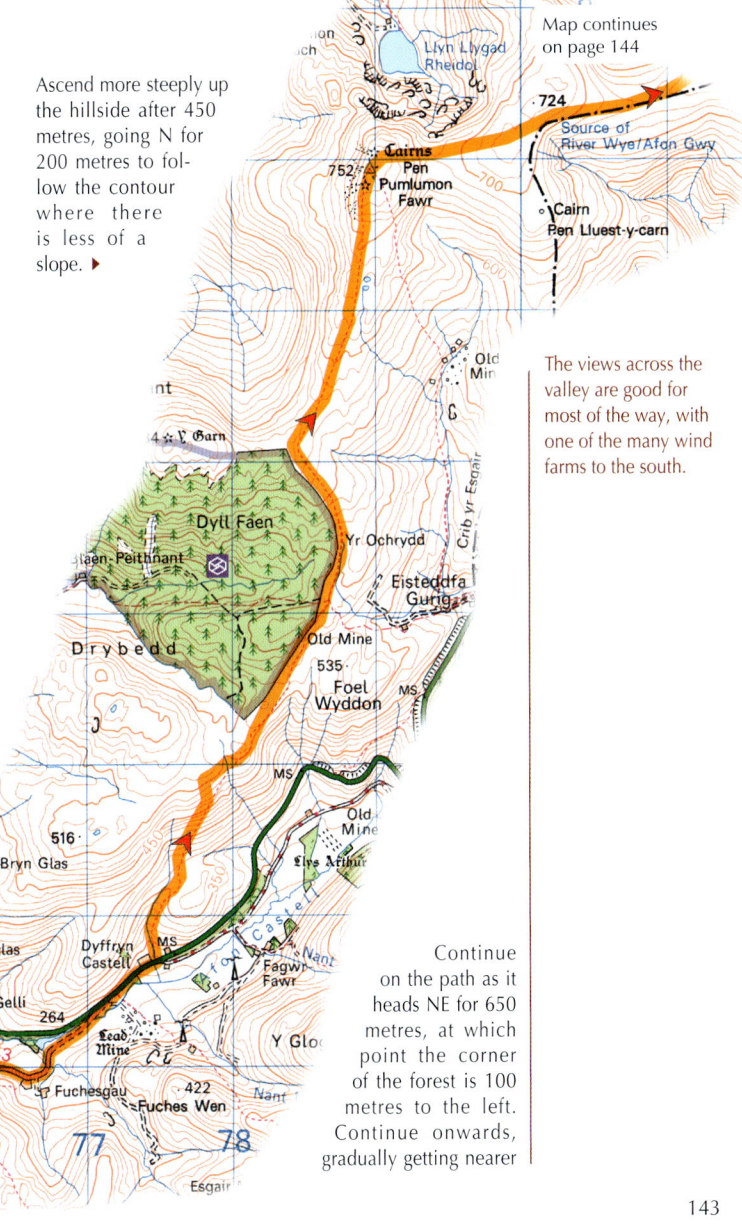

Ascend more steeply up the hillside after 450 metres, going N for 200 metres to follow the contour where there is less of a slope. ▶

Map continues on page 144

The views across the valley are good for most of the way, with one of the many wind farms to the south.

Continue on the path as it heads NE for 650 metres, at which point the corner of the forest is 100 metres to the left. Continue onwards, gradually getting nearer

143

to the forest and reaching it after 800 metres. Maps show the path entering the edge of the forest and occupying it for 200 metres, but this is overgrown by trees. Continue along a path

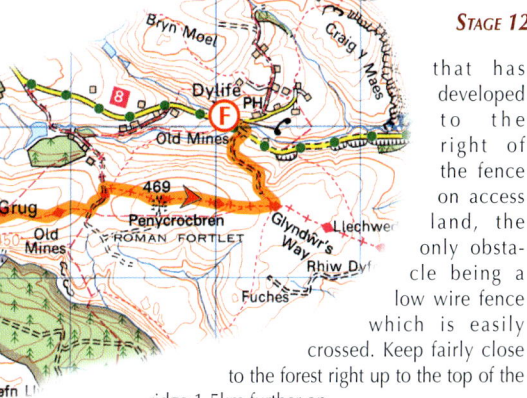

that has developed to the right of the fence on access land, the only obstacle being a low wire fence which is easily crossed. Keep fairly close to the forest right up to the top of the ridge 1.5km further on.

From the top of the ridge, wide views open up on both sides, and navigation is a simple matter of following the fence NE, gradually turning N to the summit of **Pen Pumlumon Fawr** nearly 2km ahead. This is Checkpoint 19 at 752m (2468ft).

> **Pen Pumlumon Fawr** ('large head of five peaks') is anglicised as Plynlimon. There is a large cairn just before the summit, which also has a trig point and a circular stone wind shelter. The large Nant-y-moch Reservoir and the coast can be seen from near the summit, as can Cadair Idris and several wind farms. Llyn Llygad Rheidol ('eye of Rheidol lake') can be seen by walking a little way N of the summit, although it does come into sight a little further along the route.

From the summit, follow the left side of the fence going E, passing another cairn before descending into a dip. (It is from here that Llyn Llygad Rheidol comes into view on the left and it can easily be missed when concentrating on the way ahead.) A gentle rise leads to an unnamed summit with a cairn and boundary stone, 950 metres from Pumlumon. ▶

A valley off to the right is the source of the River Wye (Afon Gwy).

Continue E, rather than following the fence, and join another fence 350 metres further on. Follow this E for 900 metres and then stay with the path as it bears left away from the fence to reach the summit of **Pen Pumlumon Arwystli**, 400 metres ahead. Head NE past two cairns and join a track by the fence after 300 metres. Follow this for 200 metres but then take a path bearing slightly left towards a stone and a fence 200 metres ahead and 50m higher up the hillside (whereas the track heads for the corner of the forest to turn downhill).

> There are seven **slate marker stones** on the higher ground over Pen Pumlumon Fawr and Pen Pumlumon Arwystli. Most have the inscription 'WWW 1865' and an upward-pointing arrow, although the inscriptions vary a little. The initials refer to Watkins William-Wynn who was a very rich landowner, owning vast areas of land in Wales, even extending across the border into Shropshire. It is, therefore, likely that they marked a boundary to some of his land.

Continue on the faint path, which is now heading almost due N near the fence and watershed for 1km to pass a small **tarn** on the left. Continue N for 550 metres, where an optional detour over a stile and along a path to the right leads to the **source of the River Severn** (Afon Hafren), 100 metres E with large marker posts. Back on the route, head NNW up the rise, where there is another boundary stone and a white stone cairn. Soon the path disappears, and it is necessary to walk over open ground for some way, although it may be possible to pick up some faint paths.

Continue slightly W of due N, heading for the stone **Carn Fawr** ('big cairn') 500 metres ahead. From here continue N, heading down the hillside by whatever route is easiest for 900 metres, the aim being to arrive at a point in the valley where it is easy to cross the stream, which runs in an underground pipe from the east and emerges at SN 8175 9139 to flow west in the open. There is a marker post at this spot, but the aim is to ensure that you are not anywhere W of this. There is a lot of boggy ground and long reeds around here, so having passed this point it is best to take the shortest route to the track around the hillside by heading NNW for 300 metres, then going W along the hillside, following the track as it swings around N overlooking **Bugeilyn** ('shepherd lake'). After 1.2km the track crosses the stream that joins the two lakes and heads upwards to reach ruined farm buildings, also called **Bugeilyn**, after 400 metres.

OS maps show a right of way cutting across to the **boathouse** by the lake, but there is little evidence of this on the ground and no easy crossing point on the stream, so it is best accessed by a track off to the right 100 metres after crossing the stream if desired.

The route passes between the two expanses of Bugeilyn lake

From the ruined buildings, continue N for 100 metres to a modern barn that is still in use and can offer some shelter from wind and rain. Head N for a further 550 metres, where the track turns right at the top of the rise with views of the small moorland tarn called **Glaslyn** ('blue lake') to the N. Follow the track as it bears right, going E for 400 metres to join Glyndŵr's Way at a junction of tracks.

Bear right and follow Glyndŵr's Way for 4.3km. It is well signposted and fairly easy to follow, but described here nonetheless. Head ESE for 450 metres, then turn right on a track down the side of the Nant Ddu ('black stream') valley (although staying on the original track is optional) with evidence of old mining activity in the form of spoil heaps and ruined buildings. After 450 metres, rejoin the original track.

Continue down to the bottom of the valley, with zigzags past old buildings, to cross a footbridge after 850 metres. Ascend on the higher of two paths along the next hillside for 800 metres then bear right at a fork, going E down the southern side of the hill for 600 metres. Turn left along the dip between two hills and continue for 200 metres before

turning sharp right and going E uphill to reach **Penycrocbren**,
a Roman fortlet, after 450 metres.

> **Penycrocbren** means 'head of the gallows' and
> is the setting for a gruesome tale: in the 1700s a
> blacksmith who had been working in the local lead
> mines murdered his wife and two children. For this
> he received the death penalty, and he was made
> to forge the iron frame in which his body was then
> hung.
>   The site has been identified as a minor Roman
> military work with a turf-built bank. There was no
> ditch, and this is presumed to be due to the rocky
> ground. It is thought that four large posts at the
> entrance supported a tower, but no trace of build-
> ings has been discovered. The site is similar to mile-
> castles found on Hadrian's Wall that held garrisons
> of soldiers.

The Star Inn can be seen to the N, but rather than taking
a steep route down, continue for another 700 metres E down
the hill to SN 864 935, where a good track turns sharp left
and heads NW downhill for 650 metres to meet the road at
Dylife. ◄ Turn left on the road and follow it for 50 metres to
SN 861 940, where a road to the right leads to the Star Inn.
The stage ends at this road junction, which is Checkpoint 20.

*For the bothy in
Hafren Forest (4.1km),
at SN 864 935
continue E following
Glyndŵr's Way.*

148

STAGE 13
Dylife to Dinas Mawddwy

Start	Minor road near Star Inn, Dylife (SN 861 940)
Finish	Red Lion Inn (Y Llew Coch), Dinas Mawddwy (SH 859 149)
Distance	37km (23 miles)
Total ascent	1470m (4820ft)
Total descent	1740m (5720ft)
Time	10–12¾hr
Maps	OS Explorer 215 and OL 23; OS Landranger 135 and 124
Refreshments	Cemmaes (off-route) and Mallwyd
Public transport	Bus services to Machynlleth and Wrexham from Commins Coch, and to Machynlleth and Dolgellau from Dinas Mawddwy and Cemmaes
Accommodation	Cemmaes 15.5km (+3.5km); Mallwyd 32.5km; Dinas Mawddwy

This section is in complete contrast to the starkness of Pumlumon, with much undulating grassy and moorland walking over two attractive passes. There is a swift descent to Commins Coch – and an alternative accommodation route for the village of Cemmaes – then lanes and tracks ascend to a traverse of the Mynydd y Cemmaes wind farm. The trail negotiates a slightly tricky forestry section, which is followed by an ascent and then a descent to Mallwyd. It then climbs and contours along the mountain before finally descending to Dinas Mawddwy.

From the road junction in **Dylife** at SN 861 940, head NE then E for 250 metres, going past the Star Inn car park to where a track takes a sharp left turn up the hillside by a clump of trees. Follow this track, turning right after 50 metres and heading N for 400 metres, then turning left to pass behind a modern farm building before going sharp right and N up a grassy bank to go through a gate. After 200 metres the track descends to cross a stream and the open moorland starts.

There is a right of way running halfway up the right-hand side of the valley ahead, and this could be followed for 500 metres as it swings NW; however, it is easier to follow a fainter

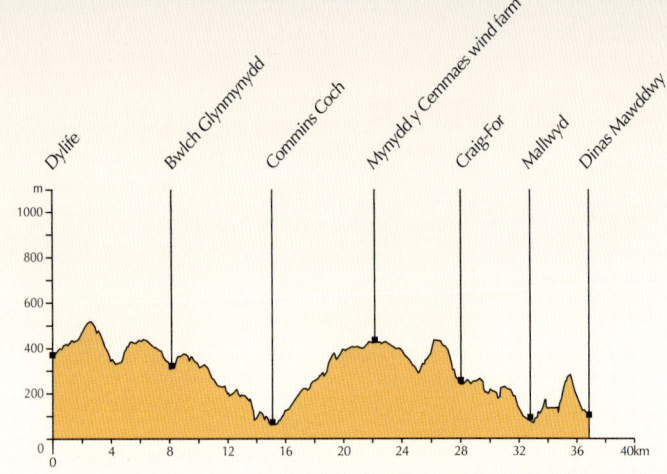

Dylife
Bwlch Glynmynydd
Commins Coch
Mynydd y Cemmaes wind farm
Craig-For
Mallwyd
Dinas Mawddwy
m
1000
800
600
400
200
0
0
4
8
12
16
20
24
28
32
36
40km

path straight up the end of the hillside, which is easily discerned from the previous raised ground. Where the path levels off somewhat at SN 863 950, head NW across gentler sloping ground to rejoin the right of way where it meets a fence.

Turn right up the hill and walk alongside the fence for a few yards to go through a gate at SN 858 953. Continue NW straight up the hillside for 650 metres to the top corner of a second field at the brow of the hill. Go through

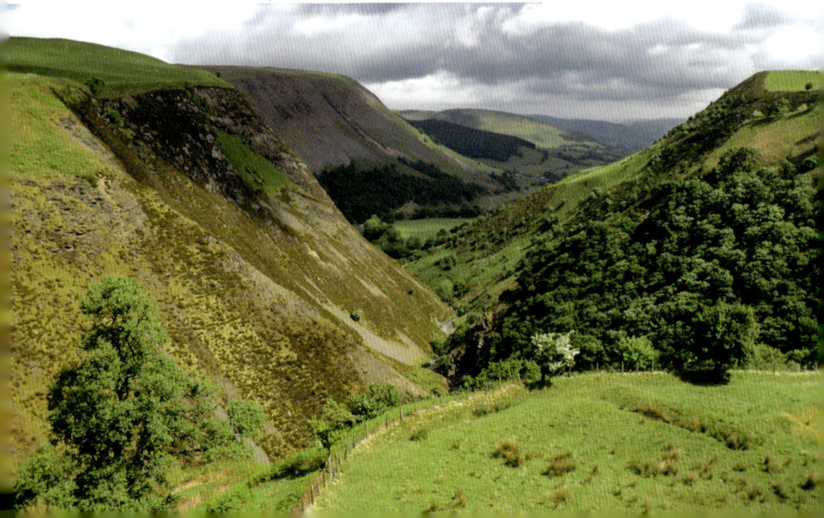

Pennant Valley near Dylife

Map continues
on page 155

Some splendid views open up across the steep-sided valley westwards in the direction of Machynlleth.

two gates that lead out onto a track which skirts around the head of a valley to the left. Follow this N as it meanders somewhat downhill on the right-hand side of the valley for 1.7km to pass some sheep pens then the steep crags of **Craig y Gath** on the left and then reach the forest at SN 849 973. ◄

Enter the forest via a gate, going sharp left and continuing SW for 100 metres on the forest track, then bear right to go obliquely uphill on a wider track, heading WNW for 300 metres. Turn sharp right at an open area with a junction of tracks, heading E for 100 metres, still going uphill. Look out for a path bearing left and going NE up the steep hillside and follow this for another 100 metres to where it joins a wider track heading NW. This meanders right and left for 250 metres to end at a turning circle where you should take a sharp right turn along a much fainter track, then veer left to exit the forest 200 metres later at SN 848 978.

In case of confusion with all the zigzags, the aim is reach the highest point of the forest, always taking the tracks that go upwards. Should you mistakenly go too far E, there is another track that will rejoin the route a few hundred metres further on.

On exiting the forest head NNE, and the next gate soon comes into view. The paths are not very clear and tend to go a little further north than the line shown on maps. The route dips to a gate after 250 metres, then climbs again, heading NE. It levels off alongside a valley to the right, coming to a corner of two fences after 450 metres at SN 853 983. The right of way then follows the left-hand side of the fence for 1.2km, but this has become overgrown and boggy with lack of use. It is much easier to follow a faint path for 100 metres through the heather on the south side of the fence to reach a clear and easy vehicle track. Follow this track for 800 metres to SN 861 987, where the path on the north side can be rejoined through a gate. ◄

There are some good views of small tarns and a steep valley on the right, and the lakes of Llynnau Caeconroi further on.

The path is much clearer now but take care to turn left after 300 metres, just before a rocky outcrop, where the route heads N down the hillside then swings E to meet the road 600 metres further on at the head of the **Bwlch Glynmynydd** pass with good views to both sides. Cross the road and enter the forest on a track that initially goes left heading NNW but soon swings right to head steadily NE up the ridge. ◄

Recent clear-felling has opened up the views to the west.

After 400 metres the track curves round the hillside, eventually heading WNW after another 400 metres. At this point, maps show it cutting across the corner of the forest, but this route is no longer passable so take a path which continues along the edge of the forest to go through a gate 200 metres further on.

Turn right to follow the edge of the forest NE. The path is not very clear for the next 900 metres, but keep close to the forest for 200 metres then contour along the hillside, heading initially N to go through a gate, then NW and NE to go through another gate at SH 868 005. Again, the path is not clear and doesn't quite agree with the map, but head N and descend into the valley through a field for 400 metres to join a clear green track raking up W through the scrub, reaching the brow after a further 400 metres.

Head WNW down the hillside, crossing a farm track and passing to the left of some trees, aiming for ruined buildings 350 metres beyond. Here, at last, is a clear farm track, turning right and heading NE at first, then turning W at the bottom of the valley after 200 metres. Follow this for 600 metres to where another track joins from the right. Bear right here,

Llynau Caeconroi near Bwlch Glynmynydd

going NW downhill across the field, cutting off the corner and rejoining the track to go N after 200 metres at the corner of a field by farm buildings. Follow the track right past the building and turn immediately left down the grassy hillside, swinging right at the bottom to meet a road after 200 metres.

Turn left along the road and follow it for 80 metres to the point at which it crosses a steam. Here the road turns left to **Maesteg** but the route turns right along a track, going N along the edge of a forest and entering it after 300 metres. Stay on the forest track as it winds back and forth along the hillside, going NW then N again. After 1.1km the track swings round to loop back left. Look out for the waymarked path that goes straight ahead down the hillside just round the bend.

Carry on straight downhill (N) for 300 metres to join a minor road at the bottom. Turn left and continue along the road for 900 metres as it follows the bend in the river to head N. Turn right at the road junction and go down to meet the main A470 road at **Commins Coch** after 100 metres. Turn right along the A470 to cross the river after 150 metres, then turn left under the railway bridge on a minor road. Follow this road as it heads N for 500 metres to SH 846 035. For anyone seeking accommodation at Cemmaes, the optional route bears left, whereas the main Cambrian Way route bears uphill to the right.

FOR ACCOMMODATION IN CEMMAES

Bear left between two lots of buildings on a track that heads N on a fairly level course. After 120 metres the track turns left to head WNW for 500 metres to **Glyntwmyn Farm**, passing trees on the hillside to the right. Bear left below the farm where the track becomes a grassy path, heading W and curving round the hillside for 550 metres. At a fork in the track bear right uphill and head N, keeping to the right-hand side of the valley for 600 metres.

On approaching the top of the ridge, cross Glyndŵr's Way and head NW then N over the top, starting to descend after 200 metres. Continue through a gate and head NNW for 100 metres. The fence across the path here is new and bypasses the old stile; you will need to cross the corner of the adjacent field via two gates to regain the line of the footpath. Then head diagonally across to join a track at the left of the field, reaching a farm at the bottom of the hill after 500 metres. Continue through the farm and bear left to join the **A470** after a further 350 metres. Turn right along the road and walk for 550 metres to **Cemmaes** and the Penrhos Arms Hotel.

Map continues on page 159

The Dovey Valley from Mynydd y Cemmaes

To rejoin the Cambrian Way, from the Penrhos Arms go back SSW along the A470 for 50 metres then turn left along a minor road and go SE then ESE for 450 metres. Turn left along a narrower road and go N uphill past some buildings, heading towards a mast 350 metres away up the hill with the road swinging NE on the way. By the mast, bear right, still climbing steadily in a generally E direction, and continue for 800 metres to where a track leads to **Tynwtra Farm**. Ignore the turning to the left 200 metres before the farm, and continue ahead towards the farm buildings.

The path is shown on the map as passing to the N of the house but there is no through access here. Instead, bear right in front of the house to pass the farm buildings and go through the gate immediately beyond them. Turn sharp left to climb through the field, heading towards the northern boundary. Walk generally E along the boundary of this and the next field, climbing steadily. Continue to follow the track, which after 300 metres goes right and then left to follow the right-hand side of the next field. After a further 400 metres the track runs parallel to the wind farm access road, which can be accessed by a gate at SH 859 057 if wished, just before the start of the line of trees. *To avoid the difficult section described below, go through the gate and follow the access road uphill as it does a large zigzag. The bend in this at SH 862 054 is where the main route is joined.* At the time of writing (2018), the right of way ahead had several obstructions, making it difficult in wet conditions. The route follows the northern edge of the small diamond-shaped wood close to the steep-sided valley of the stream. Towards the place where a ford is marked on 1:25,000 maps, low branches obstruct the boggy path, making progress difficult, but not impossible. To make matters worse, the ford has been washed away by heavy rain, so it is necessary to scramble down the steep valley and back up the other side, where a rusty old gate must be scaled. After this the going is easy up a well-defined track, climbing the hillside and heading N to rejoin the main route at the top of the hill.

From SH 846 035 continue along the road, heading NE up the hillside for 600 metres, then bear left at a fork in the road and continue for another 800 metres to where the road starts to level and turns left. ▶ Take the track ahead (Glyndŵr's Way) and continue for 650 metres to meet a minor road. Turn left and walk for 100 metres, then turn right on a track which goes E and then curves round **Moel Eiddew** for 200 metres to head NW.

For the campsite at Commins Gwalia, turn left up the road (0.4km).

The track turns sharp right, but here head N for 100 metres towards the right-hand end of a row of trees. Cross a small stream behind the trees and go through a gate to enter the corner of a field. The path goes NW, following a fence on the left (not on the current map) and heading gradually uphill to reach a gate at the far boundary 250 metres away. Continue on the path in the next field as it gradually curves round to the N past some trees along a short section of boundary, reaching a fence at SH 861 052 after 250 metres. There is no longer a stile here, but the fence is easily scaled to join a track heading along the hillside, curving round from ENE to N.

After 300 metres a bend in a much wider track is reached. This is the wind farm access road, with permissive access for walkers. ▶ The right of way shown through the diamond-shaped forest here has been blocked for many years, so the best option is to follow the wind farm road uphill to the right. Continue uphill for 200 metres to reach the easternmost corner of the forest, where the access road starts to zigzag to the right. Bear left down the bank to the forest corner, cross a stile and continue along a faint track heading NE, with fine views across the Dovey Valley to the mountains beyond. After a short while the track gives way to the open hillside, and by following this around roughly along a contour in a northerly direction the main track can be reached after about 300 metres at around SH 864 062. ▶

This is one of the places where the Cemmaes option can rejoin.

This is the second place where the Cemmaes option can rejoin.

The **wind farm** on Mynydd y Cemmaes was commissioned in 2002/03 and consists of 18 turbines of 850kw, making a total nominal output of 15,300kw. The height of each turbine hub is 40m, with three 26m-long blades. In recent years there has been much local opposition to onshore wind farms in picturesque areas, and there is now a preference for offshore wind farms or locations that have less natural beauty.

The route is clear for the next 100 metres or so (depending on where you joined it), but where it swings right towards the wind farm carry on along a faint footpath going straight ahead. This cuts off a corner and goes over the highest point of this part of the ridge to meet the access road after 200 metres. After briefly joining the road, fork left to follow the edge of the hillside for 800 metres before meeting a fence line and heading back to the access road again. The route again forks left to follow the edge of the hillside, reaching a steep-sided valley and going W after 600 metres. ◄ After another 150 metres the access road is rejoined, and this time it is followed for 1.6km. For those preferring a softer surface, a bridleway runs not far from the road for most of the way, although this is faint and difficult to make out in places.

This is one of the finest viewpoints of the Dovey Valley from Mynydd y Cemmaes, with Cadair Idris and other mountains beyond.

The use of the **bridleway** serves two purposes, offering off-road walking as well as giving the best views into the Dovey Valley for much of the way. However, in bad visibility, when there are no views, it is easier to use the wind farm access road. This simplifies route finding and is dryer underfoot – and in thick mist it is quite an eerie sensation when passing close to one of the turbines with its presence only being detected by the whooshing of its blades and the humming of its generator before its shape finally appears.

At SH 875 089, where the main track bends to the right towards the last wind turbine, follow a clear but greener track ahead up a small rise, and then a faint path bearing right towards a fence junction and gate at the forest corner. Go through the gate and head E down the hillside with the forest to the left. Paths are unclear down here, but it is best to keep 100 metres from the forest where the ground is less steep and less boggy. After 400 metres the path turns towards a waymarked entrance to the forest at SH 882 092 in a slight dip.

The faint path runs N for 170 metres, deviating to the right on occasion to avoid fallen trees. At around SH 882 093 the path turns left through a clearer area and continues for 300 metres before exiting the forest. Continue W, following the edge of the forest by a stream along **Waun Llinau**,

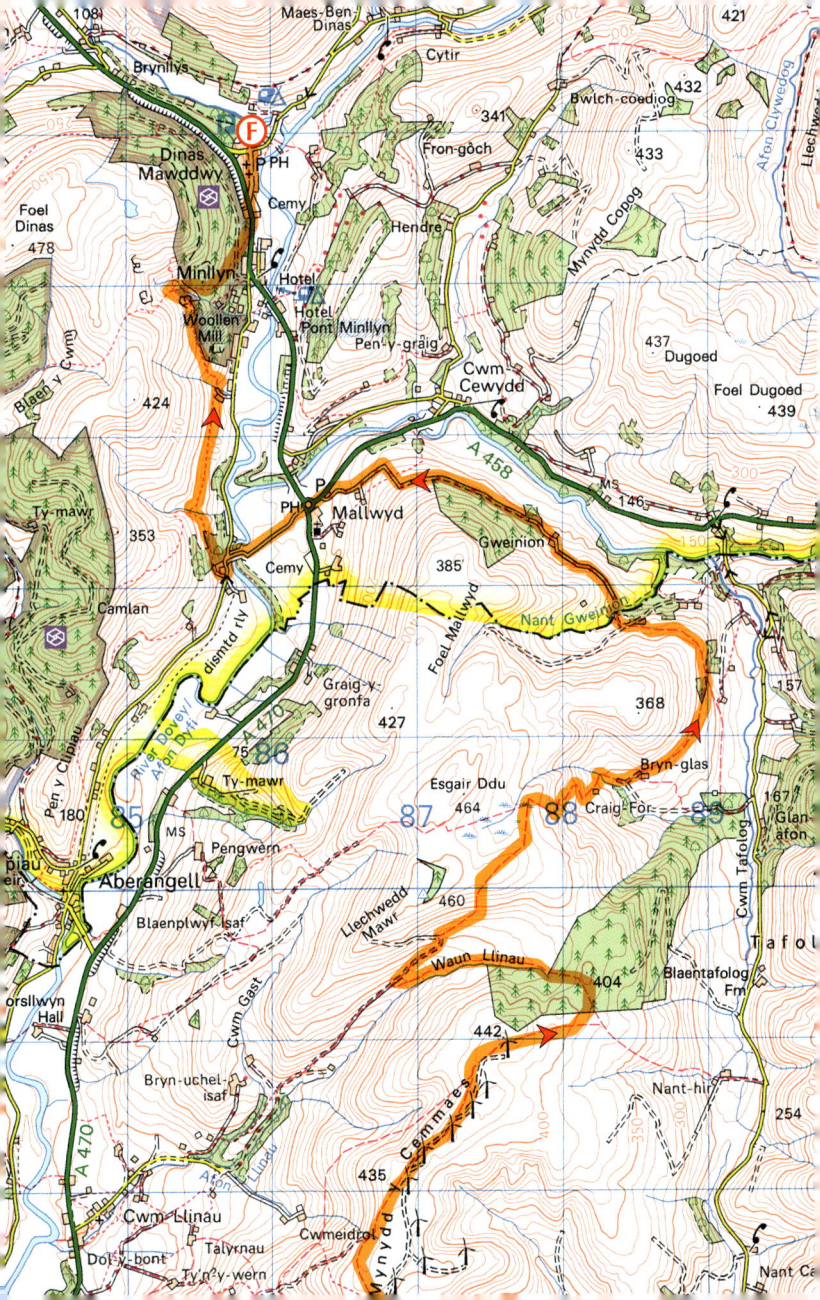

looking out for occasional marker posts. This whole area can become very boggy, but the path attempts to avoid the worst parts by keeping on the highest ground. After 450 metres the forest ends.

Looking at the map, it may be tempting to head N for 300 metres to avoid walking over 1.4km down the valley and back up the other side, but the boggy ground and thick tufty grass make for extremely difficult walking, so it may take just as long and be more tiring.

Therefore, continue W to the right of the stream for 650 metres, where the path joins a track running along the hillside to the north. Turn sharp right and follow the track NE for 450 metres. Ignore a track turning sharp left and continue ENE for another 350 metres to SH 874 098, where a way-mark points left up the steep hillside. Follow the steep path N for 150 metres, then it starts to level off and continues NE for another 150 metres to cross over a low wire fence with a small, stone-stepped stile.

Paths are again faint, but head NE along the ridge for 300 metres, then N for 300 metres, keeping above the low ground to the left. ◀ Turn right at SH 878 105, heading E then SE for 200 metres to join a stream partway down a steep valley. Turn sharp left to descend NNE along the stream for 200 metres, crossing it on the way. Zigzag right and left for a further 250 metres to reach the farm building at **Craig-For**.

Nearby are two streams; the first to the north being very steep with waterfalls, the second to the east descending a little more gently.

Follow the farm access track N and then E, ignoring a branch off to the right, to reach the ruined buildings of **Bryn-glas** after 400 metres. Here, do not take the more obvious track which forks left up the hillside, but keep further down along the boundary, where the path continues on an almost level route round the hillside for 1.6km, becoming a well-defined track after a short distance and swinging gradually round in a semicircle to head W. ◀ At SH 884 117, cross a farm track and swing N to cross two streams at fords. Then join a track, which soon becomes surfaced, and follow it for 2.6km to **Mallwyd**.

There are good views across the valley to the east from here.

Mallwyd is the first place for a long way with any facilities. It has a fuel station with a shop and café, and the high-class Brigands Inn with a bar and accommodation. A wider range of options is available in Dinas Mawddwy, only 5km ahead.

From the roundabout where the A458 joins the A470, take the small road going WSW for 650 metres to Pont Mallwyd, the bridge over **Afon Dyfi** (River Dovey). Over the bridge, turn left along the road. After 100 metres take the waymarked track on the right and follow it NNW up the hill-side with clumps of trees on either side.

After 550 metres, where the main track swings left, bear right through trees to cross a ford. Do not take the track going steeply up to the left but head N to the grassy hillside a short way ahead and join an almost level but fairly faint path. After 250 metres this becomes a clearer track with the boundary on the right for 400 metres, then it dips to cross a stream near Maes-y-camlan Farm. ▶

Follow the path through the edge of a clump of trees and cross a stile to turn left up the grassy hillside. Where the trees end, cross the fence ahead and follow a faint path NNW past spoil heaps to the fence corner at SH 855 135. Walk up alongside the fence. Here, some beautiful views appear over the Dovey Valley to the mountains beyond.

After 450 metres pass some trees on the right and bear left towards the lower part of the quarry, passing some

Heading towards Mallwyd near the end of the stage

For facilities in Minllyn (0.9km), turn right down to a minor road and then turn left along the road.

Pont Minllyn over the Dovey in Dinas Mawddwy

ruined buildings. This is Checkpoint 21A, an alternative to Checkpoint 21B in Dinas Mawddwy. For those not wishing to visit Dinas Mawddwy, the route continues up through the quarry – see Stage 14 – but to reach the village, bear right round spoil heaps and look for a stile heading into the forest almost immediately. Do not go as far as the dip where the stream enters the forest.

The track is quite easy to follow, going down through the forest for 700 metres to cross a wider forest track. Go across this in a straight line and continue for another 100 metres to join the main **A470** road. Bear left along the road and head N for 100 metres, then take the narrow road through the village that forks off to the right. The centre of **Dinas Mawddwy** is 350 metres ahead, with the Llew Coch (Red Lion) pub, church, post office and car parks.

STAGE 14
Dinas Mawddwy to Bwlch Llyn Bach

Start	Red Lion Inn (Y Llew Coch), Dinas Mawddwy (SH 859 149)
Finish	Head of Bwlch Llyn Bach on A487 (SH 756 138)
Distance	15.5km (9½ miles)
Total ascent	1170m (3830ft)
Total descent	980m (3210ft)
Time	5–6¾hr
Maps	OS Explorer OL 23; OS Landranger 124
Refreshments	None on route
Public transport	Bus services to Machynlleth and Dolgellau from Dinas Mawddwy
Accommodation	Via alternative route: Minffordd 19km; Dolffanog 19km (+1.5km); Tal-y-llyn 19km (+3km)

From Dinas Mawddwy, a path rises steeply through forest to a disused quarry. The route then continues unmarked over rough moorland and down a heathery spur before winding around high mountain ridges with spectacular views to Cadair Idris, the Aran mountains and the high Snowdonia ranges. Accommodation options can be reached via the alternative route at the end of the section.

From the Llew Coch in **Dinas Mawddwy**, follow the road S through the village for 350 metres to join the main **A470** road. After going 150 metres S on this, take the track that bears right past a building to enter the forest. Head SSW up the hillside, crossing over a main forest track after 100 metres and continuing uphill through the forest for a further 650 metres, gradually swinging round W.

Above the forest, the track enters the area of the disused quarry by old buildings at SH 853 140, which is Checkpoint 21A. ▶ A few other routes can be taken to the top of the quarry, but the one described here is less steep than some. Head WSW towards the steep valley of a small stream for 300 metres to where it climbs more steeply, then zigzag right

Walkers bypassing Dinas Mawddwy on Stage 13 should pick up the route description from this point.

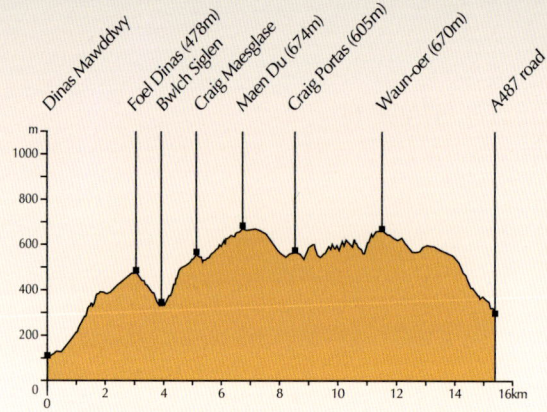

then left to reach the northern edge of the valley. Follow the valley upwards (W) for 130 metres to its head and swing S then SSW for 200 metres along a faint path heading towards the lowest point on the ridge ahead at SH 849 137. (The tramway incline shown on OS maps is more direct but steeper.) This is the place to aim for if you opt to take a different route from the one described here.

Turn right to follow the top of the ridge NW then NNW for 850 metres. There is little or no path for most of the way; aim towards the NW corner of the fence near Foel Dinas across the open moorland. Cross the stile and bear left to head NW then SW to reach the summit of **Foel Dinas** after 300 metres. From there, head SSW along the steep-sided ridge for 850 metres with the forest to the left and the steep Nant Maesglase valley to the right. ◄ A small path runs down the ridge and is quite steep in places until it levels off after swinging WSW to **Bwlch Siglen** ('shaking pass'), which is Checkpoint 22.

There are fine views across the valley to Craig Maesglase with waterfalls tumbling down the steep cliffs.

In the valley 200 metres north of Bwlch Siglen, the **Red Dragon Mine** started as a lead mine in 1852 but a 'black mineral' (possibly manganese) was found in large quantities. Struggling for finance, investors were tempted by suggestions of gold, and poured in a large amount of money to fund gold mining in 1854, only to find there was none and the mine was abandoned around 1856.

Continue W along the ridge as it climbs steeply near the forest for 700 metres to where the slope levels off somewhat.

To bypass Maesglase

If time is short or the weather is bad, Maesglase can be omitted by following the edge of the forest for 400 metres to the top of the ridge then turning right to follow the ridge fence NNW for 1.6km to rejoin the route at SH 817 148, saving 700 metres of walking.

The main route now bears right on a small path, swinging round from WNW to NNW as it crosses the head of a stream and heads towards the top of the steep cliffs of **Craig Maesglase**. The path hugs the edge of the cliffs, traversing the

Map continues
on page 167

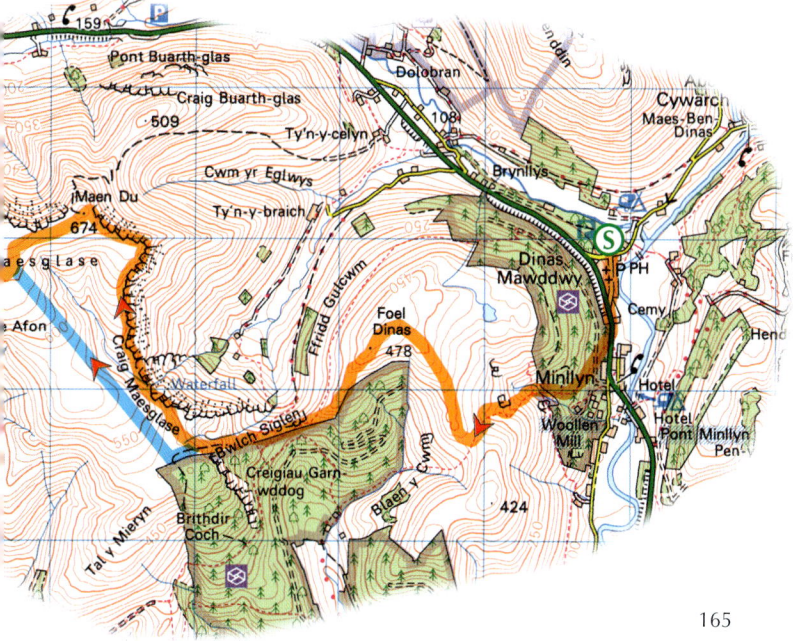

The dramatic outcrop of Craig Maesglase

There is a craggy outcrop just above the path after it crosses the stream which makes a fine rest stop with an excellent view.

steep hillside and dropping slightly to cross the stream feeding the Maesglase falls at SH 826 141. ◄

After 1km there are fewer cliffs but still a very steep mountainside to the right. Continue upwards, going N along the edge for another 600 metres to **Maesglase**. Turn left, still following the edge as it turns WNW, and continue for 450 metres to reach the summit of **Maen Du** ('black stone') at 674m (2211ft), the highest point of this stage with wide views over many of the mountains of Snowdonia.

Turn left and follow the left side of the fence for 550 metres, going WSW down a dip with a gentle rise onto Craig Rhiw-erch. Then turn left and head S for 150 metres to a fence junction at SH 817

This is where the route omitting Maesglase rejoins.

148. ◄ Cross over and continue on the right of the fence and head WSW along the ridge for 1.6km to **Craig Portas**. This is magnificent ridge walking with dramatic scenery both nearby and in the distance.

Do not be tempted to continue SW along the ridge ahead, as the route turns NW here. Cross the fence to keep close to the steep edge for 150 metres, at which point the path starts to move away from the fence. Where the edge swings NNW, head downhill and follow the ridge for 200

Map continues on page 169

285

metres to its lowest point, then rejoin the fence at the head of the valley and follow it NW uphill for 150 metres, crossing over to its western side. The path meanders somewhat as it heads NW for 1km but follows the edge of the ridge, seldom more than 50 metres from the fence except for the last 300 metres where it cuts off a corner to head W.

At SH 792 151, on the western side of **Cribin Fawr**, cross to the north of the fence, which runs downhill approximately westwards. The path along the edge of the forest ahead is overgrown with young conifers, making it difficult to get through, so it is easier to cross the low wire fence and take a meandering route on the northern side for the next 400 metres, heading steeply down to the W and trying not to stray too far from the forest. Continue WSW for 200 metres up the ridge to the trig point on the 670m (2200ft) summit of **Waun-oer** ('cold moor'), 200 metres ahead. ▶

From Waun-oer, OS maps show a path on the left side of the fence but in practice the path walked is to the right of the fence (to the north and west). Follow the fence for 2.4km: another fine section of ridge walk- ing. At SH 767 134, at the low point on the ridge between Mynydd Ceiswyn and Mynydd y Waun, turn right and t a k e

This is the second highest mountain of this stage but only by 4m. It offers splendid panoramic views of mountains near and far.

the path heading NW down the hillside for 1km to a cycle track. The path is not very clear and doesn't always follow that on the OS map, but the main aim is to head NW then W down the steepest part of the hillside, then head NW to where the cycle track goes through a gap in the stone wall, crossing two streams and a boggy area on the way.

Cross the cycle track, follow the wall WNW for 100 metres to the top of the ridge, then bear left down the steep hillside to follow a gully going WSW to meet the **A487** road after 300 metres. This is where the stage ends, at the head of Bwlch Llyn Bach.

For accommodation in Minffordd, Dolffanog or Tal-y-llyn

This alternative route enables access to accommodation options, rejoining the main route partway through Stage 15 without missing any checkpoints. Head SW down the A487 road. There is a footpath on the left leading in 350 metres to a large car park on the right.

Cross the road, go through the car park and follow the footpath parallel to the road on the right for 200 metres, where it starts to diverge from the road down the hillside. Continue for 350 metres, where it becomes a clearer track and then a minor road, eventually reaching the main road after 1.5km. It is then necessary to walk along the road for the next 400 metres to the **Minffordd Hotel**. For Dol-ffanog (1.5km) and Tal-y-llyn (3.1km) continue for 100 metres then bear right along the **B4405** road for 750 metres. Keep straight on along a minor road/cycle track for Tal-y-llyn or turn left along the B4405 for Dol-ffanog.

To return to the main route, from the A487/B4405 road junction the main southern ascent of Cadair Idris ('Idris's chair') begins. Follow the track past the car park and toilets, going WNW for 300 metres then WSW for 150 metres

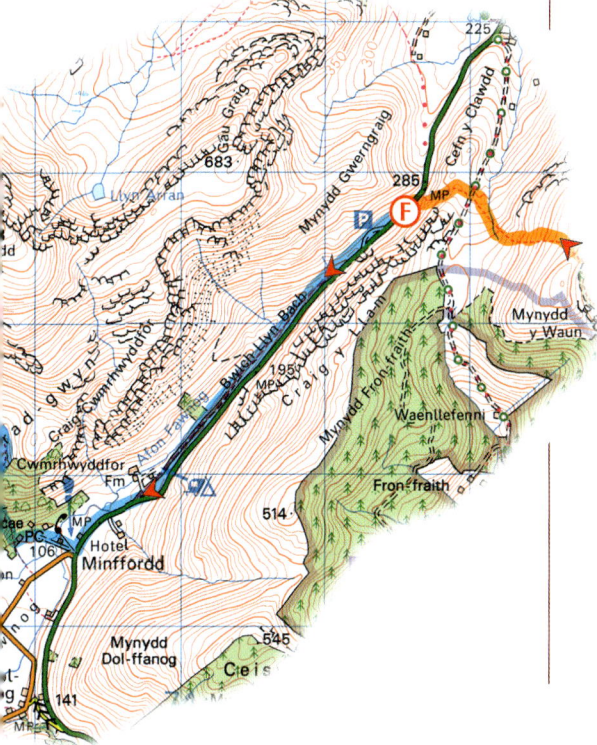

169

This overlooks Llyn Cau in Cwm Cau, a most spectacular glacial valley with steep crags on three sides.

along the valley bottom to where a well-marked track turns right and follows the Nant Cadair stream N up the steep wooded valley. Take this track, and after 350 metres the trees thin out and the route continues to meander up the valley, gradually becoming less steep over the next 800 metres. Here it starts to swing W towards **Llyn Cau** ('closed lake'), heading close to the steep craggy hillside on the left for 700 metres then turning S to climb steeply up to the ridge 400 metres ahead. ◄

Continue climbing the ridge for 1.2km as it heads W and swings round NW. Then the path forks: those with a good head for heights can stay on the route by forking right to go along the cliff edge over the summit of **Craig Cwm Amarch** overlooking Llyn Cau, while others can take a safer route 100 metres away to the left. After 350 metres the paths rejoin to head N then NE for 850 metres to reach the summit of **Penygadair** (Stage 15), were the main route is rejoined at Checkpoint 23.

STAGE 15
Bwlch Llyn Bach to Barmouth

Start	Head of Bwlch Llyn Bach on A487 (SH 756 138)
Finish	Steps near Barmouth Bridge on A496 (SH 617 156)
Distance	20km (12½ miles)
Total ascent	970m (3180ft)
Total descent	1240m (4070ft)
Time	5¾–7½hr
Maps	OS Explorer OL 23; OS Landranger 124
Refreshments	None on route
Public transport	Trains to Aberystwyth and Shrewsbury and several bus services from Barmouth
Accommodation	YHA Kings Hostel 11.5km (on alternative route); Dolgellau (+6km from YHA Kings Hostel); Barmouth

The traverse of Cadair Idris is one of the great stages of the Cambrian Way. It is the most iconic and finest of mountains in southern Snowdonia, with spectacular bird's-eye views into deep valleys and lakes and westwards to the sea. The route starts with a steep climb involving some scrambling, which levels out to a broad ridge leading to the mountain-top. There is then a long, initially rough descent, to the beautiful Llynnau Cregennen lakes and Arthog Waterfalls, and finally a footpath alongside the long wooden railway bridge over the estuary to Barmouth.

From SH 756 138, 150 metres southwest of the summit of the pass, cross the **A487** to reach an access road to an old quarry. Turn right along a footpath that runs beside the road and continue for 150 metres, going NE to the top of the pass and over a boundary fence. Continue N along the path for 50 metres, moving away from the road.

Gentler route via Gau Graig
Some parts of the main route from Bwlch Llyn Bach to the point near Gau Graig are very steep. A gentler – but 1.4km longer – ascent can be made from the NE end of the ridge by taking the footpath that follows the contour N from SH 757 140 (on the A487) for 800 metres to cross a stream near

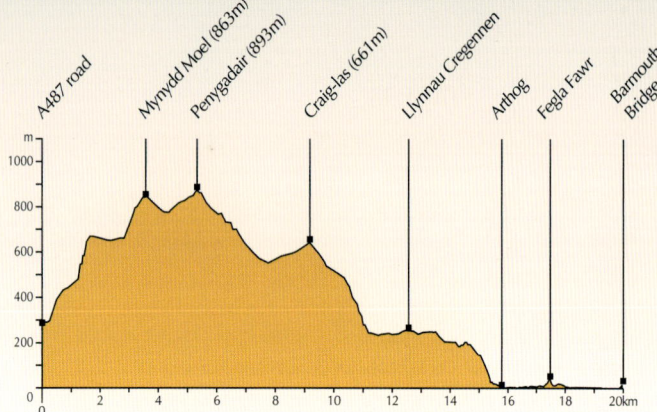

A487 road
Mynydd Moel (863m)
Penygadair (893m)
Craig-las (661m)
Llynnau Cregennen
Arthog
Fegla Fawr
Barmouth Bridge

a farm building. Follow the track which goes left of the farm access lane and climbs steadily NNW up the hillside for 300 metres to the left of the fence.

The track continues for another 450 metres before heading up the ridge. However, this route is often thick with vegetation and difficult to negotiate, so most walkers take an unofficial shortcut by heading W from SH 755 150 to cross a wall at SH 753 151, from where a small but clear path ascends the ridge. If you don't want to cut the corner, continue NNW along the track then bear WNW to reach a stream at SH 751 153

Map continues
on page 174

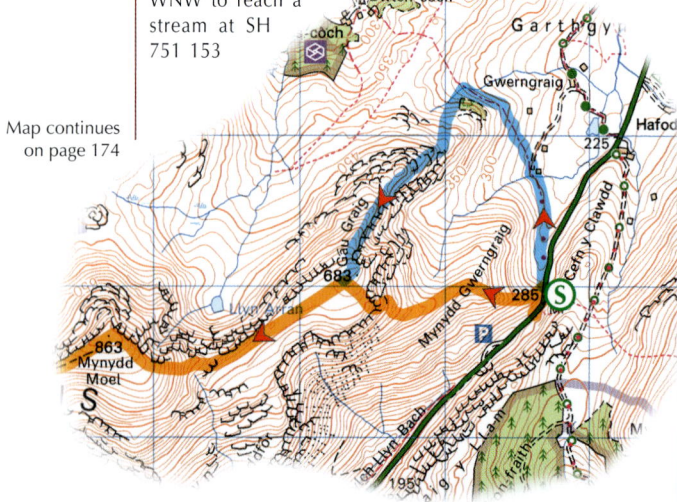

172

Penygadair provides spectacular views of the surrounding mountain scenery

after 450 metres; turn left and go S then SW, crossing two walls and picking up a path up the ridge. The ridge path takes you past **Gau Craig** to rejoin the main route at SH 743 140 after 2km. ▸

The views from this ridge are even better than those from the direct main route.

To continue on the steep route turn sharp left and head WSW for 100 metres to reach the fence again and follow it W up the steep hillside for 1km. The fence line reaches scree and the way becomes very steep, but there is a path zigzagging right to bypass the steepest part, going NNW for 80 metres then SW for 80 metres, climbing a gully and rejoining the fence. Continue to follow the fence NW for a further 300 metres over the highest point of this part of the ridge at SH 743 140, which is where the alternative route rejoins.

From here route finding is easy as it is just a matter of following the ridge-top WSW for 1km, W for 500 metres then NW for 300 metres to reach the summit of **Mynydd Moel** ('bare mountain') with a cairn at 863m (2831ft). ▸ From here the route bears left, heading down WSW near to the steep northern edge of the ridge for 800 metres, then going gently uphill for another 800 metres to some cairns. A steeper ascent then leads SW for 200 metres to the summit trig point of **Penygadair** ('head of the chair'), which is Checkpoint 23 at 893m (2927ft) and the point at which the Minffordd alternative route from Stage 14 rejoins.

There are fine views from here, particularly to the north across the Mawddach Estuary and beyond.

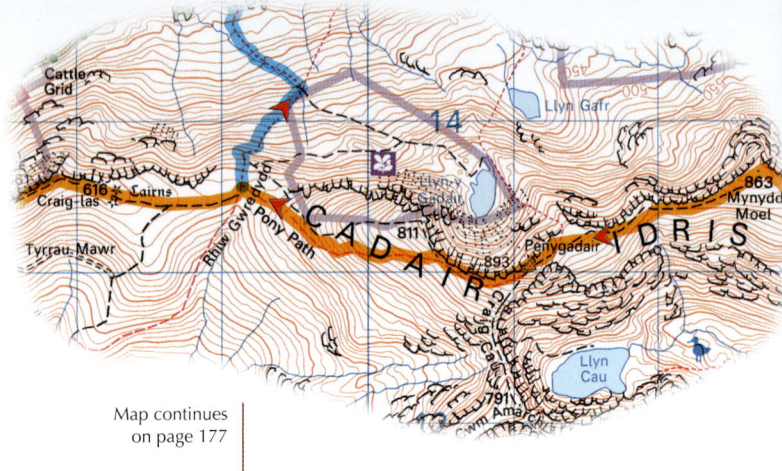

Map continues
on page 177

Penygadair is the name of the highest point of the
Cadair Idris massif. There is a mountain refuge shelter 20 metres north of the summit and spectacular
views all around, and a short descent south brings
Llyn Cau into full view. This is a very popular mountain, but few approach it from the east – most coming from the west on the Pony Path or from the south
via Llyn Cau on the Minffordd alternative route.

From the summit head WSW, following the edge of the
steep cliffs overlooking Llyn y Gadair far below to the N. Stay
on the edge as it curves round WNW for 700 metres with
impressive views below. Here the well-trodden Pony Path
bears left down the hillside. ◄ Follow the Pony Path W for
1.6km, then WNW to a junction of paths in a dip at SH 691
135. This is where the Pony Path descends to the N and is the
route taken to YHA Kings Hostel.

*If desired, the next
peak (Cyfrwy, or 'the
saddle', at 811m) can
be climbed by going
250 metres NNW.
Join the Pony Path by
heading W for 1km.*

FOR YHA KINGS HOSTEL

From the junction of paths at SH 691 135, head along the well-trodden Pony
Path as it descends steeply N for 200 metres, with a series of zigzags on the way,
before swinging NW then ENE down the steepest part of the hillside for 200
metres and then heading NE to meet a wall after 200 metres. Follow the wall NE
for 300 metres, crossing one wall to reach another. Do not take the main track
ahead but turn left through a gate in this wall and follow a lesser path heading

NW for 400 metres. Cross a wall and head NNW for 250 metres to cross another wall, then head in a northerly direction via a series of zigzags down the hillside to meet the next wall after 300 metres. Follow this wall to the left for 80 metres as it swings W, then turn N across a narrow field to join a minor road at the bottom of the hillside after 50 metres.

Turn right along the road and walk for 50 metres, then turn left along a track going NNW through a field. After 300 metres pass **Tynceunant Farm** and head NE then N to follow the eastern side of the Gwynant river as it meanders and swings NW to reach YHA Kings Hostel in **Islaw'r-dref** after 1.1km.

For accommodation in Penmaenpool, follow the minor road N for 1.5km, then follow the A493 NE for another 2km. Return to the main route by taking the Mawddach Trail, which follows the estuary for 7.2km W then SW to SH 640 148 NW of Arthog.

To rejoin the main route from YHA Kings Hostel, follow the road WNW uphill for 50 metres, where it turns sharply left and then heads S for 50 metres to a hairpin bend. Leave the road, going left on the bend and heading SSW uphill on a path through the woodland. After 250 metres rejoin the road, having cut off the corner.

Follow the road WSW for 250 metres, then leave it where it turns sharp left and continue on a track. Follow the track W for 650 metres to a point at which it starts to turn SW towards **Ty'n Ilidiart Farm**. Here take a waymarked diversion N of the farm, with the path continuing W for 170 metres and starting to climb the hillside. The path becomes steeper and after crossing two walls it heads SSW, SSE then SSW again, following the hillside around for 200 metres and approaching a wall after levelling off at SH 671 153. Either continue SW then WSW for 1.5km alongside the wall then across to the N side of the **lakes**, or take the optional variant over Pared y Cefn hîr.

Optional diversion via Pared y Cefn hîr

The 'main' route continues straight ahead, but a more interesting route is to climb the ridge to Pared y Cefn hîr by taking the faint path heading diagonally up the hillside. This follows the ridge to its end, returning to the route by the north side of Llynnau Cregennen. There are several steep scrambles along the ridge, but there are also plenty of handholds and footholds, so it is not too difficult. The views from the ridge are stunning, although this option does involve about 200m (650ft) of additional ascent and takes about 20–30min longer.

From the Cregennen lakes

A minor road is reached on the north side of the lakes 100 metres after crossing a wall. Turn left down the road and go S for 400 metres to the **car park** and toilets. Continue for another 100 metres to SH 658 142 where the main route is rejoined along the faint path heading S.

Llynnau Cregennen and the Mawddach Estuary from Craig-las

From the Pony Path, turn left where the paths join at SH 691 135 and head SW for 100 metres, looking out for a faint path

heading W up the ridge. After 150 metres the path runs W alongside the boundary for 800 metres to the minor summit of Carnedd Lŵyd. Go down a small dip and follow the boundary around for 800 metres to **Craig-las** ('blue rock'), which affords good views.

Continue to follow the boundary, now heading WSW, and gradually swing SSW downhill for 1.2km to reach a dip. Look out for a small stile over the fence; go over this and head WNW down the steep hillside. The path is not very clear but starts off close to the fence then goes left around a craggy area to a small enclosure by a wall 300 metres ahead. Cross the wall and follow the right-hand side of another wall NW for 400 metres, then cross into the corner of the field on the left. The path runs about 50 metres left of the wall for 500 metres, heading NW to come out on a minor road with the ruined buildings of **Hafotty-fâch** at the other side.

Turn right along the road and follow it for 400 metres, turning sharp left to **Llynnau Cregennen**. Continue on the road as it winds its way NW for 900 metres then swings sharp left around the southern edge of the lake. Some 150 metres later, look out for

The lakes and surrounding area are owned by the National Trust and are in a beautiful setting surrounded by mountains.

a signposted faint footpath going sharp left (about 100 metres before the car park, which has some basic toilets) at SH 658 142. This is the point at which the YHA Kings Hostel alternative rejoins. ◄

Take the footpath, heading S, and after 300 metres cross a wall and head WSW across the field a little way from the wall on the right for 350 metres, then bear right between two walls. After 100 metres the path follows a wall on the left, heading WNW for 450 metres to join a well-defined track going SSW and following the wall to the left as the gap between the walls widens. Follow this for 200 metres as it swings S, looking out for a picturesque old clapper bridge crossing the stream to the right of the track. Cross over the bridge to join another track heading WNW, and almost immediately look for a path bearing NNW towards the trees and descending beside the **Arthog waterfalls**. Follow this path all the way to the bottom of the hill to meet the A493 road 900 metres away, staying relatively close to the falls and avoiding any paths off to the left.

Turn left along the road and follow it for 30 metres, going past the church yard, then turn right to follow a track going N for 60 metres then WNW for 250 metres. Bear left, heading W for 150 metres to meet a minor road. Turn right

Clapper bridge above the Arthog waterfalls

and follow the road as it meanders alongside the estuary for 350 metres, crossing the Mawddach Trail which follows a disused railway line. Turn left on a path through the trees 50 metres after the start of the woodland, meandering NW for 200 metres to its western edge. ▸

Head NNW along the edge of the woodland for 100 metres to meet a track. Do not follow the track but take the path just before it, heading WSW for 500 metres then swinging right to a minor road beside the estuary. Bear left and follow this for 150 metres, then take a path that bypasses a row of houses by going to the S and returning to the estuary 250 metres further on.

At low tide it is normally possible to take a shortcut to the railway bridge by going along the bank of shingle, but at high tide take the path which turns left to head S over **Fegla Fawr**, joining the bridge 700 metres further on at SH 628 143. The right of way is currently overgrown but a clearer path running higher up the hillside can be taken if the obstruction persists.

Follow the bridge walkway NNW for 1.5km to the toll booth, then another 150 metres to join the road, going left for 100 metres to where steps go northwards up the opposite hillside. Barmouth Bridge is Checkpoint 24 – the end of the stage.

> **Barmouth Bridge** is a mainly wooden viaduct with a steel swing bridge for the passage of boats. It is 699 metres long and was opened in 1867 to carry a single-track railway line across the Mawddach Estuary, also carrying foot and cycle traffic for which a toll was charged until 2013. It is the longest wooden viaduct in Wales and one of the oldest in regular use in Britain. There is a fine view of Barmouth's Coes Faen clock tower from the bridge.

This woodland has been extended over the years, and it may expand further in time.

STAGE 16
Barmouth to Cwm Bychan

Start	Steps near Barmouth Bridge on A496 (SH 617 156)
Finish	Minor road by Cwm Bychan Farm (SH 646 315)
Distance	23km (14 miles)
Total ascent	1690m (5540ft)
Total descent	1530m (5020ft)
Time	8½–10¾hr (allowing 1hr extra for slow progress)
Maps	OS Explorer OL 23 and OL18; OS Landranger 124
Refreshments	None on route
Public transport	Trains to Aberystwyth and Shrewsbury and several bus services from Barmouth
Accommodation	Bronaber 16.5km (+8km); Llanbedr 16.5km (+10km); Harlech 22.5km (+8.5km)

This stage traverses the southern section of the Rhinog mountains, which are the most demanding and the most rewarding of the Cambrian Way. The terrain is steep and rocky in many places and requires good navigational skills as well as the ability to walk and scramble up and down rocky crags while carrying a heavy rucksack. There is a lot of exhilarating ridge walking with extensive views across Tremadog Bay to the Lleyn Peninsula as well as views across the Mawddach Estuary and Cadair Idris. This is also an area much less walked than other parts of Snowdonia, giving a feeling of wilderness and solitude.

The Rhinog mountains, especially further north, can be dangerous in bad weather conditions with some steep scrambling, smooth slippery rocks and protruding stones hidden by heather. This is a remote area where, in the event of an accident, there are few other walkers to give assistance and route finding is particularly difficult when visibility is poor. If bad conditions are forecast, you should seriously consider the alternative bad-weather route described in Stage 16/17A, which rejoins the main route at Moelfryn on Stage 17. There are also two possible escape routes should you have opted to proceed with the high-level route: one in this stage; the other in Stage 17.

From the A496 road 100 metres west of where **Barmouth Bridge** meets the road, head N up a steep flight of steps up the hillside to the right of the deep cleft of an old quarry.

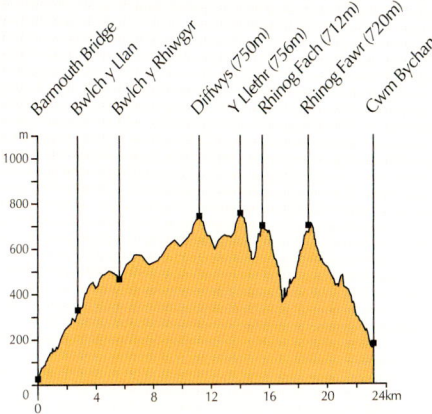

Follow the path as it zigzags right and then left to enter Cae Fadog, owned by the National Trust. After 100 metres it becomes less steep and opens out onto the grassy hillside overlooking the quarry and Barmouth Harbour.

Keep on heading uphill, going NNE for 300 metres along the path which is rather overgrown in parts, first following a wall on the left then on the right. Avoid the track bearing right through a gate towards a minor road; instead turn sharp left and walk for 70 metres, then turn sharp right and walk for another 70 metres to the wall above a clump of trees at SH 619 159. This zigzag is not shown very clearly on OS maps. ▸

Bunkorama bunkhouse can be reached by heading NNE for 650 metres, but for the main route, head N from the wall for 50 metres then up the hillside for another 50 metres, almost reaching the wall again. Bear right and head N for 150 metres then bear right along the path beneath the steep cliffs of **Garn**, heading NNE then N for 400 metres and passing through two gates to reach a minor road.

Cross over the road and take a faint path heading up NNE through bracken to a ladder stile in a cross-wall at SH 621 168. Cross the stile and continue in the same direction along the ridge for a further 900 metres, crossing two more walls then descending with a wall on your right to a crossing of paths at **Bwlch y Llan**. Continue NNE alongside the wall for a further 200 metres to the next wall.

Here, do not continue along the main path but turn left before the wall to climb the steep hillside onto the main

Views over Barmouth Bridge appear here.

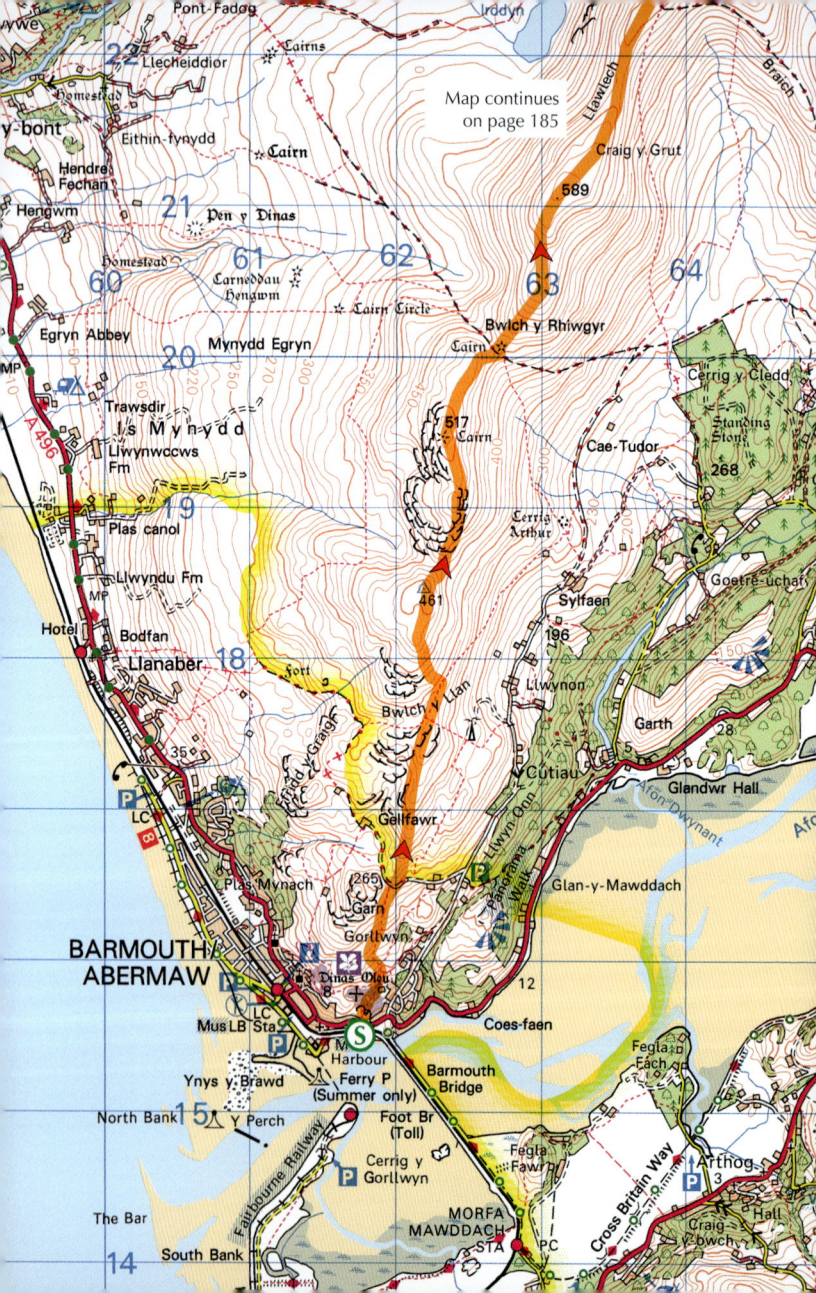

Map continues
on page 185

ridge 350 metres ahead. The aim is to keep near to the wall on the right, but it is easier to zigzag up some of the steepest parts. Near the top of the ridge, cross over the wall and keep on the right-hand side of it for 2.1km, heading N to the pass of **Bwlch y Rhiwgyr**, where the route crosses Taith Ardudwy Way. ▶ Several minor summits are taken in along the way, with fine views to the east and also to the west in some parts. The walls here are high but are crossed by a series of ladder stiles.

The bad-weather alternative leaves the main route here and follows Taith Ardudwy Way: see Stage 16/17A.

Near Bwlch y Rhiwgyr the ridge path swings to the right, going E for the last 100 metres down to the pass, where it is important to cross to the left-hand side of the wall as there are ladder stiles on this side to cross walls along the ridge. Follow the wall up the ridge, heading NE for 500 metres to the first minor summit. Route finding is easy from here as it is just a matter of following the wall along the ridge for 4.8km (3 miles) to the summit of Diffwys. The route heads roughly N, then swings round to the E before turning NNE near Diffwys.

At **Diffwys** (750m/2460ft) the trig point can be accessed by a ladder stile over the wall to the right. Return to continue along the route for 350 metres, then the path starts to drop NE by a rocky outcrop. ▶ This is mainly easy and fast ridge walking along grassy paths with magnificent views, although there are a few boggy parts here and there.

The outcrop makes a good resting point with a fine view of Llyn Dulyn and Y Llethr ahead.

A section of loose stones can be bypassed by a small detour to the left, then after another 200 metres the clear path parts company with the wall for about 300 metres to take an easier route that cuts off the corner where the ridge swings N. Rejoin the wall and continue following it N then NNW for 1.2km, going into a dip and then over **Crib-y-rhiw** ('comb of the hill'). Here the smooth grassy paths give way to

Looking ahead to Crib-y-rhiw from Diffwys

Looking back along Crib-y-rhiw to Diffwys from Y Llethr

rougher, craggier going which requires care and slows down the walking pace. Continue to follow the ridge NNW for 250 metres to another dip, then climb for 250 metres to a wall at SH 660 255.

Cross the wall and continue N then NNE for 250 metres to the summit cairn on **Y Llethr** ('steep crag') at 756m (2475ft). This is Checkpoint 25 and the highest point in the Rhinog mountains. From the summit, continue to follow the wall for a further 400 metres, starting a steady descent and looking out for a path down the steep hillside on the left. This is eroded in places and involves some scrambling as it heads N for 250 metres towards Llyn Hywel. After this steep initial descent, the path heads NE to join the wall after 150 metres on a gentler course. Continue N alongside the wall for 150 metres to the lowest part of the ridge, just east of **Llyn Hywel**.

Escape route

In case of bad weather closing in, the summits of Rhinog Fach and/or Rhinog Fawr may have to be omitted. At Llyn Hywel, follow the northern edge of the lake to join a faint path heading down NNW then NNE, past **Llyn Cwmhosan** to **Bwlch Drws Ardudwy**. To join the Taith Ardudwy Way alternative route (5.6km), turn left here and descend W to

Map continues
on page 188

Map continues
on page 186

Carreg-y-saeth

452

66

Glovyn
Lyn

Llyn Morwynion

Waterfall

249

Graigdd

Carreg
Fawr

Llyn Du

Afon

Foel Ddu

477

Rhinog Fawr

620

617

Bwlch Drws-Ardudwy

Llyn
Cwmhosan

Nantcol

414

Foel Wen

Maes-y-garnedd

Rhinog Fach

712

407

Cwm-y-Nantcol

Cairn

Llyn Hywel

Pont Cerrig

Llyn
Perfeddau

Llyn y Bi

Cefn C

Graig-isaf

Cil-
cychwyn

Y Llethr

756

Moelyblithcwm

Crib-y-rhiw

Hafod-y-
Brenhin

wydd

Llyn Dulyn

Llyn Cwm
mynach

Llyn Bodlyn

688

Cairn

Pont-Scethin

Diffwys

750

642

Craig
Aderyn

572

Mynydd
Cwm-mynach

Maes-y-garnedd Farm, then follow the road to Penisarcwm Farm and continue as per Stage 16/17A. Otherwise, head E to the cairn at the top of the pass. ▸

From the pass, drop down through a wall and take a faint path forking off to the left 80 metres later. The path heads NE over rough ground to reach, then walk alongside, then enter, forestry, arriving at a major forest track after 1.5km. Turn left and follow the track for 3.8km, then take a waymarked footpath to the left. The path briefly follows a wall and then turns and heads N to exit the (now felled) forest at a stile.

Continue N for 900 metres over featureless marshy ground to cross a stile over a fence at SH 675 323. Occasional marker posts now guide you NE for 1.8km past the barn at **Wern-fâch** and to a lane, where you turn right and walk a further 1.8km to a junction. Continue ahead for accommodation and services in Trawsfynydd, or go left to rejoin the main route at **Moelfryn** (Stage 17).

Main route

To stay on the main route, from Llyn Hywel continue NNE for 500 metres up the steep path, still following the wall, with some scrambling needed in places. The wall then swings NW and the slope eases off for 100 metres before a final steep 100-metre zigzag scramble W to the rounded

The main route over
Rhinog Fach meets the
escape route here.

*Llyn Hywel, sheltered
by Rhinog Fach's
scree slopes*

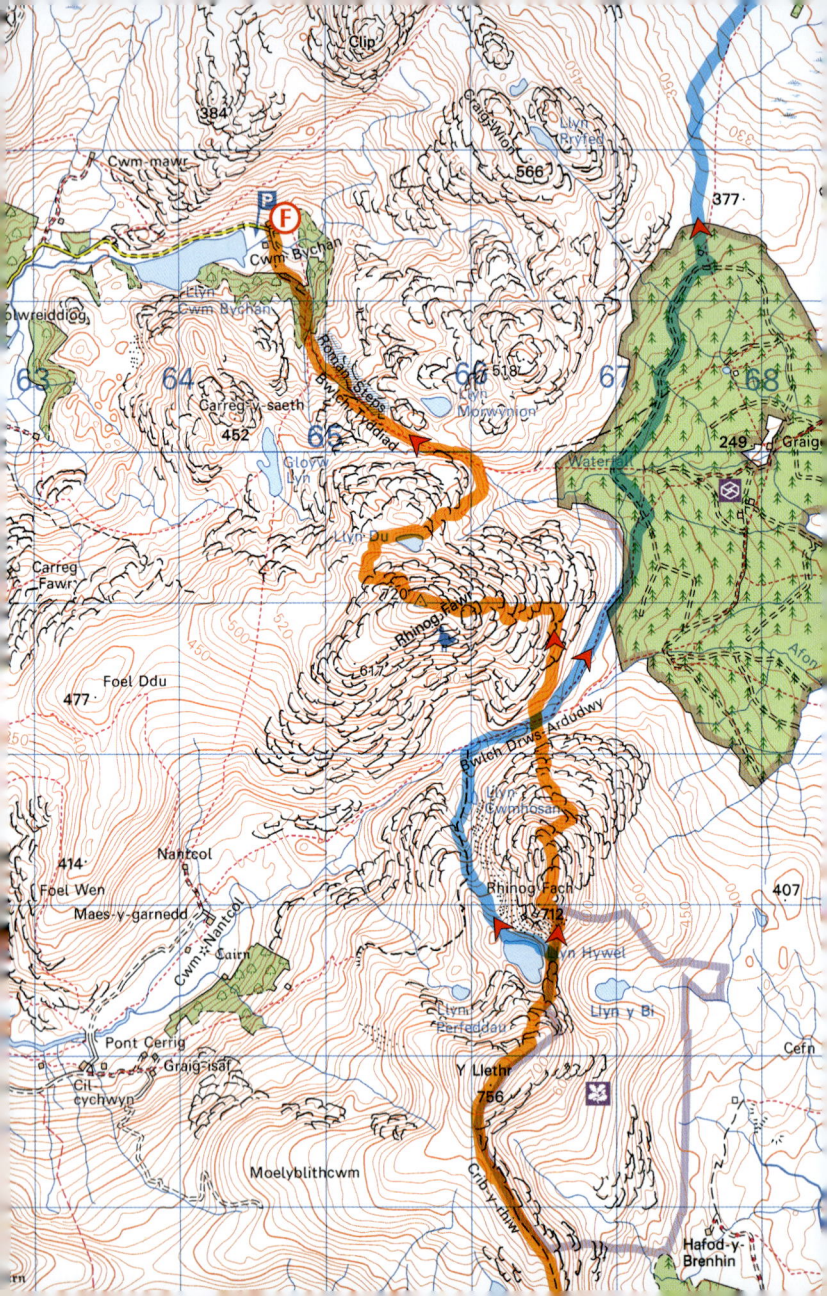

summit of **Rhinog Fach**, which is Checkpoint 26 at 712m (2333ft). ▶ There are numerous small alternatives on the route, but the aim is to keep going upwards and not to cross the wall on the right.

It is possible to retrace the path back to Llyn Hywel and follow the escape route to Bwlch Drws Ardudwy. However, a path has developed to the north which, although steep and tortuous in places, saves about 1.2km of walking. Drop NE from the summit for 100 metres then follow the ridge N for 400 metres. There is more than one possible path but most join again at SH 665 274 at the northern edge of the mountain. Do not continue N here as the path ends after a short while. Instead turn E then ENE for 250 metres, then swing round NW for 300 metres then N for 600 metres, descending steeply to the wall at the bottom of the pass of **Bwlch Drws Ardudwy** at SH 664 282. From here continue N uphill to reach the main path along the pass after 50 metres. This brings you out at the summit of the pass. ▶

There is a direct route to the summit of Rhinog Fawr by heading NW up the steep rocky mountainside, but the easier (albeit somewhat longer) route is recommended as follows. From the main path take a faint path N up the hillside about 30 metres to the left of a wall, meeting the wall where it curves left. Cross the wall either by crawling through a gap or by going around its top end, and follow a very faint path in a generally northerly direction. The path clambers over rocky terraces interspersed with damp grassy hollows. It is not easy to follow but there are small cairns marking its route, sometimes just a stone or two on a rock surface.

After 700 metres, at SH 666 290, a more substantial cairn marks where the path veers W. After a further 300 metres, at SH 663 290, the path becomes clearer as it zigzags up more steeply. Continue to head upwards for 800 metres to reach the summit trig point of **Rhinog Fawr**. This is Checkpoint 27 at 720m (2362ft).

A large number of paths have developed going northwards from Rhinog Fawr and it is not vital to take any particular one. The one described here has the advantage of following a wall for part of the way and going around the north shore of Llyn Du from W to E, which helps route finding in bad weather; although there is a more direct route that passes the E side of Llyn Du.

The best views from Rhinog Fach of Llyn Hywel and Y Llethr are from its southern edge 50 metres south of the summit.

For accommodation head E for Bronaber (8km/5 miles) or W for Llanbedr (8.8km/5½ miles).

From the summit of Rhinog Fawr take the path going W for 100 metres, which then starts descending the steep hillside and swings around towards the N, zigzagging down to a broad ledge after a further 200 metres. Cross over a clear path that runs SW to NE and head due W for 250 metres on a gentler slope to meet a wall. Follow the wall, going down NNE for 300 metres to the bottom of the hill (the path is indistinct) and turn right to go ENE round the bouldery northern shore of **Llyn Du**, reaching its eastern end after 300 metres.

For accommodation in Bronaber (7.2km/4½ miles) head E from here.

Take the path going NE for 200 metres of steady descent, then bear right to keep on descending while swinging gradually left round the hillside, eventually heading WNW to reach the pass of **Bwlch Tyddiad** after 500 metres. ◄

Follow the track along the pass WNW for 1km, first going steadily uphill then down the other side to cross a wall. (The stone slabs here are called the **Roman Steps** but they are just an old packhorse route of a more recent age.) The path turns N then swings back round W before continuing NNW again for 550 metres, then it turns N to enter woodland. The main track does not follow the line of the right of way through the woods but takes the path – shown on 1:25,000 maps as a dotted line – to the left for 250 metres then heads N through the campsite of **Cwm Bychan Farm** for 300 metres to reach the farm buildings at SH 646 315, which is the end of this stage with basic camping, car park and road access to Harlech (8.4km/5¼ miles).

Roman Steps towards Cwm Bychan

STAGE 16/17A

Bad-weather route to Moelfryn
following Taith Ardudwy Way

Start	Bwlch y Rhiwgyr (SH 627 200)
Finish	Moelfryn (SH 684 358)
Distance	28km (17½ miles) – plus 5.1km (3¼ miles) from Barmouth to Bwlch y Rhiwgyr
Total ascent	830m (2720ft) – plus 590m (1920ft) from Barmouth to Bwlch y Rhiwgyr
Total descent	1060m (3490ft) – plus 140m (460ft) from Barmouth to Bwlch y Rhiwgyr
Time	7¼–9hr – plus 2–2¾hr from Barmouth to Bwlch y Rhiwgyr
Maps	OS Explorer OL 23 and OL18; OS Landranger 124
Refreshments	None on route
Public transport	None on route
Accommodation	Llanbedr 10km (+3.5km); Coed Ystumgwern 10km (+1.5km); Harlech 17.5km (+5km); Trawsfynydd 28km (+3.5km); Maentwrog 28km (+7km)

This alternative route for Stages 16 and 17 largely follows the waymarked Taith Ardudwy Way on good tracks and roads, with the option to rejoin the main route at Cwm Nantcol or Cwm Bychan or to continue to Moelfryn. It does, however, miss a few checkpoints – but safety should of course take priority over these.

Follow the route description for Stage 16 as far as **Bwlch y Rhiwgyr** (SH 627 200). From the pass, follow the track heading NNW down the valley. After some 3.2km, at SH 610 225, turn sharp right on another track. Follow this in an easterly direction for 3.3km as it passes **Llyn Erddyn** and swings NE to a track junction at SH 637 233. Turn left, cross the packhorse bridge of **Pont-Scethin** and continue generally westwards for 1.7km to meet a wall at SH 622 238.

Here, leave the main track and continue ahead WNW, turning right after 1.1km at SH 612 243 to follow a wall for 800 metres before heading down to meet a minor road at

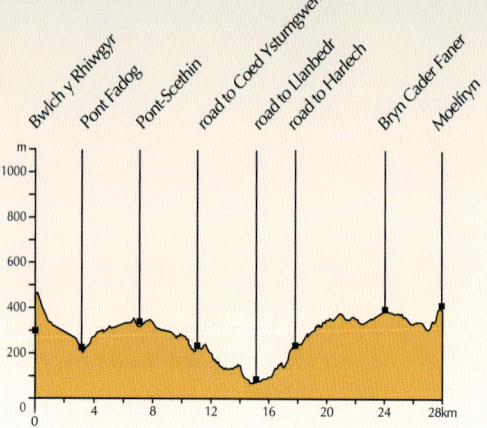

Turn left along the road for accommodation and services at Llanbedr (3.6km) or Coed Ystumgwern (1.6km).

Alternatively, continue W along the road for accommodation and services in Llanbedr (3.2km).

SH 612 253. ◄ Turn right along the road and continue for 700 metres, then as it starts to swing right past a parking area, leave it to take the signed path going straight ahead. (The main Cambrian Way route can be rejoined at Bwlch Drws Ardudwy by staying on the road and heading E for 6.4km.)

Follow waymarkers NNE downhill for 800 metres to join a minor road at SH 619 267 near **Penisarcwm Farm**. Turn left along the road and continue for 1.1km, then fork right at SH 613 272 on a clear track heading N. ◄ After 100 metres turn left at a marker post onto a fainter track meandering W and NW, soon following a wall on the left. Continue downhill on a rough track to where it becomes a surfaced track. Follow this for 700 metres as it swings W, then N through a gate, then WNW at a track junction, meeting a minor road at **Pen-y-bont** at SH 607 280.

Turn right along the road and head NNE for 700 metres to SH 610 287. The main Cambrian Way route can be rejoined by taking the road going right here and continuing to Cwm Bychan Farm (5.6km); however, to stay on the bad-weather alternative, continue ahead (N) for 500 metres, entering the campsite at **Dinas**.

Leave the main track on a path to the right, heading ENE then N past a small lake on the right. For the next 2km, the narrow path makes its way up craggy hillsides interspersed with flat marshy areas. The path heads generally N and is rough in places and faint in others, but waymarks guide you between the crags, through walls and across the marshy

Map continues
on page 194

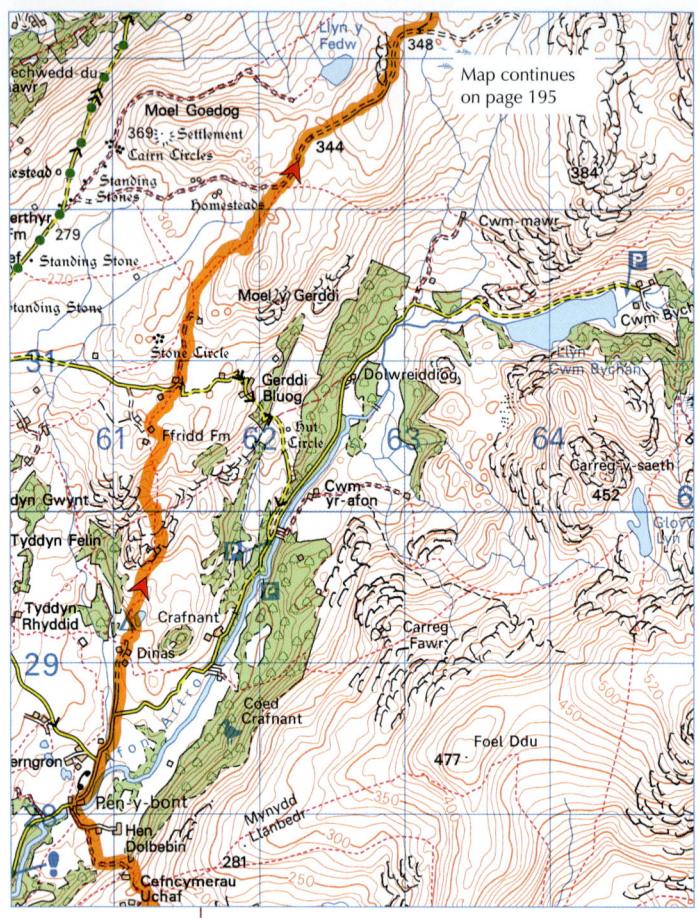

Map continues
on page 195

Turn left along
the road for
accommodation
and services in
Harlech (4.8km).

areas. The path detours briefly to the right around **Ffridd Farm** and meets a minor road at SH 614 308. ◀

Cross the road and continue N for 550 metres along a good track. Where the track turns right to Rhyd yr Eirin, cross a ladder stile in the wall ahead and continue N for 100 metres, then bear right and head NE for 400 metres to a ladder stile across a wall on the right. Continue NE across this and three

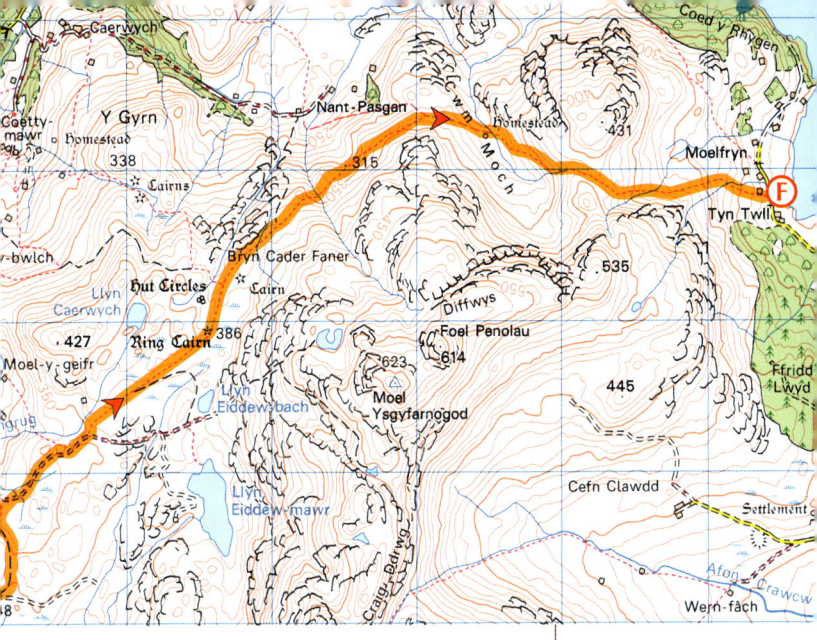

further walls, joining a clear track at SH 622 322 and continuing ahead along it. Follow the meandering track for 2.1km, taking a left fork N at SH 631 332 beyond **Llyn y Fedw**.

At SH 631 337, where the track swings left, cross a wall on the right and follow a path generally NE, soon joining a clearer track. Follow this NE for 750 metres then bear left off main track at SH 637 342 to continue N by a wall. After 100 metres, bear right going NE and continue 1.3km to a marker post at SH 646 352. ▶ Continue ahead at the waymark and follow the right of way NE, keeping right of crags and then walking with a wall on the left. Cross a stile ahead and at the next wall turn right to walk alongside it. The path veers gradually ESE and descends into **Cwm Moch**, climbing again to rejoin the main route at SH 674 358, 200 metres S of Moelfryn.

The stone circle of Bryn Cader Faner comes into view ahead.

Continue E on the path for 800 metres, with a wall on the left for most of the way, looking out for occasional waymarks. The path then exits the common and follows a rough sunken lane for 300 metres to meet a minor road close to **Moelfryn** at SH 684 358, which is Checkpoint 29. From here, pick up the main route description in Stage 17.

STAGE 17
Cwm Bychan to Maentwrog

Start	Minor road by Cwm Bychan Farm (SH 646 315)
Finish	St Twrog's Church, Maentwrog (SH 665 405)
Distance	16km (9¾ miles)
Total ascent	860m (2810ft)
Total descent	1000m (3290ft)
Time	5½–7hr (allowing 1hr extra for slow progress)
Maps	OS Explorer OL 23; OS Landranger 124
Refreshments	None on route
Public transport	Bus services from Maentwrog to Barmouth, Blaenau Ffestiniog, Dolgellau, Bangor and Aberystwyth
Accommodation	Trawsfynydd 9km (+3km); Maentwrog

The northern section of the Rhinog mountains consists of a series of rocky, often bare ledges with clefts between, some of which contain small lakes or tarns. It is a fascinating landscape but makes for challenging walking that includes some scrambling. Wayfinding is difficult with only a few cairns and little evidence that walkers have frequented the ground between rocks. There are several cliff faces to ascend but only a few places in them where easy scrambles can be made, and care is needed to find these. Allow for slow progress. The rewards are stunning views, solitude and a unique walking experience. There are alternative accommodation and bad-weather routes.

From the road by **Cwm Bychan Farm** near the car park, take the faint path to the W of the farm buildings and head NE diagonally up the hillside for 150 metres, then bear left to go directly up the hillside heading NNW then N for 250 metres. The path is still rather faint, but the aim is to join a clearer path that crosses the wall 100 metres ahead at SH 647 319. Over the wall, head ENE for 850 metres along a clearly defined path up the hillside to reach a wall.

There are two possible paths from the wall, but they join together after 150 metres. Here the main path has developed somewhat to the right of the line shown on OS maps, going NE for 300 metres then swinging NNE to reach a wall near

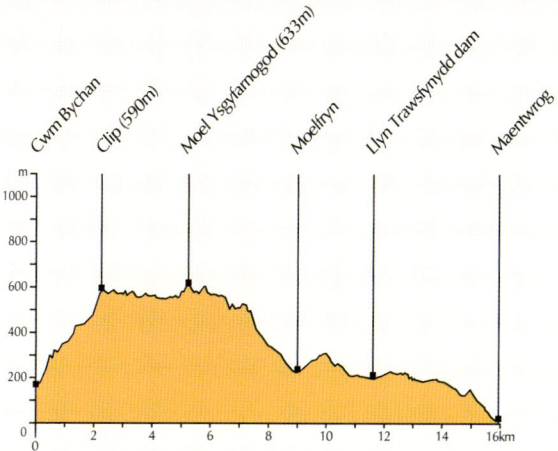

the head of the pass after a further 300 metres, rejoining the path shown on the OS map.

Escape route

In poor conditions, the northern part of the ridge can be avoided by leaving the main route at SH 657 328 before it turns to ascend Clip.

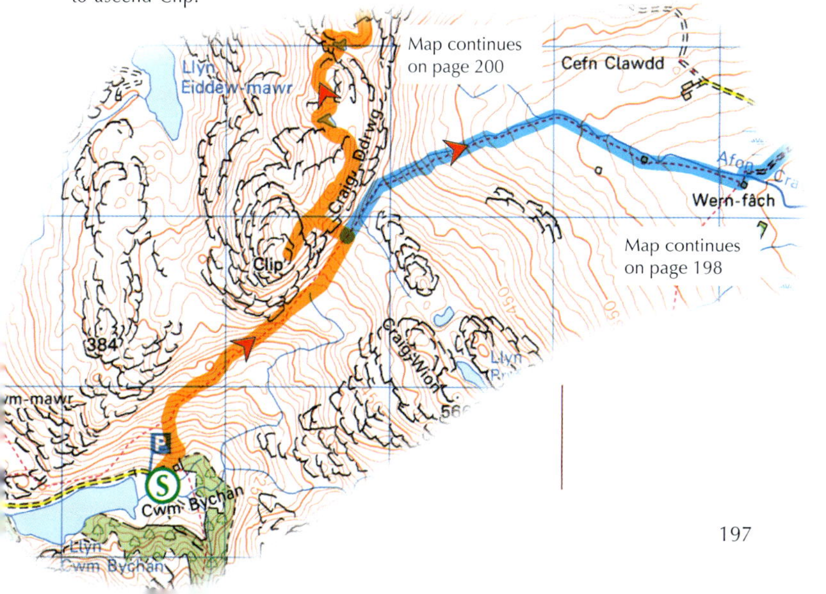

Map continues on page 200

Map continues on page 198

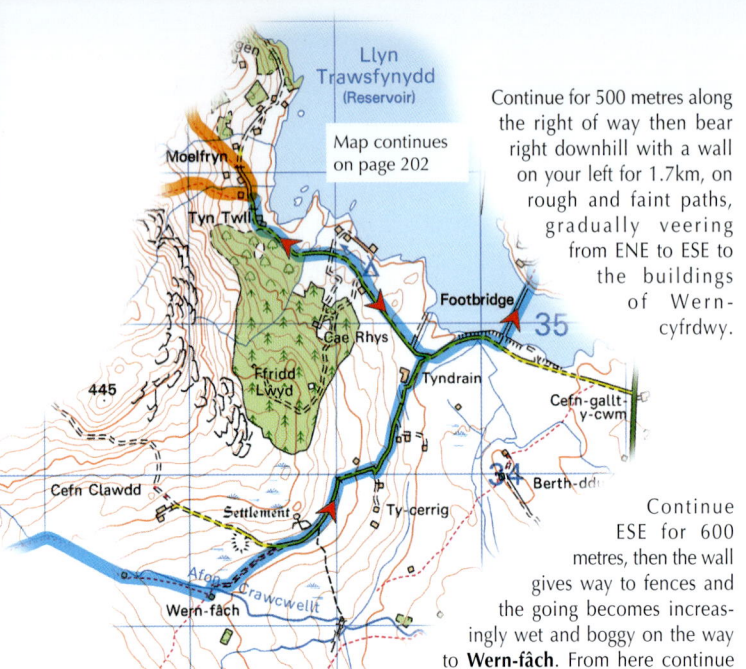

Continue for 500 metres along the right of way then bear right downhill with a wall on your left for 1.7km, on rough and faint paths, gradually veering from ENE to ESE to the buildings of Wern-cyfrdwy.

Continue ESE for 600 metres, then the wall gives way to fences and the going becomes increasingly wet and boggy on the way to **Wern-fâch**. From here continue to a lane where you turn right and walk a further 1.8km to a junction. Here, either continue ahead for accommodation and services in **Trawsfynydd** (1.6km), or turn left and follow the road to **Moelfryn** (1.8km) to rejoin the main route to Maentwrog.

Main route

Look out for a path going left up the hillside 50 metres past the wall. It is not all that clear, but try to follow it as it goes WNW towards a stile over a wall 50 metres up the steep slope. Continue up the hillside for 200 metres to the top of the ridge then turn left, heading SSW to reach the summit of **Clip** after 250 metres with a fine view of Rhinog Fawr. (There is a ledge to climb, but a place to the left is not too difficult to scramble up.) Retrace the path back along the ridge and continue NNE for 700 metres from the summit.

Here a lot of walking is over bare rocks where paths are unclear and there are numerous alternative routes. There is no right or wrong way, provided progress is made along the ridge in a northerly direction.

The next landmark is a small lake called Llyn Corn-yswch. The suggested route is to swing round NW along the ridge and descend to reach the western tip of the lake after 300 metres. Turn right and head NE for 100 metres alongside the lake, then head NNW for 400 metres, not following the wall but climbing partway up the hillside, bypassing the summit and swinging right to head NE down towards Llyn Du ('black lake'). On the ledge, before reaching the lake, turn sharp left on a path leading down for 70 metres to a wall 50 metres NW of the lake.

After crossing the wall, do not take the path going N but turn sharp right along a path heading E past the northern side of the lake. Follow the path as it contours round the hillside and starts to swing left after 250 metres to head N for 100 metres. Descend N for 100 metres to the valley bottom and then follow the path uphill, going NW for 100 metres. From here there are a few faint paths, but the aim is to head up the broad valley to the N towards a dip in the ridge 300 metres ahead, swinging NNE and joining a clearer path towards the ridge top. Turn right along the path and go ESE for 100 metres to reach the trig point and pile of stones at the summit of **Moel Ysgyfarnogod** ('bare hill of hares'). This is Checkpoint 28 at 623m (2044ft). ▶

There is a magnificent panoramic view of the coast, most of the Snowdonian mountains, part of Llyn Trawsfynydd and the Rhinog mountains.

Snowdon's iconic summit can be seen from Moel Ysgyfarnogod

Map continues
on page 202

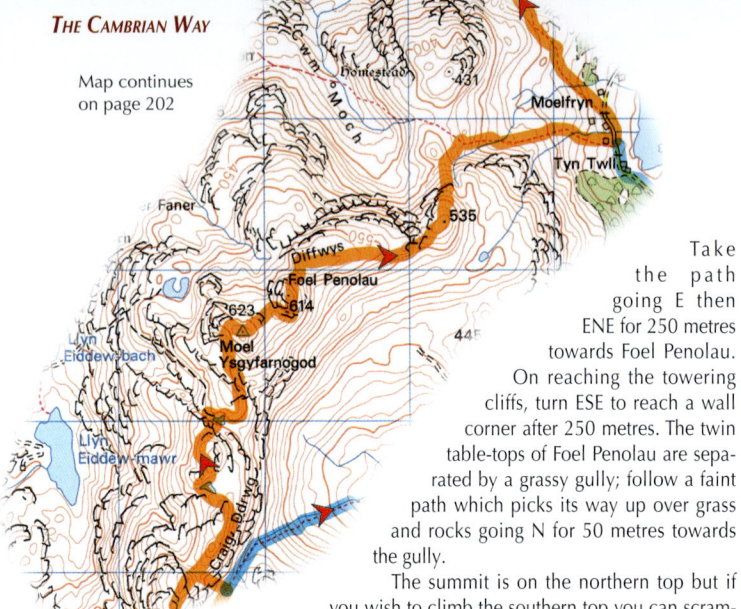

Take the path going E then ENE for 250 metres towards Foel Penolau. On reaching the towering cliffs, turn ESE to reach a wall corner after 250 metres. The twin table-tops of Foel Penolau are separated by a grassy gully; follow a faint path which picks its way up over grass and rocks going N for 50 metres towards the gully.

The summit is on the northern top but if you wish to climb the southern top you can scramble up from here or walk through the gully for an easier clamber from the west side. Otherwise, continue up the gully where a faint path leads N to reach the northern top after 100 metres. This is the actual summit of **Foel Penolau** at 614m (2014ft). ◀

From the summit the cairn on the top of nearby Diffwys is quite visible.

Continue N down a steep path which swings right to reach the bottom of a valley to the NW after 200 metres. Head N for 100 metres to the summit of **Diffwys** at 557m (1827ft), then head E and gradually descend for 500 metres.

The route along Diffwys is mainly over slabs of bare rock with only faint traces of a footpath, but a line of small cairns helps to mark the way. The important thing is to aim towards the southern edge of the mountain as this is where the only easy descent is possible.

Continue E as the route descends more steeply, going obliquely down the hillside to meet a wall after a further 150 metres. Follow the wall, and a scramble down a gully leads into a dip after 200 metres. Cross the wall ahead and go 250 metres in a NE direction to the summit of Moel y Gyrafolen at 535m (1755ft). On reaching the summit cairn, turn N and follow a faint path which comes and goes on flat rocky areas for 120 metres. Do not stray E as there are very steep, pathless heathery slopes with rocky drops. The correct path leaves the top at SH 6722 3542 (accuracy is quite critical here ' hence the eight-figure grid reference) and is marked by a small pile of stones with good views to the west and north. The path starts unexpectedly with a rocky step but can be seen more clearly continuing below. Follow a reasonably clear zigzag route N for 300 metres with the occasional cairn or stone marker to help.

Cross a wall and take a faint path NE down the gentle slope to meet a track close to where it crosses a wall 200 metres ahead at SH 674 358. Turn right over the wall and follow the path E for 800 metres, with a wall on the left for most of the way, looking out for occasional waymarks. The path then exits the common and follows a rough sunken lane for 300 metres to meet a minor road close to **Moelfryn** at SH 684 358, which is Checkpoint 29. ▶

This is where the Stage 16 escape route rejoins the main route, and where Stage 16/17A ends.

For accommodation in Trawsfynydd

The main route heads towards Maentwrog, but for accommodation or services in Trawsfynydd turn right and continue SE along the road for 2.3km, bearing left at a road junction to head towards the **footbridge** across the reservoir. Cross the bridge, which is 450 metres long. Follow the track as it heads N then E for 400 metres to a lane which bears left to reach the centre of **Trawsfynydd** after a further 300 metres. Here

Views from Llyn Trawsfynydd include the Moelwyn mountains

Map continues
on page 204

you'll find Llys Ednowain (self-catering hostel), a pub, shop and B&Bs.

To rejoin the main route, take the minor road N out of the village for 500 metres to cross the **A487** road. Take the lane going NE; after 100 metres this becomes a footpath which

heads N for 300 metres. The next 350 metres are tree-lined as the path swings right to cross a stream then swings left to go N again. Continue for 350 metres to join a farm lane; bear left onto this and walk for 50 metres, but make sure to take the first turning left which leads to the **A487** after 70 metres.

Go straight across the road and along a track, heading WSW for 80 metres before bearing right along a cycle track that follows the edge of the reservoir N then W past the **disused power station**. It then heads N again and NW to end after 3.8km at SH 687 386. Keep straight on along a wide track, heading NNW then WNW for 900 metres to reach **Bryntirion** at SH 680 391, avoiding any right turns on the way. This is where the main route is rejoined for the rest of the way to Maentwrog.

To continue on the main route from Moelfryn, turn left along the road and go N for 200 metres then bear left up a track and go NW for 850 metres, climbing steadily along the hillside, entering access land and swinging N then NW again. This is now a wide track designated as a traffic-free cycle route, although the old path runs alongside for much of the way.

After crossing a wall at the highest point, follow the track as it heads NNW then NW with woodland on the right. The route comes alongside the boundary wall of the wood after 400 metres. Follow the wall NW for 200 metres to where the woodland ends by a wall. Bear right and go N for 100 metres to where the wide track bears left. It is possible to follow this if preferred, but the route carries on ahead for 150 metres along a faint path, then it goes NW for 100 metres before swinging W for 200 metres and coming close to the wide track again. ▶ Swing NW then N round the top of the leat to join the wide track as it heads E then NNE to cross to the other side of the dam after 600 metres.

The reason for coming this far west is that the leat feeding water into the reservoir is deep and fenced off.

Beyond the dam, follow the track NE for 120 metres then ESE for 130 metres and look out for a path going left through the forest. Follow the path for 500 metres, going NNE then N to where it joins a wider track. Follow this NNE for 100 metres then bear left from the wide track, heading generally N then NE for 250 metres to exit the forest by some overhead **power lines**.

Pass to the left of a pylon, heading NNE, to reach a wall on the right and follow this to enter farmland after 120 metres. Keep following the wall on the right, still going

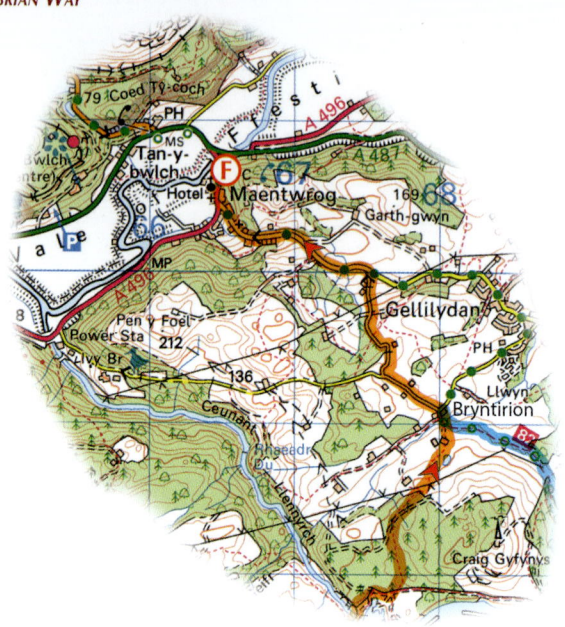

NNE, to enter the next field and continue to its far-right corner to join the farm access road after 300 metres. Follow this N for 200 metres to meet a minor road at **Bryntirion** (SH 680 391). The Trawsfynydd alternative rejoins the main route here. Turn left along the road and continue WNW for 450 metres, then bear right at the fork to head in a northerly direction for 800 metres, going downhill to join another road. Bear left to head downhill in a westerly direction for another 800 metres, then the road swings NNW for 300 metres to join the **A496**. The stage ends by the church in **Maentwrog**, 100 metres N along the A496. There is B&B accommodation in the village as well as pubs.

STAGE 18

Maentwrog to Beddgelert

Start	St Twrog's Church, Maentwrog (SH 665 405)
Finish	A498 bridge, Beddgelert (SH 590 481)
Distance	22km (13½ miles)
Total ascent	1340m (4390ft)
Total descent	1320m (4320ft)
Time	7–8¾hr
Maps	OS Explorer OL 23 and OL 17; OS Landranger 124 and 115
Refreshments	Tanygrisiau
Public transport	Bus services from Maentwrog to Barmouth, Blaenau Ffestiniog, Dolgellau, Bangor and Aberystwyth; bus services from Beddgelert to Caernarfon and Porthmadog; Sherpa bus service around six main walking routes on Snowdon – see www.gwynedd.llyw.cymru/en
Accommodation	Tanygrisiau 4km (+2km); Blaenau Ffestiniog 4km (+4km); Beddgelert; YHA Snowdon Bryn Gwynant 22km (+7km – see Stage 19)

This stage gives a taste of high Snowdonia, with numerous lakes and tarns and steep mountains on which wayfinding can be difficult in low cloud. There are spectacular views of most of the Snowdonia National Park, Tremadog Bay and the Lleyn Peninsula. The route also encounters the impressive pumped-storage electricity dam at Ffestiniog, and the popular narrow-gauge Ffestiniog and Welsh Highland Railways.

From the A496 road by St Twrog's Church in **Maentwrog**, go N for 250 metres to cross the bridge over Afon Dwyryd and join the **A487** for 300 metres, heading NNW. Where the road turns left near **Tan-y-bwlch**, take the minor road heading ENE along the Vale of Ffestiniog. Follow the road for 300 metres and then bear left through a gate onto a narrow but clear path with a fingerpost and a sign indicating the Coedydd Maentwrog reserve.

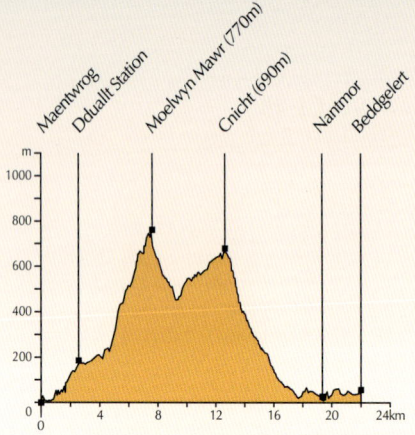

Follow the path NNE up through woodland for 100 metres. Ignore a post with a waymark signing the right of way to the left and continue ahead, following the path NE for 200 metres. At SH 666 414, leave the reserve through a gate to soon join a right of way that continues ahead across a bridge over a stream near a house. Go a few yards down the house's access drive to where the footpath turns left off the drive into a field by a short post with a waymark which is not clearly visible from this direction of approach.

Head NNW up through bracken for 50 metres and into woodland. The path then turns right, heading ENE for 450 metres to cross a footbridge over a waterfall. Go up through a gate where a fingerpost points up a tarmac driveway and follow this for 350 metres, heading ENE to Plas y Dduallt. Where the driveway turns right, follow the fingerpost on the left to climb through a field to ladder stiles, crossing the **Ffestiniog Railway** at SH 675 418 after 150 metres.

The **Ffestiniog Railway** was built to transport slate from the quarries in Ffestiniog to the port of Porthmadog. Work on the narrow-gauge line commenced in 1832, but it was only initially used for wagons going downhill using gravity, with empty wagons being hauled back by ponies. It was not until 1863 that the first steam locomotives were used, but by 1872 a main line railway reached

Blaenau Ffestiniog, taking most of the slate to other destinations and leaving the Ffestiniog Railway more dependent on tourists – thus it became less profitable. At the outbreak of war in 1939, the railway closed and the lines were removed to provide steel for the war effort.

Continue ENE for 400 metres on a path that has been cleared of vegetation but is boggy in places, and go under a viaduct that carries the loop line across the railway. Continue for another 130 metres alongside the line to cross a ladder stile and reach the platform of **Dduallt Station**.

The interesting feature at Dduallt is the **loop in the line**, which was not part of the original railway. When the dam was built on Tanygrisiau Reservoir the water flooded the then-unused railway line. When it was reopened the line had to be relocated higher up. Consequently, the extra height had to be accommodated and a loop was built at Dduallt to achieve this. Another interesting feature here is the topograph on the small hill to the east of the station, giving fine views of the surrounding area.

Map continues on page 208

Head NNE along the platform and then NE, dropping to join a track that heads uphill following the right-hand side of the railway line, first going N then NNW to the point where the railway enters a tunnel after 1km. Continue N for 400 metres to the top of the hill, cross a wall, and descend for 350 metres towards the reservoir.

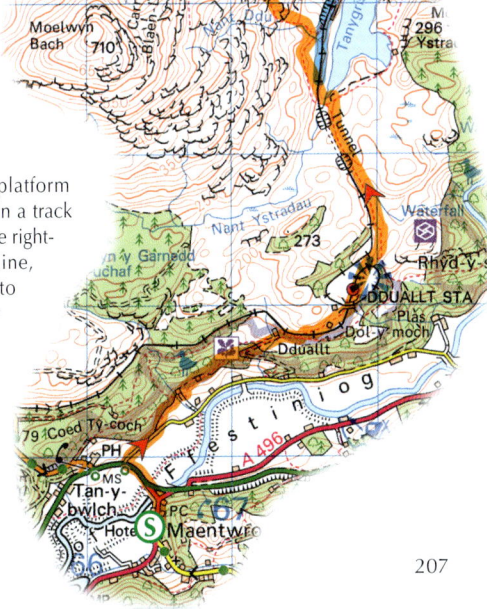

For accommodation in Tanygrisiau or Blaenau Ffestiniog

This route can also be taken as a gentler ascent to Llyn Stwlan, although it is 3km longer. Continue N towards the reservoir. ◄ After 150 metres keep left at a fork, still heading N parallel to the railway, and continue for 600 metres. Bear left on a path that keeps closer to the railway, passing to the left of the **power station** and then crossing the railway line after 200 metres. After going N for another 200 metres the path joins a minor road and heads NE for 400 metres to reach a fork, with access to the **railway station** on the right and Bryn Elltyd Guest House sharp right by the reservoir.

Take the left fork (this is the access road to the dam of Llyn Stwlan, the upper storage reservoir), crossing the railway line and heading NE for 400 metres to a car park where a road turns off to the right over a bridge and right again into **Tanygrisiau** village and onwards to Blaenau Ffestiniog (2.4km) for those seeking accommodation there. Otherwise, to rejoin the main route, continue up the access road as it swings round left to double back on itself, heading steadily up the hillside for 1.7km. The road commences a series of zigzags up the steep hillside; after 500 metres, before reaching an even greater set of zigzags to the dam ahead, look out for a path to the left crossing **Afon Stwlan** by a footbridge near some ruined buildings. Cross the bridge and head SW for 100 metres to meet the main route at SH 668 443.

To stay on the Cambrian Way, take an easily missed waymarked path turning sharp left to cross the railway line via two ladder stiles at SH 676 434. Then take a clear, waymarked path heading NNW up the

Maps show the water covering the track here but most of the time it is clear and if not, there is a path above the water line.

Map continues on page 213

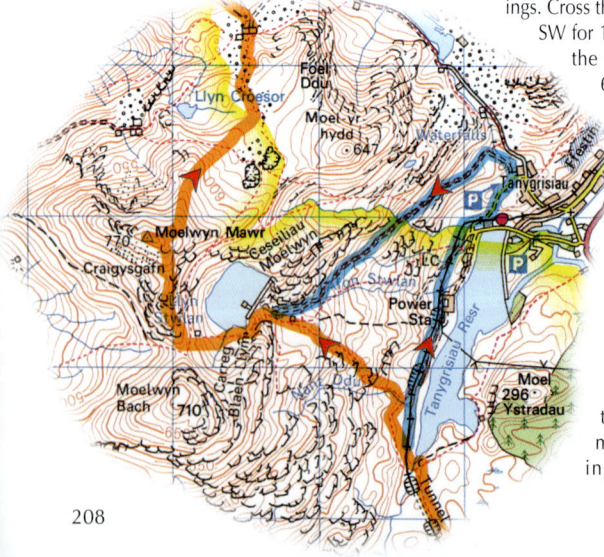

hillside for 400 metres, somewhat above the route shown on maps, to go through a gap in the wall. Turn right here to head NNE, following the left side of the wall and passing the disused Moelwyn mine to cross **Nant Ddu** ('black stream') via a waymarked footbridge after 130 metres.

Ignore a second waymark to the right on the other side of the stream and instead go ahead up a steep slope, zigzagging to a yellow-topped post, not visible from the bottom of the slope. Swing left to follow the path WNW along the valley to the right of the stream for 350 metres. Here there is a level area where a wall starts. Follow the left of the wall WNW for 400 metres, going up another steep slope before levelling off again with the dam of Llyn Stwlan looming up ahead. The wall bears right, but continue WNW to join a fence alongside old quarry workings after 200 metres. ▶

Follow the fence WNW for 200 metres, but do not go right up to the dam; instead look for a steep gully on the left 50 metres before the dam. The gully requires some scrambling, but it is not too difficult.

The route continues by going SSW for 100 metres after crossing a low wall. Turn right over some stone outcrops and pass the southern edge of the **reservoir** after going

Walkers who have visited Tanygrisiau and taken the access road up to the dam can rejoin the main route here, at SH 668 443.

The Cambrian Way provides excellent views onto neighbouring reservoirs

W for 300 metres, then continue for a further 300 metres up the steep slope towards the ridge just north of Bwlch Stwlan, passing a disused quarry on the right. (If the low area near the dam is boggy, take a loop around the higher ground to the S.) On reaching the pass, turn right to head N along **Craigysgafn** ('gentle crag'), following a steep path that requires some scrambling and zigzagging in places. There are stunning bird's-eye views from here of Llyn Stwlan and the Tanygrisiau reservoir beyond.

Llyn Stwlan is the upper reservoir of the **Ffestiniog pumped-storage hydroelectric power station**, the Tanygrisiau reservoir being the lower one. At off-peak times water is pumped from the lower to the upper reservoir, and when power is needed at peak times the flow is reversed, about 72% of the power being regained. Providing power quickly at peak times is of very high value, so the wasted energy is well worthwhile.

There are fine views of the route ahead to the north, and of Moelwyn Bach and the coast to the south.

After 300 metres the path levels off for 300 metres, although it is still rough and craggy, before another steep 300-metre ascent leads to Moelwyn Mawr's rounded ridge. An easy walk of 150 metres WNW takes you to the trig point on the summit of **Moelwyn Mawr**, which is Checkpoint 30 at 770m (2527ft). ◀

From the trig point, head back E for 100 metres and take a path to the left that descends ENE then NE for 150 metres. Follow the ridge in a northerly direction for 250 metres, then the path starts to swing gradually NW to the right of the hill-side towards tips and old quarry workings below. After a further 600 metres, cross a wire fence via a stile.

Continue NE, swinging round to pass to the left of Rhosydd Quarry and its tips, and join a clearer path (which is the right of way) going N through quarry workings down two inclines to reach a level area of the main quarry after 550 metres. (If it is very wet at the bottom of the second incline, go along the ridge to the left.) There is a large flat area of spoil with numerous ruined quarry buildings which attract walkers coming from both E and W to explore the area.

The route ahead goes over access land with many paths that are not marked on maps, and those that are marked do

not always agree with what's on the ground. The main aim is to reach the lowest part of the ridge leading to Cnicht at SH 657 477, which is about 1.9km NNW. The following describes a route that tries to avoid boggy ground, has paths that are fairly clear most of the way, and features a few landmarks such as a fence to follow if visibility is poor. However, if in doubt, just keep heading generally NNW until a path up to the ridge can be seen.

Head NNW across the spoil for 100 metres, avoiding the main track which goes NNE down past a building and some waterfalls (although it is interesting to take a look at them). Instead, stay on the level to the left of the main track and then head WNW to join a path going up the hillside with the stream that feeds the waterfalls about 100 metres over to the right. Follow this for 300 metres to where it meets a fence at SH 662 465, at which point a right of way crosses.

Cross the fence, which is very low here with some posts missing (2018), and follow the left side of the fence N uphill for 400 metres until you join one of the other paths and there is a gate. (This gate could be used should the fence ever be repaired in the future, although a stile should be provided at the point where you would cross the fence.) The path starts to move gradually away from the fence to the left, staying N for

200 metres and going along the edge of higher ground left of **Llyn Cwm-corsiog**. Continue N for 150 metres down into Cwm Corsiog and then a further 200 metres over the gentle ridge ahead, bearing right from the right of way which heads NNW. This brings you into another dip with a craggy buttress looming ahead.

A few alternative routes cross the buttress, but the one described here has the clearest paths. If in doubt, take any one of the gullies or craggy ledges with an obvious path, heading roughly N while scrambling around rocks and crags. Beyond the buttress, a clearer path is visible heading onto the Cnicht ridge. The lower route heads over a lower ledge at SH 660 473 (200 metres W); another that is closest to the right of way but less clear further on starts at SH 661 473 (100 metres W). Our route starts at SH 661 473, where rocks and boulders are scattered a little way up the valley to the right.

Cross the rocky area and take the steep path going NNW up a gully in the buttress. After climbing above the rocks, the path swings NW and levels off after 150 metres but the route is still quite craggy and meanders somewhat. Continue ahead, going NNW for 200 metres then W for 130 metres, as the path descends to rejoin the alternative routes and right of way at SH 659 476. Head NW down the clear path to cross a stream after 130 metres then go up to reach a cairn at the top of the ridge after 170 metres.

Once on the ridge, route finding is much simpler as it is just a matter of following the ridge left and heading SW for 1.6km to climb to the summit of Cnicht. There is more than one path in places and it doesn't matter which is taken as they all end up in the same place. However, after 1km it is worth keeping on paths to the left as they bypass some of the craggy outcrops and avoid some scrambling. What looks like the summit here is actually another crag before the summit, and it is again better to keep to the left. The real summit is now in sight and a short climb round to the right leads to the top. **Cnicht** ('knight') is Checkpoint 31 at 690m (2265ft) and offers panoramic views with mountains and lakes all around. There are several spots offering shelter from the wind for a rest stop. ◄

Cnicht is often called the 'Welsh Matterhorn' because of its appearance from the south, although it is tiny compared with the real Matterhorn.

The descent of Cnicht is very steep with zigzags and scrambling in places, so a great deal of care should be taken.

From the summit, head WSW and then follow the path as it bears to the left. Some scrambling is needed at a steep section not far below the summit where the best route is down an open chute to the left (SE) side of the ridge.

The path drops and soon reaches a grassy shoulder.

Looking across to the next objective – Cnicht

Map continues on page 215

213

Descend the ridge SW, picking the easiest ways through the rocky crags and trying not to stray too far to the right as there are rocky cliff faces. About 1km from the summit, the path rounds the right-hand side of a craggy outcrop and reaches a ladder stile over a wall on the right. Cross the stile and follow a path going SW down the ridge for 750 metres.

Bear right, going 100 metres W into the valley to join a path heading SW and follow this for 600 metres to a wall, where a gate leads onto a rough track. Turn sharp right along the track and follow it generally NW and W for 1.5km, then SW for 400 metres and finally NE for 100 metres to join a road at a T-junction by some houses. Cross the road and follow the side-turn opposite, heading initially W and following the lane as it winds its way for 2km to **Nantmor** in a roughly NW direction. ◀

Turn right along the **A4085** and walk for 100 metres, then turn right uphill towards the car park. After 50 metres, before reaching the railway viaduct, turn left up the hillside then left again and head W on a path through the woods to reach **Pont Aberglaslyn**, which is Checkpoint 32A, after 300 metres (Checkpoint 32B is listed for historic reasons on an alternative route – now blocked – to Bryn Gwynant hostel).

Nantmor has a station on the Welsh Highland Railway line. It was reopened in 2009 as part of the extension to Porthmadog.

The attractive Pass of Aberglaslyn near the end of the stage

There are attractive waterfalls under the bridge. Do not cross the bridge but turn right before it and follow the right-hand riverbank path N through the **Pass of Aberglaslyn**.

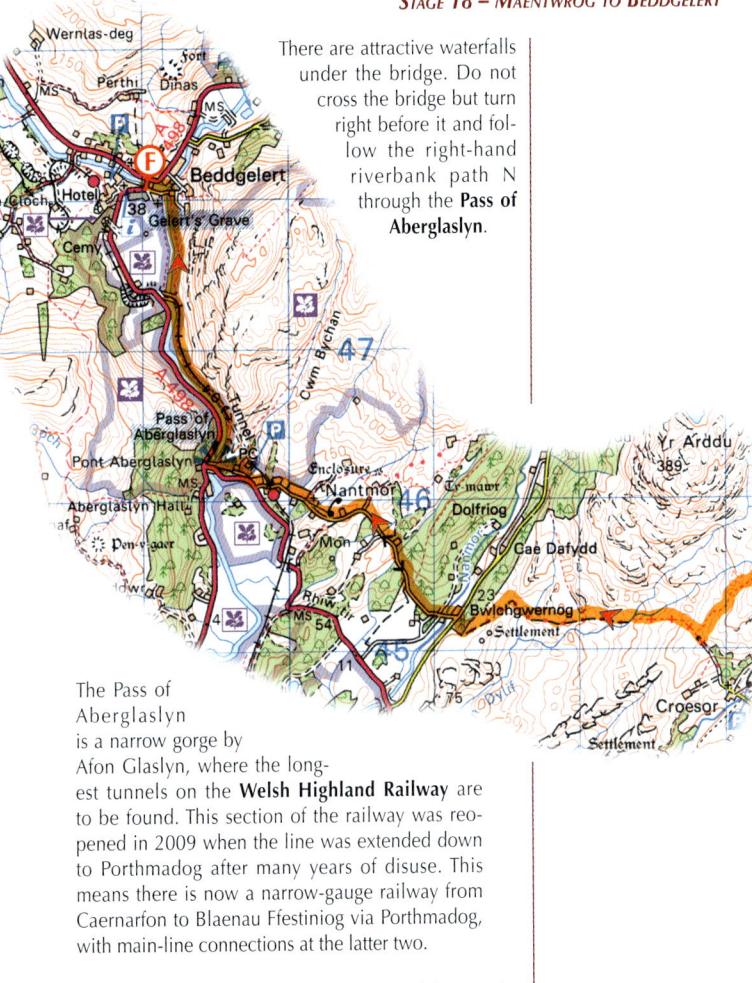

The Pass of Aberglaslyn is a narrow gorge by Afon Glaslyn, where the longest tunnels on the **Welsh Highland Railway** are to be found. This section of the railway was reopened in 2009 when the line was extended down to Porthmadog after many years of disuse. This means there is now a narrow-gauge railway from Caernarfon to Blaenau Ffestiniog via Porthmadog, with main-line connections at the latter two.

After 1.3km a bridge crosses the river, and this can be used by those wishing to visit Gelert's Grave which is on the W side of the river. The railway, previously above and to the right of the path, also crosses the path and the river here to run alongside the road.

Gelert's Grave overlooked by the Snowdonian Mountains

The legend displayed by the 'grave' tells the tale of the dog **Gelert**, which was slain in the 13th century by its master Llywelyn the Great who thought it had killed his infant son. In fact the blood Llywelyn had found was from a wolf that Gelert had killed to protect the child, who was unharmed. Llywelyn, in remorse, buried the dog in a public place. However, the 'grave' only dates back 200 years. Beddgelert means 'the grave of Gelert'.

For those not wishing to go into the village, turn right before the footbridge and go NE along the riverbank – see Stage 19.

Otherwise continue N along the riverside path for 800 metres to the point at which Afon Colwyn from the left joins Afon Glaslyn from the right. Cross the footbridge on the left and continue W for 100 metres to the A498 in **Beddgelert**, which is the end of this stage. ◄

STAGE 19
Beddgelert to Pen-y-Pass

Start	A498 bridge, Beddgelert (SH 590 481)
Finish	Pen-y-Pass (SH 647 556)
Distance	17.5km (10¾ miles)
Total ascent	1390m (4560ft)
Total descent	1060m (3490ft)
Time	5¾–7¾hr
Maps	OS Explorer OL 17; OS Landranger 115
Refreshments	Snowdon summit
Public transport	Bus services from Beddgelert to Caernarfon and Porthmadog; Sherpa bus service around six main walking routes on Snowdon – see www.gwynedd.llyw.cymru/en
Accommodation	YHA Snowdon Bryn Gwynant 5km (+2km); Llanberis 12.5km (+7km); YHA Snowdon Pen-y-Pass; Capel Curig 17.5km (+9km)

For most walkers this is the highlight of the whole route, passing over Snowdon, the highest mountain in England and Wales. On a clear day the views in all directions are wide-ranging and impressive. Snowdon is a classic mountain with steep rugged ridges, sheer cliff faces and bird's-eye views of the lakes and tarns below. The walk is initially a flat valley walk but then ascends the lower section of the Watkin Path and steepens considerably up the south ridge of the mountain. In mist, care must be taken to select the correct descent to Pen-y-Pass.

From the southern end of the A498 road bridge in **Beddgelert**, head E along the riverside for 100 metres to cross the footbridge, then continue NE along the riverside for 400 metres to join a minor road. Turn right along the road and follow it ENE for 1km, passing to the right of **Cae-du caravan and camping park**. At the end of the camping park, leave the road to take a path along the left-hand side of the field and continue for 200 metres, still going ENE, to meet the access road to the **Sygun Copper Mine** near a large car park.

Turn left and walk for 30 metres, then, before reaching the bridge, turn right to join a wide track heading E. Follow

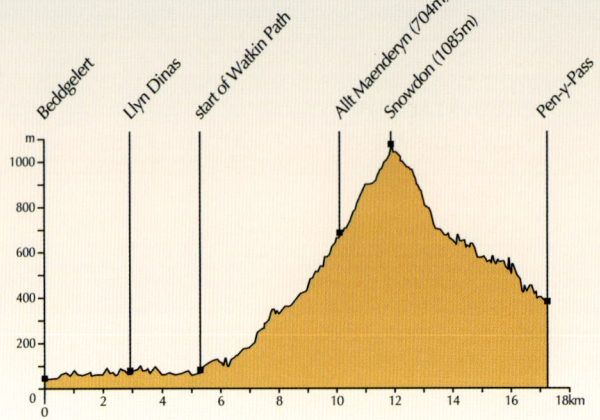

this for 900 metres along the bottom of the hillside, gradually swinging NE then back E to reach **Llyn Dinas** ('lake of the fort'). Follow the path round the edge of the lake for 600 metres, heading ESE and swinging round to ENE. Then the track swings ESE away from the lakeside to follow the bottom of the hillside for 800 metres, swinging back ENE and then heading NNE. It then swings right around woodland for 100 metres before turning left again, becoming a farm lane and passing by **Llyndy Isaf Farm**, heading in a northerly direction for 400 metres, then swinging gradually right round the bottom of the hillside to the NE and meeting a minor road after 250 metres.

For YHA Snowdon Bryn Gwynant

There used to be access to Bryn Gwynant from a track along the hillside to the west – hence the inclusion of Checkpoint 32B in Appendix A for historic reasons – but this is now blocked with little prospect of being reopened. The only reasonable access now is via its main entrance on the A498. Some main road walking en route to the hostel is avoided by going ENE along the road for 450 metres. Just after the road swings right, turn sharp left on a track past **Plas Gwynant** and continue for 450 metres then bear right on a path heading N round the hillside for 300 metres to join the **A498** road and follow this for the remaining 1.1km to **Bryn Gwynant**. To return to the main route, go down the main driveway from the hostel, heading W for 250 metres to exit onto the A498 road. Follow the road in a westerly then southwesterly direction for 1.5km to rejoin the main route at the start of the Watkin Path, just after crossing Afon Glaslyn.

To continue on the main route, turn left along the minor road for 200 metres, heading NW to cross a bridge and join the main **A498** road with Bryn Dinas camping pods to the left. Turn right and head NNE for 250 metres to the point where the main Watkin Path to Snowdon bears left up the hillside, just past Bethania. ▸ This path was built through woodland circa 2007 and is still not correctly shown on OS maps 11 years later; however, it is well marked and there is no mistaking it as it heads N through the woods for 700 metres to SH 626 512, where it rejoins the original track.

The track initially heads N but soon

This is where Bryn Gwynant hostellers rejoin the route.

Map continues on page 220

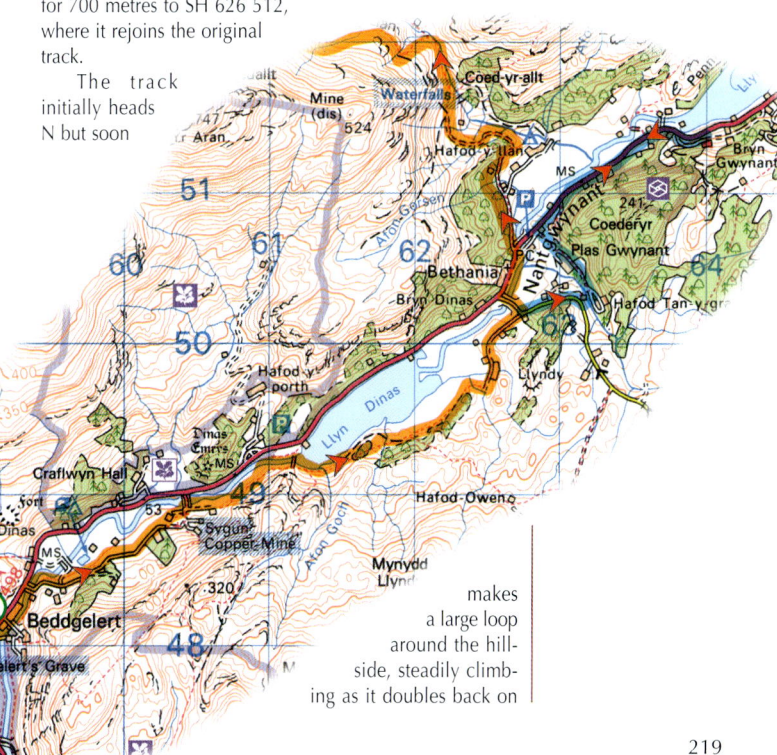

makes a large loop around the hillside, steadily climbing as it doubles back on

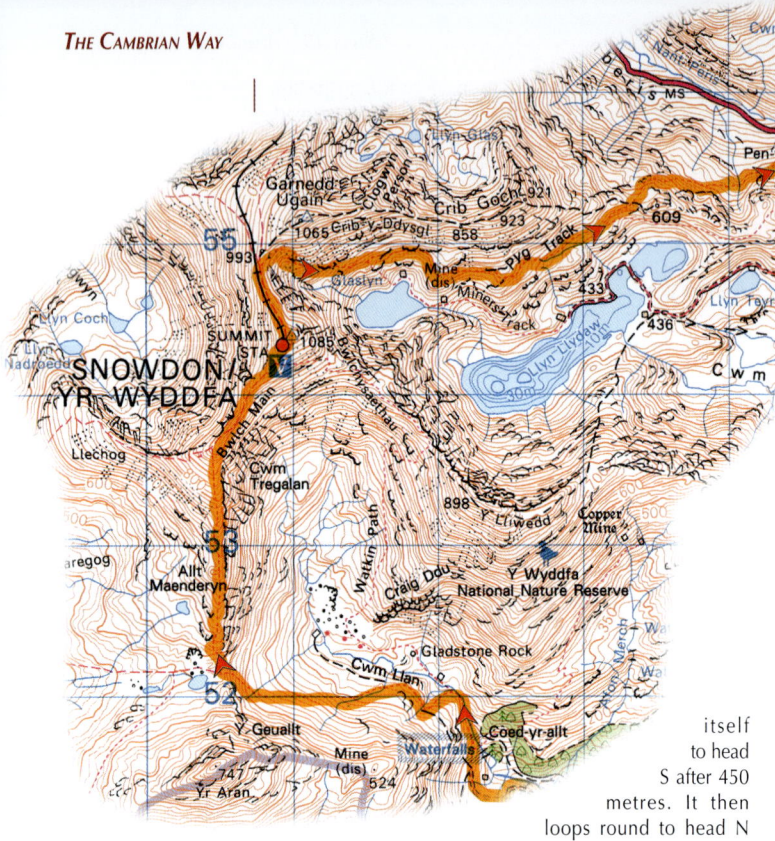

itself
to head
S after 450
metres. It then
loops round to head N
again after 300 metres with fine views
over Afon Cwm Llan and its **waterfalls**. Continue N for
650 metres until the track bears left and starts to level off.

The **Gladstone Rock** lies further along the Watkin
Path. This was where Prime Minister William
Gladstone, at the age of 83, addressed the people
of Snowdonia in 1892 on 'Justice for Wales'. The
gathered crowd sang Welsh hymns and the Welsh
national anthem *Hen Wlad Fy Nhadau* (Land of
my Fathers). There is a plaque commemorating this
on the rock, which can be visited via a 400-metre
detour NE.

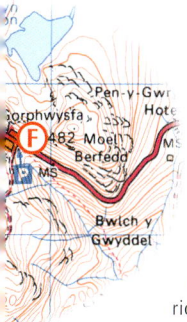

The Watkin Path goes straight on but look out for a path heading WSW up the hillside at SH 621 520. Follow this for 300 metres to join the route of an old tramway. Turn right and follow the tramway along a level for 250 metres, then bear left on a path going obliquely W up the hillside for 1.3km, swinging NW near the top at Bwlch Cwm Llan. Head N up the ridge to the left of the wall for 100 metres; the path gets steeper and zigzags up the ridge for 1.7km to the minor summit of **Allt Maenderyn**.

Here the path levels briefly, then it continues upward for 950 metres to **Bwlch Main** ('thin pass') where, as the name suggests, there is a short but very narrow part of the ridge. ▶ Continue NNE for 450 metres with the path becoming steeper before the slope eases off. The **Hafod Eryri visitor centre** at last comes into sight 300 metres ahead and is reached after a steady climb. Another short climb of 50 metres leads to the actual summit of Yr Wyddfa (**Snowdon**), which is Checkpoint 33 at 1085m (3560ft) – the highest point in Wales and England.

The visitor centre is also the terminus of the Snowdon Mountain Railway, which carries passengers from Llanberis. However, most of the

The Rhyd Ddu Path joins from the SE here.

Start of the Bwlch Main ('thin pass') ascent of Snowdon

half-million visitors per year arrive on foot. The centre is only open when trains are running – from late spring until the end of October – and is closed when trains are cancelled in bad weather. See https://snowdonrailway.co.uk. The visitor centre is just below the actual summit of **Snowdon**, where a viewing platform has been built up spiral steps commanding a magnificent panorama, with all four countries of the UK visible on occasional very clear days. One bank holiday saw two-hour queues for the viewing platform – although all the views are visible from its base! To avoid any problems, the checkpoint is on the natural summit.

From the summit head NNW, following the right-hand side of the railway for 550 metres to reach Bwlch Glas ('blue pass'), where a large vertical stone marks the head of the Pyg Track – 'Pyg' being an abbreviation of Pen-y-Gwryd ('head of the River Gwryd').

THE WELSH 3000S

There are 14 or 16 Welsh mountains over 3000ft (914m), depending on whether those with very little prominence (in italics) are included. The Cambrian Way climbs nine of them (in bold) but others can be climbed optionally on alternative routes or detours. **Snowdon/Yr Wyddfa**, 3560ft (1085m); Garnedd Ugain/Crib y Ddysgl, 3494ft (1,065m); Crib Goch, 3028ft (923m); Elidir Fawr, 3031ft (924m); Y Garn, 3106ft (947m); **Glyder Fawr**, 3284ft (1001m); *Castell y Gwynt*, 3188ft (972m); **Glyder Fach**, 3261ft (994m); Tryfan, 3009ft (917m); **Pen yr Ole Wen**, 3208ft (978m); **Carnedd Dafydd**, 3425ft (1044m); **Carnedd Llewelyn**, 3490ft (1064m); Yr Elen, 3156ft (962m); **Foel Grach**, 3202ft (976m); *Carnedd Gwenllian*, 3038ft (926m); **Foel-fras**, 3090ft (942m). Note that Crib Goch is potentially very dangerous, especially on descent, and is best approached from the east, returning down the Pyg Track to the start. It should only be attempted in good weather, by experienced walkers, without a heavy pack. Those wishing to climb it might opt to stay an extra night at Pen-y-Pass and travel light.

From Bwlch Glas, bear right down the well-made **Pyg Track** which curves round from NE to ESE down the steep mountainside for 250 metres then does a large zigzag SW for 150 metres before heading eastwards again. After 500 metres a number of paths turn off down the steep hillside towards

The majestic view from Bwlch Glas at the head of the Pyg Track

Glaslyn ('blue lake') to join the Miners' Track, which also leads to Pen-y-Pass. ▶

Continue meandering along the hillside. The slope eases off although there are still a few obstacles to clamber over. After 2km a much smaller path bears right to join the Miners' Track not far from where it reaches Pen-y-Pass, but the main route continues ENE for 300 metres then makes a short rise to the pass of Bwlch y Moch.

Head N from the pass, soon swinging NW then N again for 150 metres. The track is still clear but is more rugged as it starts to descend quite steeply for a while and swings in an easterly direction to reach the car park at **Pen-y-Pass** after 1.5km – the end of this stage. The youth hostel is just across the road and is often full, but the Sherpa bus services connect with Llanberis, Pen-y-Gwryd and Capel Curig as well as many other places with accommodation.

The YHA benefitted from a large gift by **Tony Drake** and there is a room dedicated to him and display panels in tribute to him in the Pen-y-Pass hostel.

The Pen-y-Gwryd Hotel, 1.5km E of here, was where **Hillary and Tenzing** trained for the first successful ascent of Mount Everest in 1953. Members of the team stayed during their training and it subsequently became a place of pilgrimage for mountaineers from all over the world.

The Miners' Track is another popular route. It is gentler after the initial steep descent but 1.3km longer.

STAGE 20
Pen-y-Pass to Llyn Ogwen

Start	Pen-y-Pass (SH 647 556)
Finish	A5 road at Idwal Cottage (SH 650 604)
Distance	8.5km (5½ miles)
Total ascent	810m (2670ft)
Total descent	870m (2860ft)
Time	4–5hr (allowing 1hr extra for slow progress)
Maps	OS Explorer OL 17; OS Landranger 115
Refreshments	None on route
Public transport	Sherpa bus service around six main walking routes on Snowdon – see www.gwynedd.llyw.cymru/en
Accommodation	YHA Idwal Cottage (Llyn Ogwen); Capel Curig 8.5km (+8km)

This is a short stage because much of it is steep and rugged, on sections that are like lunar landscapes. It starts with a steep climb. Views are breathtaking but careful route finding is necessary in cloud or mist.

From the car park at **Pen-y-Pass** go left along the road for 50 metres, heading WNW past the buildings, then take a sign-posted footpath heading N to cross a wall after 30 metres. Follow the path as it heads NNW for 300 metres to reach a minor summit, meandering slightly on the way. (The path is not very well trodden as most people approach these mountains from the north.)

The route swings round W as it descends into a dip and passes to the right of a small tarn after 100 metres before continuing W for another 50 metres. Bear right and head NW for 200 metres on any one of the few paths going in roughly the same direction, then go WNW for 200 metres. Here the path starts to become steeper as it ascends NNW on the craggy hillside for 300 metres to a ledge before turning right for 200 metres and heading NE onto a minor summit at **646m** (2119ft).

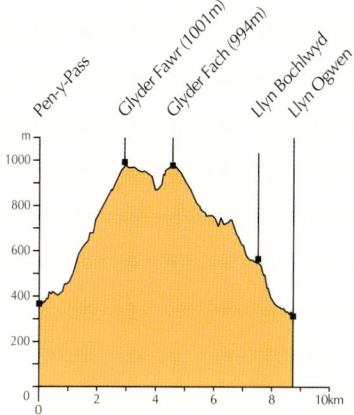

Bear left to head N for 250 metres, going up another steep scramble, after which the path turns left for 60 metres before resuming its northerly direction for the remaining 1km of steady ascent to the summit of **Glyder Fawr**, which is Checkpoint 34 at 1001m (3284ft). ▶

From the summit head E for 350 metres over stones and boulders, passing strange-looking outcrops of vertical rocks.

There are two rocky mounds, the first one being the summit, and an almost complete lack of vegetation all around.

The distinctive rocky mass of Castell y Gwynt and Glyder Fach, seen from Glyder Fawr

The very steep northern edge gives fine views of Llyn Idwal, Nant Ffrancon and Pen yr Ole Wen.

The path can be seen for a while but is then marked by a series of cairns over the rocks. An easier path then leads in an easterly direction along a grassy ridge for 550 metres to **Bwlch y Ddwy Glyder** ('pass of the two Glyderau'). ◀

Towards the end of the ridge, as it starts to descend, there is a fork in the path. Bear right on a smaller path, which is easier, and follow it for 300 metres. The direct route to the summit of Glyder Fach is blocked by the very steep rocky outcrop of Castell y Gwynt ('castle of the wind'), so the route skirts round this on its southern side, avoiding the area of rocks and boulders. Resist the temptation to climb northwards too soon – wait until a more obvious path is visible going NNE. There are still a few boulders to clamber over, but the way soon becomes easier and then levels out onto a wide stony plateau after 150 metres with Castell y Gwynt to the left and Glyder Fach to the right. ◀

The ascent of Castell y Gwynt is easier from this side, although it still involves some rock climbing.

Head ENE over stony ground where it is just possible to make out a path a little way from the northern edge of the plateau. After 100 metres look out for the Cantilever Stone on the right – a large slab of rock balancing on a pivot.

Despite its precarious appearance, the **Cantilever Stone** is quite stable. However, it has been seen and heard rocking when a group of five or six people have jumped up and down on it in unison. This is very dangerous and should not be attempted.

Cantilever Stone on Glyder Fach

Continue for another 100 metres past the summit of **Glyder Fach**, then take an easier route to scramble to the summit from the E. This is Checkpoint 35 at 994m (3261ft). From the summit, head ENE for 250 metres along the ridge, starting to descend from the stony plateau. There is a path to the left going NNE towards Bwlch Tryfan, but avoid this and continue along the path going eastwards for 300 metres. It is still stony but has cairns to mark the way where it is unclear as it descends near to the steep edge on the left.

The descent to Bwlch Tryfan by the path going NNE on a direct route is discouraged as it is very steep and badly eroded. Instead, the route taken goes ESE down a gentler slope then doubles back along a lower path which is still steep in places, to reach Bwlch Tryfan from the east. In years to come it is possible that a stepped path could be built, making the direct route acceptable.

The path becomes clearer beyond the stoniest part as it heads ESE for 300 metres. Avoid the first path descending N as this is still steep and eroded, and continue E for a further 200 metres. The slope becomes gentler and reaches the Miner's Track.

Turn left down the steep hillside, heading first N then soon WNW, for 200 metres as the path levels off. Avoid the path downhill to the right and continue NW along the hillside for a further 500 metres. Again, avoid paths to the right and continue NW on a path ascending the hillside for 150 metres to cross the wall at Bwlch Tryfan.

Optional ascent of Tryfan

Tryfan is one of the most rugged and iconic mountains in Wales. To climb it, descend W from the wall for 40 metres then turn right, heading in a northerly direction for 350 metres and following a reasonably clear path along the western side of the ridge, avoiding the rugged crest. This still involves some scrambling and clambering over rocks, but nothing too difficult. Bear right, going NE for 150 metres to reach the Adam and Eve rocks on the summit of **Tryfan** at 917m (3009ft). This is 550 metres of slow walking with 180m (590ft) of ascent. Return by the same route.

Welsh Black bull near Idwal Cottage

From the wall, descend NW along the clear path for 950 metres to pass to the east (left) of **Llyn Bochlwyd** ('lake grey cheek'). The path is steep at first but gets easier as it makes its way to fords at the bottom of the lake and swings NNW. ▶

Cross the stream from the lake and head N down the steep path to the left of the Nant Bochlwyd stream for 350 metres, then the slope eases off somewhat. Continue NNW for 500 metres to join the main track from Llyn Idwal. Follow the main track NW for 400 metres to reach the A5 road at the western tip of **Llyn Ogwen**, where this stage ends. Idwal Cottage visitor centre and **youth hostel** are 50 metres to the left.

A lot of path work has been completed lower down and more is in progress higher up.

STAGE 21
Llyn Ogwen to Conwy

Start	A5 road at Idwal Cottage (SH 650 604)
Finish	Conwy Castle (SH 783 775)
Distance	30.5km (19 miles)
Total ascent	1580m (5180ft)
Total descent	1870m (6120ft)
Time	9–11½hr
Maps	OS Explorer OL 17; OS Landranger 115
Refreshments	Possibly an ice cream van at Sychnant Pass, 27km from start
Public transport	Sherpa bus service around six main walking routes on Snowdon – see www.gwynedd.llyw.cymru/en; trains and bus services at Conwy
Accommodation	YHA Rowen 21km (+2.5km); YHA Conwy and B&Bs in Conwy

This is the longest stretch of high-level walking on the whole route, with 7km at over 900m (2950ft) and including six of the 16 'Welsh 3000' mountains. Carnedd Llewelyn is only 21m lower than Snowdon. In fine weather there are spectacular views all the way down to the magnificent Conwy Castle, a fitting end to the journey. There is a diversion for accommodation but after the earlier steep ascents the rest of the route is not too challenging and should be achievable by the now-hardened mountain walker. There is a bad-weather basic refuge on Foel Grach, 10.5km from the start.

From the A5 by the **youth hostel** at Idwal Cottage, head NNW along the road for 170 metres and cross the bridge at Ogwen waterfall where Afon Ogwen flows down a steep valley. Just past the bridge, turn right along a path that leads along the north side of **Llyn Ogwen**.

Do not take the direct route to the summit of Pen yr Ole Wen as this is very steep and eroded. Doing so would omit Checkpoint 36, which is the reason for having this checkpoint.

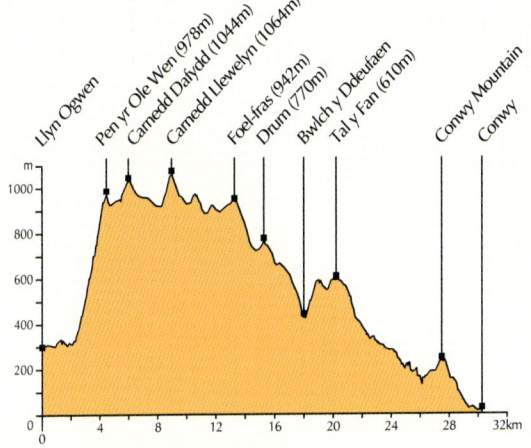

The lakeside path is very rocky at first with some scrambling over boulders, but as it approaches the lake after 170 metres is becomes easier. The path then stays fairly close to the lake for 700 metres as it heads E, then it swings further up the hillside heading NNE then ENE for 300 metres before continuing in an easterly direction for 800 metres with a number of boggy patches along the way.

Just before a farm, **Afon Lloer** ('river of the moon') runs down the hillside. There are several marker posts to show the way up the hillside and a number of other paths. Turn left beside the river and cross a footbridge 100 metres to the N. This is Checkpoint 36 near **Tan y Llyn Ogwen** at SH 667 609.

Head NE for 100 metres then N for 250 metres to cross the river again at SH 667 612, and continue upwards for another 550 metres by the left side of the river to cross a wall. Continue to follow the river N for 150 metres, then swing left round the hillside and start to ascend W on the ridge. This becomes steeper and rockier for the next 800 metres as the path zigzags upwards in a westerly direction to reach a grassier section of path. Follow it WNW along the edge of the ridge for 400 metres to the rounded summit of **Pen yr Ole Wen**, at 978m (3208ft) the first of the 3000-footers. ▶

There are fine views out to the surrounding peaks and down to Ffynnon Lloer ('well of the moon'), the lake in the steep-sided Cwm Lloer.

Nant Ffrancon and Y Garn from Pen yr Ole Wen, with Snowdon behind

Follow the ridge round the head of the cwm, first dropping then ascending again as the path swings round from NW to ENE to reach a stone wind shelter after 1.3km. Continue NE for 200 metres to **Carnedd Dafydd**, which is Checkpoint 37 at 1044m (3425ft) with more cairns offering shelter. There is little or no vegetation around here, but the paths are still clearly visible over the stony surface.

From the summit, descend E for 300 metres to the edge of **Cefn Ysgolion Duon** ('black ladders ridge') and follow this E for 850 metres to where there is a marvellous view of the river meandering down the long, steep-sided valley towards Bethesda. Continue ENE over stony ridges for 700 metres, then turn NNE along a narrow ridge for 750 metres before a steep ascent N for 650 metres leads to the summit of **Carnedd Llewelyn**, which is Checkpoint 38 at 1064m (3490ft) – the highest point of the Carneddau. This also has a wind shelter. ◄

The summit of Carnedd Llewelyn is rather flat, so the best views can be had from around the edges.

From the summit, head N for 100 metres then follow the ridge NE for 500 metres as it descends over stony ground with rocks and boulders in places and where the path is not always clear. Once beyond this steep rocky descent, the clear path is easier to follow and gentler as it heads NNE for 500 metres to the lowest part of the broad ridge. The path swings N for 400 metres as it heads up the left side of Foel Grach, then it swings round right to head E and reach the summit cairn after a further 130 metres. **Foel Grach** is another 3000-footer at 976m (3202ft) and is again flat-topped and stony.

The northeast side of Foel Grach is steep and craggy, so the path goes NNW for 50 metres and then scrambles E over rocks for another 50 metres. ▶ Head in a northerly direction down the broad

At the bottom of the rocky slope there is a mountain refuge shelter with benches inside.

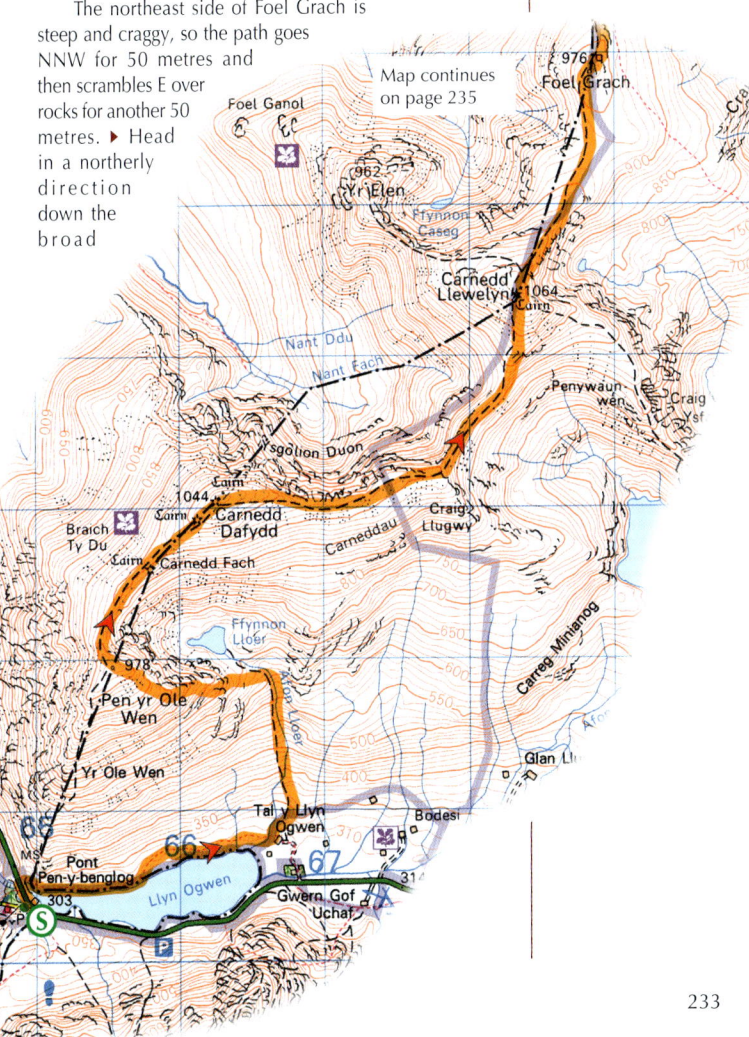

Map continues on page 235

233

ridge for 650 metres, avoiding smaller paths to the left and right. There are a few boggy patches that may have to be skirted around after rainfall and the route then ascends N for 300 metres to reach the summit of **Carnedd Gwenllian** at 926m (3038ft).

> **Carnedd Gwenllian** was named Carnedd Uchaf ('highest cairn') until 2009 when it was renamed in memory of Princess Gwenllian (1282–1337), only child of Llywelyn ap Gruffudd, after whom Carnedd Llewelyn was named. The princess was the last of the royal blood line and was kept in a priory for protection after her father was killed in battle when she was an infant. She was born in the village of Abergwyngregyn 7km away on the coast and she died aged 54 without ever knowing her real identity.

From Carnedd Gwenllian, head NE down the ridge for 600 metres and then up towards the next summit for 600 metres to meet a wall. Follow this N for 400 metres to the summit of **Foel-fras** at 942m (3090ft). A stony path runs close to the wall but the trig point is up to the left of this. ◄

Foel-fras is the last of the 3000-footers on the Cambrian Way.

Head NNE, staying fairly close to the wall for 150 metres. Continue to follow the wall as it turns right, descends ENE along the ridge for 1.3km and becomes a fence, gradually curving NNE. In keeping with the fence, ascend NNE for 550 metres to reach **Drum** ('summit'), where there is a wind shelter over the fence to the right.

It is possible to follow the fence from here, but easier to follow a parallel track running about 50 metres to the left. Follow the track N for 700 metres until it starts to swing left down the hillside. Do not continue on the track but take a small path that heads N to rejoin the fence after 300 metres at the minor summit of **Carnedd y Ddelw**.

Follow the fence NW for 400 metres and bear right, heading NNE then NE for 700 metres to the start of a wall. Follow the wall NE for 750 metres as it descends steeply to cross a Roman road at **Bwlch y Ddeufaen** ('pass of the dual stones'). ◄

There is a car park and access road 800 metres SE of here.

> It may have appeared from higher up that all the climbing was over and that it was now mainly downhill, so it can come as a surprise to find that

Map continues
on page 237

here is still over
400 metres of **ascent**
before the end of the walk
- some of it steep.

Follow the wall ENE beneath the
power lines and up the steep hillside for

270 metres (although it is possible to take an easier route up the steepest part by zigzagging to the left), then follow it N for 170 metres to where the route becomes less steep. Still following the wall, go round to the right heading ENE then E for 1km, going over **Foel Lwyd** and descending to a pass. The path meanders through wild bilberry and heather, moving away from the wall in places over stony ground.

Tal y Fan only just qualifies as a true mountain, at almost exactly 2000ft, and is the last one on the route.

It is possible to follow either side of the wall from here to the summit of Tal y Fan, 450 metres NE, although most people remain on the left-hand side. Some scrambling is needed in places up the craggy hillside and there is a lesser summit before the main one. Cross the wall via a stile to reach the trig point of **Tal y Fan**, which is Checkpoint 39 at 610m (2000ft) and gives fine views across the Conwy Valley. ◄

Return to the northern side of the wall and continue to follow it ENE along the craggy ridge for 300 metres. Here the path departs from the wall for 200 metres to avoid one particularly steep crag. Beyond that, continue to follow the wall for 200 metres to a dip 80 metres before the wall swings right.

For YHA Rowen

To reach the youth hostel, follow the path to the left of the wall ENE for 80 metres to the top of the hill, then continue to follow the wall fairly closely going SE for 150 metres. The path is now unclear, but the aim is to head eastwards down the hillside for 600 metres to join the right of way at SH 744 728. This part of the route is on access land, but this soon ends so it is necessary to follow the right of way.

Head SSE, crossing two walls 100 metres apart, and continue down the middle of the field for 600 metres – although the path is unclear. The right of way then seems to end and the direct route to the nearby youth hostel is blocked off, so it is necessary to head 200 metres ENE to join another right of way in the next field. Heads S on this for 130 metres to join the minor road leading to the hostel. ◄ Turn right up the very steep road and continue WSW for 150 metres to reach YHA Rowen in **Rhiw**.

The right of way should continue past the parish boundary, but the next parish failed to update maps.

To rejoin the main route, retrace steps to SH 744 728 at the top right-hand corner of the third field. Instead of climbing back onto the ridge, the route now cuts across to join the main route on its way down towards the standing stone of Maen Penddu. Head NW along faint paths for 500 metres to reach a wall around a large enclosure. Follow to the left of the wall as it starts to descend NW, continuing for 250 metres to SH 739 734 where the main route is rejoined.

From the dip, turn left down the hillside along a faint path and go NNE for 130 metres, then E for 170 metres to join a path that runs NNE past a small quarry on the left 250 metres further down (there are a few alternative paths leading to the same place). ▶ Continue NNE downhill towards a large enclosure for 150 metres, reaching SH 739 734 – where the YHA Rowen option rejoins – and bear left to head for the **standing stone** of Maen Penddu ('stone of black head'), 200 metres N.

Turn right along the wide quarry access track and follow this for 500 metres, going E for a short way then NE. The track swings steadily NNE over 200 metres then heads N and follows a wall on the right.

There is a small bad-weather shelter in the old quarry buildings, accessed by taking a track to the left at SH 739 733.

Map continues on page 238

237

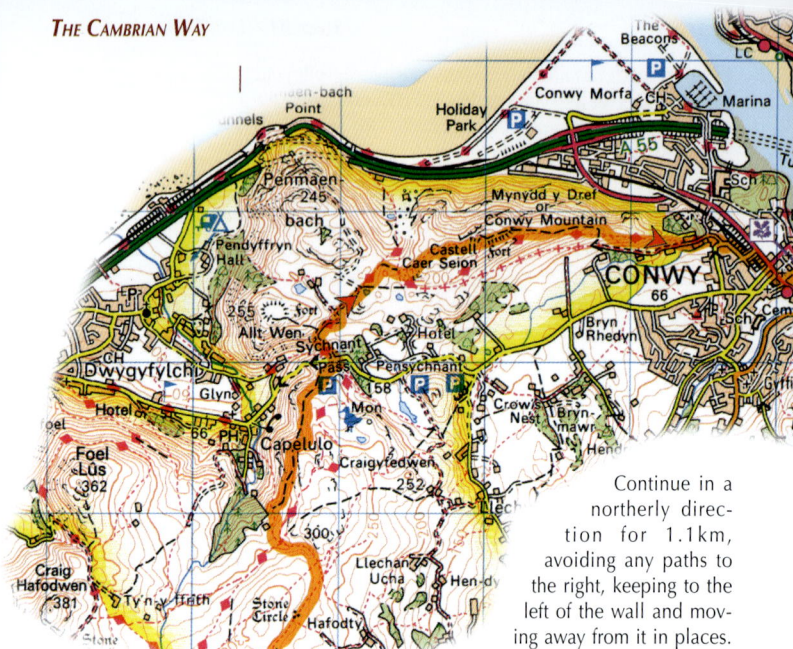

Continue in a northerly direction for 1.1km, avoiding any paths to the right, keeping to the left of the wall and moving away from it in places. Stay on the track as it swings NNE again for 450 metres and stays nearer to the wall. At SH 748 754, take a smaller path bearing left towards a pass between the hills to the left. ◄

A few paths head towards Llyn y Wrach ('lake of the witch'), which often dries out in fine weather.

After 300 metres continue downhill on a clear track, passing to the right of the lake and swinging W then WNW to cross the North Wales Path (NWP) long-distance route after 200 metres. Head towards the wall 100 metres to the NW and follow it N for 100 metres, then descend a narrow lane with walls on both sides, going NNW for 100 metres. Where the walls end, do not continue on the main track that goes downhill, but bear right along a narrow path that follows a contour along the hillside for 1km in a northerly direction. It is a little tortuous in places but gives excellent views of the coast and nearby hills.

Continue to follow the path as it bears right at a rocky outcrop (which makes a good viewpoint) and heads NE for 350 metres to join the NWP, turning sharp left and continuing for 30 metres to reach the car park at Pensychnant, the head of the **Sychnant ('dry stream') Pass**.

Maps show **Echo Rock** nearby, but the rock is actually beside the road 100 metres west of the car park. It used to be a vertical rock face giving a good echo from the hills to the north, but road widening reduced the echo to a very feeble one.

Cross the road and follow the wide track for 200 metres, going NW along the head of the valley then climbing the hillside. Continue along the main track for another 250 metres as it winds around going NNE then E and NW, still following the NWP, to reach a junction of paths. Turn right and head NE for 300 metres to reach another junction of paths, and continue straight ahead towards the hillside for 200 metres. Turn right, still on the NWP, and head ESE for 100 metres. Here the NWP turns right but the Cambrian Way heads in a northeasterly direction to climb the ridge along its left side. There is more than

Conwy Mountain, with Great Orme seen beyond

Conwy Castle, standing proud at the end of Cambrian Way

one path but they converge as they head towards the Iron Age **hill fort** near the summit of **Conwy Mountain**, which is Checkpoint 40 at 247m (810ft), after 600 metres.

Despite its limited height, **Conwy Mountain** has many of the features of a good mountain: rocky crags and panoramic views. There are a few other paths here, taking in various excavations around the hill fort with noticeboards giving details.

Continue E along the ridge, following it downhill and rejoining the NWP. Conwy Castle looms larger and larger, heralding the journey's end, and after 900 metres the path starts to drop to the right of the ridge, going through trees before emerging onto a road after another 600 metres.

Bear left along Mountain Road and go E through a housing estate for 130 metres, then bear right, still on Mountain Road as it swings SSE to meet Cadnant Park after 130 metres. Turn left and walk E for 70 metres, then go right and walk SE for 130 metres to reach a road bridge going NE across the railway. Cross the bridge, turn right along Bangor Road and continue for 280 metres, passing through a gateway in the town walls and heading into the town centre. It is possible to continue along Rose Hill Street, but the route turns left down the High Street and follows it for 200 metres, then right along Castle Street for another 200 metres, to arrive at a roundabout by the NW corner of the magnificent 13th-century **Conwy Castle**, a UNESCO World Heritage Site and Checkpoint 41; a fitting end to the Cambrian Way.

CONWY

Conwy is an historic walled market town on the estuary of Afon Conwy. The historic castle and walls were built on the instruction of Edward I of England between 1283 and 1289 after he conquered Wales, and they remain well preserved to the present day. Until 1826, when Thomas Telford completed the construction of a suspension bridge, Afon Conwy had to be crossed by ferry. This was important because Conwy was on the stage coach route from London to Holyhead en route to the ferry to Ireland. The bridge, being near to the castle, was built in a similar style with matching turrets, but it no longer carries traffic since the building of a modern road bridge alongside it. From 1848 to 1849 Robert Stephenson built a railway bridge constructed of metal tubes along the other side of the Telford bridge, with a railway station inside the castle walls. As part of the building of the A55 expressway, Britain's first immersed tube tunnel was completed in 1991, going under the estuary and bypassing the town.

There are a number of other interesting places to visit in Conwy, including Aberconwy House, a 14th-century merchant's house; Plas Mawr ('great hall'), a fine example of Elizabethan architecture; and 'The Smallest House in Great Britain', which has been occupied since the 16th century and can be visited by the public.

If you have completed the whole route – even if you had to miss some of it out due to bad weather or fatigue – it is time to congratulate yourself for having undertaken one of the most challenging long-distance walks in Britain. Reaching the end deservedly merits great satisfaction, although there may also be some sadness that it is finished. If so, you can tell yourself that the real satisfaction is in the walk itself and experiencing the beauty of the Welsh mountains and countryside, even though there may have been some challenging moments. Perhaps this is the time to start thinking about walking the Cambrian Way again – even if it is only to visit sections that were spoiled by adverse weather. You could consider making it part of a circular walk by linking it in with the Wales Coastal Path and Offa's Dyke Path. There are also many other beautiful parts of Wales to be explored.

The Cambrian Way Trust welcomes feedback from those who have completed the walk, so do please email us with this at info@cambrianway.org.uk.

APPENDIX A
The checkpoints

Checkpoints have been included to cater for Tony Drake's wish that the route should be walked in a continuous line from point to point. There is nothing physically at these checkpoints; they just represent key points along the route and are a way of marking progress. It is entirely up to the walker as to whether they adhere to this, and in the case of bad weather, sense should overrule the idea that any particular point should be reached.

Note: the checkpoints shown in italics are retained from earlier guides as optional alternatives for those wishing to follow different routes.

Checkpoint number	Grid reference	Location
1	ST 181 765	Cardiff Castle
2	ST 131 826	Castell Coch
3	ST 224 900	Mynydd Machen
4	ST 242 926	Twmbarlwm
5	SO 270 119	Blorenge
6	SO 272 188	Sugar Loaf
7	SO 255 315	Capel-y-ffin
8	SO 225 351	Twmpa
9	SO 216 299	Waun Fach
10	SO 207 243	Pen Allt-mawr
11	SO 193 156	Eglwys Faen
12	SO 012 216	Pen y fan
13A	SN 881 191	Fan Gyhirych *or*
13B	*SN 908 144*	*Blaen Nedd Isaf Junction*
14	SN 825 218	Fan Brycheiniog
15	SN 767 447	Rhandirmwyn Bridge
16	SN 740 610	Garn Gron
17	SN 808 720	Domen Milwyn
18	SN 727 782	Pontbren Pwlca
19	SN 790 869	Pen Pumlumon Fawr
20	SN 861 940	Dylife
21A	SH 853 140	Minllyn Quarry *or*
21B	*SH 859 149*	*Dinas Mawddwy*

Checkpoint number	Grid reference	Location
22	SH 837 137	Bwlch Siglen
23	SH 711 130	Penygadair (Cadair Idris)
24	SH 617 156	Barmouth Bridge
25	SH 661 258	Y Llethr
26	SH 665 270	Rhinog Fach
27	SH 657 290	Rhinog Fawr
28	SH 658 346	Moel Ysgyfarnogod
29	SH 684 358	Moelfryn (road junction)
30	SH 658 449	Moelwyn Mawr
31	SH 645 466	Cnicht
32A	SH 594 462	Pont Aberglaslyn *or*
32B	*SH 640 514*	*Bryn Gwynant YH*
33	SH 610 544	Snowdon
34	SH 643 579	Glyder Fawr
35	SH 657 583	Glyder Fach
36	SH 666 608	Tal y Llyn Ogwen
37	SH 663 630	Carnedd Dafydd
38	SH 684 644	Carnedd Llewelyn
39	SH 729 726	Tal y Fan
40	SH 760 778	Conwy Mountain
41	SH 783 775	Conwy Castle

APPENDIX B

Glossary of Welsh words and places on the Cambrian Way

Throughout the guide, where an obvious translation of names of places and other features is possible, it is shown in brackets.

Welsh	English
aber	river mouth
adar	birds
afon	river
allt	hillside
bach, fach	small
ban, fan	peak
bychan, fechan	small
Beddgelert	grave of Gelert
blaen	foremost (valley head)
bont	bridge
bryn	hill
bugeilyn	sheep pasture
bwlch	mountain pass, gap
Cadair Idris	Idris's chair
cadno	fox
caer	fort
Capel-y-ffin	chapel on the border
carn, garn	cairn, heap of stones
carneddau	cairns
caseg	mare
castell	castle
Cemmaes	bend in river
cnewr	meandering stream
cnicht	knight
coch, goch	red
coed	trees, woodland

Welsh	English
Commins Coch	red commons
craig, graig	crag, cliff
crocben	gallows
dau, ddau, dwy, ddwy	two
dduallt	black hillside
diffwys	wilderness, precipice
dinas	fortress, city
Dolgellau	meadow of (monks') cells
domen	mound, heap, dunghill
drum	ridge, summit
drws	narrow pass, door
du, ddu	black
Garreg Ddial	stone of revenge
goch	red
graig	crag, cliff
gwaun, waun	moor, meadow
gwen, gwyn, wen	white
gwryd	length of outstretched arms
tomen, domen	mound, heap, dunghill
Dwygyfylchi	two round forts
dwyryd	two fords
Dyffryn Castell	valley of the river Castell
Dylife	floods
eglwys	church

Welsh	English
esgair	ridge, leg
faen	stone
fan	peak
fawr	large
fechan	small
ffordd	road
foel	bare hill
fynach	monk
Gabalfa	place of the ferry
gallt	slope, hillside
Garn Gron	round cairn
gelli	grove
glan	riverbank
glas	blue/green
hafod	summer dwelling
Harlech	beautiful rock
hendre	winter dwelling
is	lower
isaf	lowest
Libanus	Lebanon
llan	sacred ground, church
Llanddeusant	church of two saints
llethr	slope
lluest ty mawr	camp (farm) of big house
llwyn onn	ash grove
Llwyn-y-celyn	holly grove or bush
llyn	lake
llywynog, cadno	fox
maen, faen	stone
Maentwrog	stone of Twrog
maes	field
Maesteg	fair field

Welsh	English
Mallwyd	grey field
mawr, fawr	large
Minffordd	edge of road
moel, foel, moelfre	bare hill
Myddfai	meadow of the round hollow
mynach, fynach	monk
mynydd, mynyddoedd	mountain, mountains
nant	brook
neuadd	hall
newydd	new
oer	cold
ogof agen allwedd	keyhole cave
ogof	cave
oleu	light
pant	dip, hollow
pantyfedwen	hollow of birch trees
pen	head, peak or top
Pen y Fan	top of the peak
Pengenffordd	head of ridge road
Penmaenmawr	head of large rock
Pennant	head of stream or valley
Pen-y-Gwryd	head of Gwryd stream
plas	mansion
poeth	hot
pont, bont	bridge
Pontarfynach	bridge over the river Mynach (Devil's Bridge)
Ponterwyd	bridge of poles

Welsh	English
Pontrhydfendigaid	bridge of the blessed ones (monks)
pontsticill	bridge of the stile
Pumlumon (Plynlimon)	five peaks
pwll	pit, pool
pysgotwr	fisherman
rhaeadr	waterfall
rhandirmwyn	land of minerals
rhiw	hillside
rhos	moorland
rhyd	ford
Rowen	white pebbles
sarn	paved way
scwd	waterfall
sychnant	stream that dries up
tal	end
talwrn	spot, field

Welsh	English
Talyllyn	end of the lake
Torpantau	break in the hollows
Trawsfynydd	across the mountain
Tryfan	three peaks
twymyn	feverish
tŷ	house
tŷ bach	little house (toilet)
Tŷ'n-y-cornel	house in the corner
uchaf	highest
waun	moor, meadow
waun oer	cold moorland
wen	white
Yr Wyddfa	the grave (Snowdon summit)
ysgyfarnogod	hares
ystrad	wide valley bottom
Ystradfellte	valley of the river Mellte (lightning)

Welsh plurals

There is no standard ending for plurals in Welsh. Some are more common than others, but each one has to be treated individually. Mountain ranges often have a large mountain and a small mountain that share a name, such as Glyder Fawr and Glyder Fach – referred to collectively as Y Glyderau (Y meaning 'the'). However, Rhinog Fawr and Rhinog Fach can either be called Y Rhinogau or Y Rhinogydd, while Moelwyn Mawr and Moelwyn Bach are Y Moelwynion, and the several Carnedd mountains are Y Carneddau. Anglicising names by simply adding an 's' causes offence to some Welsh speakers, so is best avoided.

Mutations

Welsh grammar is very complex and there is widespread use of mutations where the initial letter or letters of a word can change depending on a number of factors such as gender or preceding words, which is why you see bach and fach, both being the same word for 'small', with fach being the mutated form. Bach here is describing a masculine noun and fach a feminine noun. Similarly, there is mawr and fawr for 'large', and du and ddu for 'black'. These use just one of the of three types of mutation and just one of the 44 reasons for mutation that are listed in the BBC's booklet Learning Welsh.

APPENDIX C
Useful contacts

A great deal of useful information about the Cambrian Way is to be found on the **Cambrian Way website**, www.cambrianway.org.uk, where there is a detailed accommodation list, news items about footpath obstructions and diversions, GPX files of the route for downloading, background information and history of the Way, an extensive photo gallery and much more.

Transport services

There are frequent changes in timetables and services, and even franchises for bus and rail are subject to change. By far the best way to get information is to go to www.traveline.cymru, where you can enter start and finish points to find details of public transport services. Traveline Cymru also takes calls on 0800 464 00 00. Tickets are not sold through the website, but other websites such as www.nationalrail.co.uk and www.thetrainline.com can be used to purchase rail tickets. There are often large discounts for tickets on longer journeys, especially at off-peak times and when booking in advance. An allocation of heavily discounted tickets is generally made available several weeks ahead, and the cost increases closer to the journey time. However, the cheapest tickets apply to one specific journey time only and they are not normally refundable or transferrable.

Bus fares are generally paid to the bus driver on local services, although coach services operate on longer journeys and tickets can be booked online from National Express – www.nationalexpress.com – and other companies.

Tourist information

In Wales, many of the local tourist information centres have closed, the exceptions being those that operate in busy tourist towns or cities or in a popular tourist attraction such as one of the major castles. Tourist information can be obtained by going to the website of Visit Wales or one of the national park authorities listed below.

Visit Wales
www.visitwales.com

Brecon Beacons NP
www.beacons-npa.gov.uk
www.breconbeacons.org

Brecon Beacons NP Society
www.breconbeaconsparksociety.org

Snowdonia NP
www.snowdonia.gov.wales

Snowdonia Society
www.snowdonia-society.org.uk

Cambrian Mountains
www.thecambrianmountains.co.uk

Pentir Pumlumon
www.pumlumon.org.uk

National Trust Wales
www.nationaltrust.org.uk (search 'Wales')

Hostels, bunkhouses and bothies
Independent Hostel Guide
https://independenthostels.co.uk

YHA (with online booking)
www.yha.org.uk

Elenydd Wilderness Hostels (with online booking)
www.elenydd-hostels.co.uk

Walkers' associations

Long Distance Walkers Association
www.ldwa.org.uk

Ramblers Cymru
www.ramblers.org.uk/wales

Local authorities and public bodies
These websites include some information about local events, attractions and accommodation.

Cardiff Council
www.cardiff.gov.uk

Caerphilly County Borough Council
www.caerphilly.gov.uk

Torfaen County Borough Council
www.torfaen.gov.uk

Monmouthshire County Council
www.monmouthshire.gov.uk

Powys County Council
www.powys.gov.uk

Carmarthenshire County Council
www.carmarthenshire.gov.wales

Ceredigion County Council
www.ceredigion.gov.uk

Gwynedd Council
www.gwynedd.llyw.cymru

Conwy County Borough Council
www.conwy.gov.uk

Natural Resources Wales
https://naturalresources.wales

APPENDIX D
Accommodation list

This list includes all types of accommodation from campsites to bothies, bunkhouses, hostels, B&Bs, pubs with rooms and hotels. It also includes tourist information websites, as they give details of accommodation providers. Accommodation and services frequently change, and such lists can soon become out of date; however, the Cambrian Way website (www.cambrianway.org.uk) is updated whenever changes come to light. It also gives more details than can be included in this guide, as well as listing other facilities and services. Please note that in Wales wild camping is permitted only with the landowner's permission.

Stage 1 – Cardiff to Machen

Cardiff

Cardiff Castle tourist information
Old Library
The Hayes
CF10 1AH
tel 029 2087 8101
www.visitcardiff.com

YHA Cardiff Central
East Tyndall Street
CF10 4BB
tel 0800 0191 700
www.yha.org.uk/hostel/
yha-cardiff-central

NosDa Hostel
53–59 Dispenser Street
Riverside
CF11 6AG
tel 02920 378866

The River House Hostel
59 Fitzhamon Embankment
Riverside
CF11 6AN
tel 02920 399810
https://riverhousebackpackers.com

Riverside B&B
1 Coldstream Terrace
CF11 6LJ
tel 02920 210378
www.riversidebandb.co.uk

Elgano Hotel
58 Cathedral Road
CF11 9LL
tel 02920 377148
http://elgano.co.uk

Austins Guesthouse
11 Coldstream Terrace
CF11 9LJ
tel 02920 344060
https://hotelcardiff.com

Cardiff Caravan and Camping Park
Pontcanna Fields
CF11 9XR
tel 02920 398362
www.cardiffcaravanpark.co.uk

Caerphilly

Tourist information
tel 02920 880011
www.visitcaerphilly.com

Y Fron Guesthouse
The Twyn
CF83 1JL
tel 02920 882896
www.yfron.co.uk

Ty Castell Guesthouse
48 St Martin's Road
CF83 1E
tel 0798094883
www.tycastellguesthouse.co.uk

Rudry

The Coach House B&B
2 Twyn Sych
CF83 3EF
tel 02920 884772

Draethen

The Hollybush Inn
NP10 8GB
tel 01633 441326
grid ref ST 220 873
www.hollybushdraethen.co.uk

Stage 2 – Machen to Pontypool

Crosskeys

The Solar Strand Hotel
High Street
NP11 7BY
tel 01495 360026
www.thesolarstrandhotel.com

Cwmcarn Forest Campsite
Nantcarn Road
Cwmcarn
NP11 7FA
tel 01495 272001
grid ref ST 229 935
https://your.caerphilly.gov.uk/
cwmcarnforest (select 'camping')

Cwmbran

Gelligravog Farmhouse B&B
Belle Vue Lane
Upper Cwmbran
NP44 5AT
tel 01633 871147
www.gelligravog.co.uk

Pontypool

Ty Shon Jacob Farm B&B
Coch-y-North Lane
Tranch
NP4 6BP
tel 01495 757536
www.accommodationinpontypool.
co.uk

Pontypool Premier Inn Hotel
Ty'r Felin
Lower Mill Field
NP4 0RH
tel 0871 5278890
www.premierinn.com

Stage 3 – Pontypool to Abergavenny

Blaenavon

Goose and Cuckoo Inn
Upper Llanover
NP7 9ER
tel 01873 880277
https://thegooseandcuckoo.co.uk

The Lion Hotel
41 Broad Street
NP4 9NH
tel 01495 792516
www.thelionhotelblaenavon.co.uk

Abergavenny

Abergavenny tourist information
www.abergavenny.org.uk

Park Guesthouse
36 Hereford Road
NP7 5RA
tel 01873 853715
www.parkguesthouse.co.uk

The Guest House
2 Oxford Street (off Hereford Road)
NP7 5RP
tel 01873 854823
www.theguesthouseabergavenny.co.uk

The Great Western B&B and Bunkhouse
24 Station Road
NP7 5HS
tel 01873 859125
www.greatwesternabergavenny.com

Middle Ninfa Bunkhouse and Campsite
Llanellen
NP7 9LE
tel 01873 854662
grid ref SO 285 116
http://middleninfa.co.uk

Smithy's Bunkhouse
Lower House Farm
Pantygelli
NP7 7HR
tel 01873 853432
grid ref SO 305 178
www.smithysbunkhouse.f9.co.uk

Pyscodlyn Farm Caravan and Camping
Site
Llanwenarth Citra
NP7 7ER
tel 01873 853271
grid ref SO 266 155
http://pyscodlyncaravanpark.com

Stage 4 – Abergavenny to Capel-y-ffin

Llanthony

Half Moon Inn
NP7 7NN
tel 01873 890611
http://halfmoon-llanthony.co.uk

Capel-y-ffin

Grange Trekking Centre B&B and
Camping
NP7 7NP
tel 01873 890215
grid ref SO 251 315
http://grangetrekking-wales.co.uk

Grwyne Fawr Bothy
near Capel-y-ffin
grid ref SO 227 312
www.mountainbothies.org.uk

Stage 5 – Capel-y-ffin to Crickhowell

Pengenffordd

The Dragons Back Pub and Bunkhouse
LD3 0EP
tel 01874 711353
www.thedragonsback.co.uk

Crickhowell

Porth Y Berllan
Brecon Road
NP8 1DG
tel 01873 810964
www.porth-y-berllan.co.uk

The Bear Hotel
NP8 1BW
tel 01873 810408
www.bearhotel.co.uk

Dragon Inn
High Street
NP8 1BE
tel 01873 810362
https://dragoninncrickhowell.com

Riverside Caravan and Camping Park
New Road
NP8 1AY
tel 01873 810397
https://riversidecaravanscrickhowell.
co.uk

Park Place Guest House
The Legar
Llangattock
NP8 1HH
tel 01873 810878
www.parkplaceguesthouse.co.uk

YHA Llangattock Mountain Bunkhouse
Wern Watkin
Hillside
Llangattock
NP8 1LG
tel 01873 81230
grid ref SO 215 153
www.yha.org.uk (search 'Llangattock')

Stage 6 – Crickhowell to Storey Arms

Talybont-On-Usk

YHA Brecon Beacons Danywenallt
LD3 7YS
tel 0345 371 9548
grid ref SO 107 206
www.yha.org.uk (search 'Danywenallt')

Abercynafon Lodge B&B
LD3 7YT
tel 01874 676342
grid ref SO 080 175
email jill.carr7@btinternet.com

Belvedere B&B
Station Road
LD3 7JE
tel 01874 676264
grid ref SO 118 228
www.belvedere.biz

Usk Inn
Station Road
LD3 7JE
tel 01874 676251
grid ref SO 118 229
www.uskinn.co.uk

The Travellers Rest Inn
LD3 7YP
tel 01874 676333
grid ref SO 117 224
www.travellersrestinn.com

Star Inn
LD3 7YX
tel 01874 676635
grid ref SO 114 226
www.thestarinntalybont.com

The White Hart Inn and Bunkhouse
LD3 7JD
tel 01874 676227
grid ref SO 115 225
www.whitehartinntalybont.co.uk

Talybont Farm Camping
LD3 7YJ
tel 01874 676674
grid ref SO 114 227
www.talybontfarmcamping.co.uk

Storey Arms/Libanus/Heol Senni

YHA Brecon Beacons
Libanus
LD3 8NH
tel 0345 371 9029
grid ref SN 973 225
www.yha.org.uk/hostel/
yha-brecon-beacons

Tai'r Bull Inn
Libanus
LD3 8EL
tel 01874 622600
grid ref SN 995 260
www.tairbull.co.uk

Maeswalter B&B
Heol Senni
LD3 8SU
tel 01874 636629
grid ref SN 931 236
www.maeswalter.co.uk

Stage 7 – Storey Arms to Glyntawe

Brecon

Brecon Beacons tourist information
www.breconbeacons.org/
brecon-tourist-information

The Grange Guest House
22 The Watton
LD3 7ED
tel 01874 624038
www.thegrange-brecon.co.uk

The Borderers Guesthouse
47 The Watton
LD3 7EG
tel 01874 623559
www.borderers.com

Ystradfellte

Maes-yr-onnen B&B
Mrs Morgan
CF44 9JE
tel 01639 722343
grid ref SN 929 135

The New Inn Pub, Bunkhouse and
Camping
CF44 9JE
tel 01639 720211
grid ref SN 930 135
www.waterfallways.co.uk

Glyntawe

Pentre Stables B&B
Pen-y-cae
SA9 1GJ
tel 01639 730639
grid ref SN 840 153
www.pentrestables.co.uk

Ancient Briton Pub and B&B
Brecon Road
Pen-y-cae
SA9 1YY
tel 01639 730273
grid ref SN 839 133
http://ancientbriton.co.uk

Craig Y Nos Castle (group
accommodation)
Brecon Road
Pen-y-cae
SA9 1GL
tel 01639 731167
grid ref SN 839 133
www.craigynoscastle.com

Gwyn Arms (pub and meals)
Pen-y-cae
SA9 1GP
tel 01639 730310
grid ref SN 847 165

Dan yr Ogof Caves Campsite
Glyntawe
SA9 1GJ
tel 01639 730284
grid ref SN 839 160
www.showcaves.co.uk

Stage 8 – Glyntawe to Llandovery

Llanddeusant

YHA Llanddeusant
The Old Red Lion
SA19 9UL
tel 0345 371 9750
www.yha.org.uk (search 'Llanddeusant')

Cuckoo Camping
Glanrhyd-Clydach
Gwynfe
SA19 9RB
tel 01550 740617
grid ref SN 727 216
https://www.ukcampsite.co.uk (search
name 'cuckoo camping')

The Wildman Woods Camping
Gorsddu
SA19 9UW
tel 01550 740149
mob 07974 684 604
grid ref SN 787 241
www.thewildmanwoods.com

Llandovery

Pencerrig B&B
59 New Road
SA20 0EA
tel 01550 721259

Penygawse Guest House
12 High Street
SA20 0PU
tel 01550 721727
www.penygawse.co.uk

The Drover's B&B
8 Market Square
SA20 0AB
tel 01550 721115
www.droversllandovery.co.uk

The King's Head
1 Market Square
SA20 0AB
tel 01550 720393
http://kingsheadllandovery.co.uk

Erwlon Camping Park
Brecon Road
SA20 0RD
tel 01550 721021 or 01550 720332
www.erwlon.co.uk

Stage 9 – Llandovery to Tŷ'n-y-Cornel

Cynghordy

Llanerchindda Farm Guest House
SA20 0NB
tel 01550 750274
grid ref SN 807 427
www.cambrianway.com

Rhandirmwyn/Pumsaint

Royal Oak Inn
Rhandirmwyn
SA20 0NY
tel 01550 760201
grid ref SN 786 437
www.theroyaloakinn.co.uk

Brynawel B&B
The Dray
Rhandirmwyn
SA20 0NS
contact via Airbnb website
www.airbnb.co.uk (search
'Rhandirmwyn' then show all)

Aberdar Country Cottage
Cwrt-y-cadno
Pumpsaint
SA19 8YH
contact via website
www.airbnb.co.uk/rooms/11896536

Rhandirmwyn Campsite
tel 01550 760257
grid ref SN 779 436
www.campingandcaravanningclub.
co.uk (search 'Rhandirmwyn')

Doethie and Upper Tywi Valleys

Ty'n-y-Cornel Hostel
Llanddewi-Brefi
Tregaron
SY25 6PH
tel 01980 629259
grid ref SN 751 534
www.elenydd-hostels.co.uk

Dolgoch Hostel
Dolgoch
Tregaron
SY25 6NR
tel 01440 730226
grid ref SN 806 561
www.elenydd-hostels.co.uk

Moel Prysgau Bothy (remote forest
location)
grid ref SN 806 612
www.mountainbothies.org.uk

Stage 10 – Tŷ'n-y-Cornel to Claerddu

Tregaron

Y Talbot Hotel
SY25 6JL
tel 01974 298208
https://ytalbot.com

Pontrhydfendigaid

The Red Lion Hotel
Bridge Street
SY25 6BH
tel 01974 831232

Black Lion Hotel
Mill Street
SY25 6EB
tel 01974 831624
www.blacklionhotel.co.uk

Claerddu

Claerddu Bothy
north of Teifi Pools
tel 01597 831663
grid ref SN 793 687

Stage 11 – Claerddu to Ponterwyd

Devil's Bridge

Hafod Hotel
SY23 3JL
tel 01970 890232
www.thehafod.co.uk

Woodlands Camping
SY23 3JW
tel 01970 890233
http://woodlandsdevilsbridge.co.uk

Ponterwyd

George Borrow Hotel
SY23 3AD
tel 01970 890230
grid ref SN 746 805
www.thegeorgeborrowhotel.co.uk

Ffynnon Cadno Guest House
SY23 3AD
tel 01970 890224
grid ref SN 741 806
www.ffynnoncadno.co.uk

Nant Syddion Bothy
3km southeast of Ponterwyd
grid ref SN 773 791
www.mountainbothies.org.uk

Stage 12 – Ponterwyd to Dylife

Dylife

Y Star Inn
SY19 7BW
tel 01650 521345
grid ref SN 863 940
www.starinndylife.co.uk

Hafren Forest Bunkhouse
Staylittle
Llanidloes
SY19 7DB
tel 07871 740514
grid ref SN 873 904
https://independenthostels.co.uk (search
'Hafren Forest')

Stage 13 – Dylife to Dinas Mawddwy

Pennant

The Old School House B&B
SY19 7BL
tel 01650 521486
grid ref SN 879 976
www.theoldschoolhousewales.co.uk

Commins Coch, Cemmaes

Penrhos Arms
SY20 9PR
tel 01650 511243
www.penrhosarms.com

Mallwyd

Brigands Inn (hotel)
SY20 9HJ
tel 01650 531999
www.brigandsinn.com

Dinas Mawddwy

Ty Derw B&B
Old Road
SY20 9LR
tel 01650 531318
grid ref SH 857 136
www.tyderw.co.uk

The Buckley Arms
Minllyn
SY20 9LP
tel 01650 531261
http://thebuckleyarms.co.uk

Y Llew Coch (The Red Lion)
SY20 9JA
tel 01650 531247
grid ref SH 858 148
www.yllewcoch.co.uk

Celyn Brithion Campsite
SY20 9LP
tel 01650 531344
http://celynbrithion.co.uk

Stage 14 – Dinas Mawddwy to Bwlch Llyn Bach

Minffordd/Dolffanog

Gwesty Minffordd Hotel
Minffordd
LL36 9AJ
tel 01654 761665
grid ref SH 733 116
http://minffordd.com

Dolffanog Fawr Guest House
Dolffanog
LL36 9AJ
tel 01654 761247
grid ref SH 729 105
http://dolffanogfawr.co.uk

Dol Einion Camp Site
Dol Einion
LL36 9AJ
tel 01654 761312
grid ref SH 729 113
http://tal-y-llynheritagecentre.co.uk

Tal-y-llyn

The Old Rectory on the Lake
Dolffanog
LL36 9AJ
tel 01654 782225
grid ref SH711 097
www.rectoryonthelake.co.uk

Dolgellau

Dolgellau tourist information
www.visitsnowdonia.info/dolgellau-34.
aspx

Ivy House B&B
Finsbury Square
LL40 1RF
tel 01341 422535
www.ivyhouse-dolgellau.co.uk

Hyb Bunkhouse
2–3 Heol y Bont (Bridge Street)
LL40 1AU
tel 01341 421755
https://independenthostels.co.uk (search
'Hyb')

**Stage 15 – Bwlch Llyn Bach to
Barmouth**

Penmaenpool/Islaw'r-dref

George III Hotel
Penmaenpool
LL40 1YD
tel 01341 422525
www.robinsonsbrewery.com/
georgethethird

Tyddyn Mawr Farmhouse B&B
Cader Road
Islaw'r-dref
LL40 1TL
tel 01341 422331
grid ref SH 703 154
www.wales-guesthouse.co.uk

Gwernan Hotel
Islaw'r-dref
LL40 1TL
tel 01341 422488
grid ref SH 704 159
www.gwernan.wales

YHA Kings Hostel
Islaw'r-dref
LL40 1TB
tel 0345 371 9327
www.yha.org.uk/hostel/yha-kings

Arthog

The Slate Shed B&B
Craig Wen
LL39 1YP
tel 01341 250482
grid ref SH 655 157
www.slateshed.co.uk

Graig Wen Camping
Craig Wen
LL39 1YP
tel 01341 250482
grid ref SH 655 157
www.graigwen.co.uk

Garthyfog Farm Camping
LL39 1AX
tel 01341 250254
grid ref SH 636 139
www.snowdonialogcabins.co.uk

Barmouth

Dros y Dŵr B&B
6 Porkington Terrace
LL42 1LX
tel 01341 280284
www.barmouthbandb.co.uk

Lawrenny Lodge B&B
Aberamffra Road
LL41 1SU
tel 01341 280466
www.lawrennylodge.co.uk

Môr Wyn Guest House
21 Marine Parade
LL42 1NA
tel 01341 280185
www.barmouthguesthouse.com

Wavecrest Guest House
8 Marine Parade
LL42 1NA
tel 01341 280330
www.wavecrestbarmouth.co.uk

Min Y Mor Hotel
Marine Promenade
LL42 1HW
tel 01341 280555
www.minymor.com

Bunkorama Camping and Bunkhouse
Gwastad Agnesoff Panorama Road
LL42 1DX
tel 01341 281132
www.bunkorama.co.uk

Stage 16 – Barmouth to Cwm Bychan

Bronaber

Cae Gwyn Farm B&B and Camping
LL41 4YE
tel 01766 540245
grid ref SH 713 297
www.caegwynfarm.co.uk

Rhiw Goch Bunkhouse
LL41 4UY
tel 01766 540374
www.logcabinswales.co.uk/
accommodation

Penrhos Isaf Bothy
near Ganllwyd, 1km east of A470
grid ref SH 737 238
www.mountainbothies.org.uk

Llanbedr and Harlech

Maelgwyn House B&B
Ffordd Isaf
Harlech
LL46 2SW
tel 01766 780087
www.maelgwynharlech.co.uk

Gwynfryn Farm B&B
Llanbedr
LL45 2NY
tel 01341 241381 (evenings)
www.gwynfryncottages.com

The Victoria Inn
Llanbedr
LL45 2LD
tel 01341 241213
www.vic-inn.co.uk

Nantcol Waterfalls Campsite
Cefn Uchaf
Llanbedr
LL45 2PL
tel 01341 241209
grid ref SH 608 271
www.nantcolwaterfalls.co.uk

The Mill Campsite
Llanfair
Llanbedr
LL45 2NH
mob 07909 682938
grid ref SH 589 268
http://llanbedrcampingandcaravan.
co.uk

Cwm Bychan

Cwm Bychan Farm Campsite
Llanbedr
LL45 2PH
tel 01630 657001
grid ref SH 646 315

Dinas Farm Camping
Llanbedr
LL45 2PH
tel 01341 241585
grid ref SH 611 291
www.dinas-farm.co.uk

Stage 17 – Cwm Bychan to Maentwrog

Trawsfynydd

Old Mill Farmhouse B&B
Fron Oleu
LL41 4UN
tel 01766 540397
http://oldmillfarmhouse.co.uk

Llys Ednowain Hostel
LL41 4UB
tel 01766 770324

Cae Adda Cottage and Camping
LL41 4TS
email caeaddacamping@gmail.com
grid ref SH 690 355
www.caeadda.com

Maentwrog

The Grapes Hotel
LL41 4HN
tel 01766 590365
www.grapeshotelsnowdonia.co.uk

Glanddwyryd B&B
Glan Dwyryd
LL41 4HN
tel 01766 590288
http://glanddwyryd.weebly.com

The Oakeley Arms Hotel
Tan-y-bwlch
LL41 3YU
tel 01766 590277
grid ref SH 660 409
http://oakeleyarms.co.uk

Plas Tan y Bwlch (study centre and B&B)
LL41 3YU
tel 01766 590324
grid ref SH 655 406
www.eryri.llyw.cymru/study-centre

Llechrwd Riverside Campsite
Llechrwd Farm
LL41 4HF
tel 01766 590240
www.llechrwd.co.uk

Maentwrog Bunkhouse
Felen Rhyd Fach
LL41 4HY
tel 01766 590231
grid ref SH 657 393
https://independenthostels.co.uk (search
'Maentwrog')

Stage 18 – Maentwrog to Beddgelert

Llan Ffestiniog

Treks Bunkhouse
Y Cefn
LL41 4PS
mob 07796172318
grid ref SH 714 421
www.treksbunkhouse.co.uk

Blaenau Ffestiniog

Dolawel Guest House
Rhiwbrydfir
LL41 3HS
tel 01766 830511
www.dolawel.co.uk

Bryn Elltyd Eco Guest House
Tanygrisiau
LL41 3TW
tel 01766 831356
www.ecoguesthouse.co.uk

Cell B Hostel
Park Square
LL41 3AD
tel 01766 832001
http://cellb.org

Beddgelert

Royal Goat Hotel
LL55 4YE
tel 01766 890224
www.royalgoathotel.com

Colwyn Guest House
Caernarfon Road
LL55 4UY
tel 01766 890276
www.beddgelertguesthouse.co.uk

Beddgelert Campsite
Caernarfon Road
LL55 4UY
tel 01766 890288
grid ref SH 578 491
www.beddgelertcampsite.co.uk

Cae Du Campsite
LL55 4NE
tel 01766 890345
grid ref SH 598 487

Stage 19 – Beddgelert to Pen-y-Pass

Nant Gwynant

YHA Snowdon Bryn Gwynant
LL55 4NP
tel 0345 371 9108
www.yha.org.uk (search 'Bryn Gwynant')

Bryn Dinas Camping Pods
LL55 4NH
tel 01766 890351
grid ref SH 625 502
www.bryndinascampingpods.co.uk

Hafod y Llan Campsite
LL55 4NQ
email wynn.owen@nationaltrust.org.uk
grid ref SH 629 513
www.nationaltrust.org.uk (under 'Holidays', search 'Hafod y Llan')

Pen-y-Pass and Pen-y-Gwryd

YHA Snowdon Pen-y-Pass
Pen-y-Pass
LL55 4NY
tel 0345 371 9534
www.yha.org.uk (search 'Pen-y-Pass')

Pen-y-Gwryd Hotel
Nant Gwynant
LL55 4NT
tel 01286 870211
www.pyg.co.uk

Llanberis

YHA Snowdon Llanberis
Llwyn Celyn
LL55 4SR
tel 0345 371 9645
grid ref SH 574 596
www.yha.org.uk (search 'Llanberis')

Beech Bank B&B
2 High Street
LL55 4EN
tel 01286 871085
www.beech-bank.co.uk

Mount Pleasant B&B
High Street
LL55 4HA
tel 01286 870395
www.mountpleasant-llanberis.com

Glyn Afon Guest House
72 High Street
LL55 4HA
tel 01286 872528
http://llanberisbedandbreakfast.co.uk

Stage 20 – Pen-y-Pass to Llyn Ogwen

Ogwen/Capel Curig

YHA Idwal Cottage
Bethesda
LL57 3LZ
tel 01286 872528
www.yha.org.uk (search 'Idwal')

Gwern Gof Uchaf Campsite/Bunkhouse
Capel Curig
LL24 0EU
tel 01690 720294
grid ref SH 673 603
www.tryfanwales.co.uk

Gwern Gof Isaf Campsite
Capel Curig
LL24 0EU
tel 01690 72027
grid ref SH 685 601
https://gwerngofisaf.co.uk

The Rocks Hostel
Capel Curig
LL24 0EL
tel 01690 720225
grid ref SH 726 579
www.therockshostel.com

Bron Eryri B&B
Capel Curig
LL24 0EE
tel 01690 720240
grid ref SH 733 572
www.snowdoniabednbreakfast.com

Bryn Tyrch Inn B&B
Capel Curig
LL24 0EL
tel 01690 720223
grid ref SH 724 579
www.bryntyrchinn.co.uk

Tyn-y-Coed Inn
Capel Curig
LL24 0EE
tel 01690 720331
grid ref SH 732 574
www.tyn-y-coed.co.uk

Stage 21 – Llyn Ogwen to Conwy

Carneddau

Dulyn Bothy
grid ref SH 705 664
www.mountainbothies.org.uk

Rowen

Conwy Valley Barn (bunkhouse and camping)
Pyllau Gloewen Farm
Tal-y-Bont
tel 01492 660504
mob 07956 851425
grid ref SH 769 697
www.conwyvalleybarn.com

YHA Rowen
Rhiw Farm
LL32 8YW
tel 0345 371 9038
grid ref SH 747 721
www.yha.org.uk (search 'Rowen')

Conwy

YHA Conwy
Larkhill
Sychnant Pass Road
LL32 8AJ
tel 0345 371 9732
www.yha.org.uk (search 'Conwy')

Bryn B&B
Sychnant Pass Road
LL32 8NS
tel 01492 592449
www.bryn.org.uk

Gwynfryn B&B
4 York Place
LL32 8AB
tel 01492 576733
www.bedandbreakfastconwy.co.uk

Castlebank Hotel
Mount Pleasant
LL32 8NY
tel 01492 593888
https://castlebankhotel.co.uk

NOTES

DOWNLOAD THE ROUTES
IN GPX FORMAT

All the routes in this guide are available for download from:

www.cicerone.co.uk/990/GPX

as GPX files. You should be able to load them into most formats of mobile device, whether GPS or smartphone.

When you go to this link, you will be asked for your email address and where you purchased the guide, and have the option to subscribe to the Cicerone e-newsletter.

www.cicerone.co.uk

CICERONE

Trust Cicerone to guide your next adventure, wherever it may be around the world...

Discover guides for hiking, mountain walking, backpacking, trekking, trail running, cycling and mountain biking, ski touring, climbing and scrambling in Britain, Europe and worldwide.

Connect with Cicerone online and find inspiration.

- buy books and ebooks
- articles, advice and trip reports
- podcasts and live events
- GPX files and updates
- regular newsletter

cicerone.co.uk